This book contends that Newman's
idea of the Church both anticipates the
conclusions of Vatican II and reflects
a tradition common to Newman,
Coleridge and F. D. Maurice. It is a
tradition which still lives in the
questions it raises—What is the place
of the laity? How ought the Church
to regard the universities? And what
is its regulating principle—the pope,
the theologians, or the nation?
Positions now adopted by philosophers
and secular theologians are also
foreshadowed in Coleridge's conception of religious language and
Maurice's criticisms of Newman. The
Conclusion, besides generalising the
three relationships of church and
society covered by the book, shows
how they bear upon our present-day
discussion of culture and society.

NEWMAN AND THE
COMMON TRADITION

NEWMAN

AND THE

COMMON TRADITION

A STUDY IN THE LANGUAGE
OF CHURCH AND SOCIETY

BY

JOHN COULSON

CLARENDON PRESS · OXFORD

1970

Oxford University Press, Ely House, London W.1

GLASGOW NEW YORK TORONTO MELBOURNE WELLINGTON
CAPE TOWN SALISBURY IBADAN NAIROBI DAR ES SALAAM LUSAKA ADDIS ABABA
BOMBAY CALCUTTA MADRAS KARACHI LAHORE DACCA
KUALA LUMPUR SINGAPORE HONG KONG TOKYO

MADE AND PRINTED IN GREAT BRITAIN
BY WILLIAM CLOWES AND SONS, LIMITED
LONDON AND BECCLES

PREFACE

The Common Tradition

How ought we to talk about Church and society? This is the general question to which each part of this book is addressed; but its argument is specifically grounded upon the contention that, to a much greater extent than is supposed, there exists an idea of the Church common to the Anglican tradition of Coleridge and F. D. Maurice and to the Roman tradition which is discovered and re-expressed in the documents of the Second Vatican Council. It is Newman, however, who provides its fullest and most satisfactory exposition.

Part One shows how this common tradition—that the Church manifests the presence of Christ sacramentally to the world—rests upon a conception of religious language which arises as a direct counter to prevailing rationalism; but it also shows how closely akin Coleridge's conception of symbol and sacrament is to that theory of language which theologians now derive from the later Wittgenstein.

In *Part Two* Newman's idea of the Church is related not only to its origins in the common tradition but to that European one preserved in Möhler, Blondel, and von Hügel. The dramatic and narrative form of its exposition is made necessary because Newman's idea develops as a personal response to a series of challenges, at first from the Church he was to leave, and then from the Church he joined.

Part Three shows that Maurice, in his criticisms of the Roman Catholic idea of the Church and of Newman in particular, anticipates the kind of objections which would nowadays be put by secular theologians. But Newman also anticipates such objections; and it is argued that his idea of the Church and Maurice's are, in essentials, compatible.

The *Conclusion* generalizes the three relationships of Church to society covered by the book, and relates them to our present discussions on culture and society. Two claims are made: that the common tradition is confirmed and supported by the documents of Vatican II; and that an open, pluralist society still requires a sacramental conception of the Church such as is to be found in Coleridge, Newman, and Maurice.

Acknowledgements

This book has grown out of researches into what at first seemed simple and isolated questions—what is the place of the laity in the Church? Did Newman change his mind about the Catholic university?

And what, after his disappointment with Vatican I, were his final thoughts on the Church? And it is fitting that my first acknowledgement should be to the members of Newman's own Oratory at Birmingham for their continual hospitality and for their permission to print what has hitherto remained unpublished. To Fr. Stephen Dessain, the founder of contemporary Newman studies, I owe more than my thanks can adequately express.

In 1966 we held the first Oxford Newman symposium. It helped me to see the conclusions to which my material was pointing; and I wish to acknowledge the help I have received from fellow Newman scholars, particularly from such European experts as Mgr. Maurice Nédoncelle and Père J. H. Walgrave, O.P. In order that I might develop my argument into a book, Abbot B. C. Butler gave me leave to read for a D.Phil, at Oriel College, Oxford; and I wish to record my gratitude to him, to Abbot N. W. Passmore, to Dom Aelred Watkin and members of the Downside Community, since without their advice and assistance I could not have carried out this work. Oxford had already shown me kindness in the help I had received from Fr. A. M. Allchin and the Pusey House Library. I was now to receive invaluable criticism and aid from my supervisors, Professor I. T. Ramsey (now Bishop of Durham) and Canon David Jenkins, and from the Chaplain of Oriel College, Dr. F. W. Dillistone. These Oxford friendships have become for me the conclusive evidence for what I have called the common tradition.

I should like to thank the publishers of my preliminary studies listed in the bibliography—Geoffrey Chapman Ltd., Darton, Longman and Todd Ltd., and Sheed & Ward Ltd.; and where citation of such material has been necessary I wish to render due acknowledgement.

The general issue of church and society treated by this book has been hammered out in the successive Downside symposia listed in the bibliography; and in addition to thanking my fellow symposiasts I would also like to thank the following, who have read and criticized the manuscript:—Fr. Joseph Appleyard, S.J., Fr. Laurence Bright, O.P., Mr. Alexander Dru, Dom Illtyd Trethowan, Miss Meriol Trevor, and Dr. Alec Vidler. My thanks are also due to Mr. and Mrs. John Farrell for making the Index, and to Mrs. Catherine Farley for her careful typing.

And lastly, because not least, I wish to record an indebtedness which I can never properly repay to my wife, to Mrs. Gladys Wright, and to Fr. Michael Hollings, M.C.

JOHN COULSON

Bristol
December 1969

CONTENTS

Part One
THE COMMON TRADITION

Part Two
NEWMAN'S IDEA OF THE CHURCH

I

II
THE *VIA NEGATIVA*

CONTENTS

III

THE FINAL AND EXPLICIT FORM

Part Three

CRITICISM

MAURICE'S IDEA OF THE KINGDOM

ABBREVIATIONS

(for full titles and particulars *see* Bibliography)

PART ONE: S. T. COLERIDGE

AR	*Aids to Reflection* and *Confessions of an Inquiring Spirit*.
BL	*Biographia Literaria*.
C & S	*On the Constitution of Church and State* and the two *Lay Sermons*, ed. H. N. Coleridge.
CN	*The Notebooks*, ed. Kathleen Coburn.
Friend	*The Friend*.
Lit. Rem.	*The Literary Remains*, ed. H. N. Coleridge.
Log.	*Coleridge on Logic and Learning*, ed. A. D. Snyder.
Phil. Lect.	*Philosophical Lectures, 1818–1819*, ed. Kathleen Coburn.
TM	*Coleridge's Treatise on Method as published in the Encyclopaedia Metropolitana*, ed. A. D. Snyder.
TT	*Table Talk and Omniana*.

PART TWO: J. H. NEWMAN

Apo	*Apologia pro Vita Sua*, the two versions of 1864 and 1865, ed. W. Ward.
Arians	*The Arians of the Fourth Century*.
A.W.	*Autobiographical Writings*, ed. Henry Tristram.
Campaign	*My Campaign in Ireland*.
D.A.	*Discussions and Arguments on Various Subjects*.
D.E.M.S.	*Discursive Exercises on Metaphysical Subjects* (MS).
Dev.	*An Essay on the Development of Christian Doctrine*, ed. C. F. Harrold.
*Diff.*i.ii.	*Certain Difficulties felt by Anglicans in Catholic Teaching*.
D.M.C.	*Discourses addressed to Mixed Congregations*.
*Essays.*i.ii.	*Essays Critical and Historical*.
GA	*An Essay in aid of a Grammar of Assent*, ed. C. F. Harrold.
*H.S.*i.ii.iii.	*Historical Sketches*.
Idea	*The Idea of a University defined and Illustrated*.
Jfc.	*Lectures on the Doctrine of Justification*.
K.Corr.	*Correspondence of John Henry Newman with John Keble and others, 1839–45*, ed. at Birmingham Oratory.

Letters	*The Letters and Diaries of John Henry Newman*, ed. C. S. Dessain.
L.M.S.	*Letter on Matter and Spirit* (1 September 1861) (MS).
Miracles	*Two Essays on Biblical and on Ecclesiastical Miracles.*
*Moz.*i.ii.	Anne Mozley ed., *Letters and Correspondence of John Henry Newman during his life in the English Church.*
O.	Symbol used to differentiate unpublished from published material in the archives of Birmingham Oratory.
O.C.T.F.	*On Consulting the Faithful in matters of Doctrine*, edited J. Coulson.
O.U.S.	*Fifteen Sermons preached before the University of Oxford.*
P.S. (I–VIII)	*Parochial and Plain Sermons.*
Pres. Pos.	*Present Position of Catholics.*
S & N	*Discourses on the scope and nature of University Education.*
S.S.D.	*Sermons bearing on Subjects of the Day.*
Stray Essays	*Stray Essays on Controversial Points.*
S.V.O.	*Sermons preached on Various Occasions.*
Tract	*Tracts for the Times.*
*V.M.*i.ii.	*The Via Media of the Anglican Church.*
V.V.	*Verses on Various Occasions.*
*W.*i.ii.	Wilfrid Ward, *The Life of John Henry Cardinal Newman.*

PART THREE: F. D. MAURICE

H.	*The Epistle to the Hebrews . . . Three Lectures . . . (and)* a review of Mr. Newman's Theory of Development.
KC (1838),i.ii.iii.	*The Kingdom of Christ*, first ed. of 1838.
KC I.II.	ibid., new edition based on the second edition of 1842, ed. A. R. Vidler.
Life i.ii.	Frederick Maurice, *The Life of Frederick Denison Maurice.*
TE	*Theological Essays.*
WR	*What is Revelation?*

Note. In works cited in the footnotes the place of publication, if not stated, is London.

PART ONE

THE COMMON TRADITION

I

COLERIDGE, BENTHAM, AND THE FIDUCIARY USE OF LANGUAGE

In 1836 Newman was exhorted by Mr. (later Sir James) Stephen to devote himself exclusively to answering the Benthamite challenge to religion—'the most subtle enemy which Christianity had ever had'. In the ensuing discussion Newman wondered if Stephen's position were not too Coleridgean to be effective. It was, he felt, to regard 'the Church, sacraments, doctrines, etc., rather as symbols of a philosophy than as *truths*—as the mere accidental types of principles'. Newman brought forward the argument from Tradition, to be told by Stephen that 'he would be a papist if he could'.[1] Here, three years after Keble's claim to have discovered a national apostasy, are the polarities of the discussion which has continued into our own time about the truth of the Christian claim and to what extent existing institutions are essential to its mediation. Here also is the shadow of Newman's solution to the problem in terms of a visible and united Church.

Two years later, in August 1838, Mill produced his essay on Bentham to be followed by its companion essay on Coleridge in March 1840. For Mill these are the two seminal minds of the period: 'whoever could master the premises and combine the methods of both, would possess the entire English philosophy of his age'.[2] Bentham took his stand outside received opinions and institutions, Coleridge inside. For Bentham the question to ask of what we accepted was why is it true, if it is true? and for Coleridge what is the truth which the continued existence of an opinion or institution implies? And it is in terms of this contrast as it is manifest in attitudes to language that we can best begin to appreciate that common tradition which informs the writing of Coleridge, Newman, and Maurice on Church and society.

Bentham derives ultimately from Descartes and from the axiom

---

[1] Mozley, ed., *Letters and correspondence of John Henry Newman* (1891), vol. ii, pp. 155–6. (*Moz.*)

[2] J. S. Mill, *Bentham and Coleridge*, ed. F. R. Leavis (1962), p. 102.

that since we are liable to perpetual deception by the evidence of our senses, there can be one criterion only of certain knowledge—'that all which I clearly and distinctly perceive is of necessity true'.[1] The minds of Bentham and his predecessors—Bacon, Hobbes, the rational theologians, and the Deists—are formed by this method of doubt, as is their critique of language, which begins with an attack upon poetry and ends with one upon religion—if our primary response to language is analytic, the metaphors and symbols of poetic and religious statement, where they are inconsistent with clear and distinct ideas, are meaningless.

Coleridge perpetuates the older, alternative tradition—that a language is a living organism whose function is to reconcile the past and present experiences of a community. For him the primary response to language is not analytic, but fiduciary. In religion, as in poetry, we are required to make a complex act of inference and assent, and we begin by taking *on trust* expressions which are usually in analogical, metaphorical, or symbolic form, and by acting out the claims they make: understanding religious language is a function of understanding poetic language.

Such are the assumptions which inform the practice of Elizabethan writers and account for their ability to move, without apparent change of mode, from pithy metaphors to affirmations which profoundly engage us. The homely vigour of Hooker's reference to Calvin as 'their minister's foreign estimation hitherto hath been the best stake in their hedge' is not contrived, but is a natural means of reference in a society which is still highly personal and very close to the primitive position where words are directly related to actions; and in such a closely knit, face-to-face society it is possible to move on to such affirmations as 'the general and perpetual voice of men is as the sentence of God Himself'[2] without any sense of modal change. Thus, when Donne speaks of the effects of habitual immorality as 'every sin casteth another shovel of brimstone upon him in Hell', he is not using a mere illustration. It is the language of a society in which the objects of faith have become as objects of sight. It cannot without transformation become a medium for clear and distinct thinking.

It was this work of transformation which Bacon deliberately set himself to accomplish. His desire is to produce a language fit for

[1] Descartes, *Meditations*, V (Everyman, 1946), p. 125.
[2] Richard Hooker, *The Laws of Ecclesiastical Polity* (1888), pp. 13 and 81.

the new science, and in *The Advancement of Learning* (written when Descartes was only ten years old), he inveighs against knowledge which is 'steeped and infused in the humours of the affections'. His use of images and metaphors is restricted to illustrating for the reader what is already quite clear to the author; and he regards this, not as a means of deepening our understanding, but merely as a game which, if taken too seriously, will divert our attention to the form of our statements, its images, rhythms, and other deceitful adornments, and by doing so will produce 'a contract of error'. It is to avoid this that Bacon adopts his distinctively aphoristic style, putting forward what he has to say in a short, almost abrupt manner since, by this means, he is 'representing a knowledge broken, which invites men to enquire further'. Aphoristic writing is not likely to be betrayed into the flowing period, or the seductive image. It is a prose purged of irrelevant associations, so that words may be able to stand clearly and unequivocally for the realities to which they correspond. Bacon's deepest suspicions are aroused by the suggestive powers of words which, 'as a Tartar's bow, do shoot back upon the understanding of the wisest'.[1] But such strictures upon everyday language take on an ironically contemporary ring when, in 1604, the year in which Shakespeare wrote *Othello* and two years before *King Lear*, Bacon complains in *Novum Organum* of words which 'stand in the way' and 'resist change'.[2] It is not surprising, therefore, to find him saying of poetry that 'it cometh of the lust of the earth'; and since it is not 'tied to the laws of matter, it may at pleasure join that which Nature hath severed and sever that which Nature hath joined, and so make unlawful matches and divorces of things'.[3]

For a time writers were, so to speak, bilingual; and accustomed as they still were to doing much of their thinking by images and to developing their thoughts by extended analogies, they had to translate this native and immediate awareness into the requirements of the new plain prose. They were exhorted to do this by Thomas Sprat, the historian of the Royal Society, who was famous for his castigation of poetry and ornate writing.

---

[1] Francis Bacon, *Essays, including his moral and historical works* (1892), pp. 133, 218, 222–3.
[2] *Novum Organum* (New York, 1908), LIX, p. 38.
[3] Bacon, *Advancement*, pp. 184, 186.

'Who can behold, without indignation', he says, 'how many mists and uncertainties these specious tropes and figures have brought on our knowledge?' He insists that 'this vicious abundance of phrase, this trick of metaphors, this volubility of tongue' shall be eliminated in favour of a 'mathematical plainness', and that we must prefer the 'language of artisans, countrymen and merchants, before that of wits or scholars. . .'.[1] Eloquence must be banished 'as a thing fatal to peace and good manners', and for its power in the past 'to make all things look more venerable than they were'.[2] It is, once again, interesting to note when this was being said. It was in 1667, barely thirty years after the first collected edition of Donne's poetry had appeared and when Dryden was establishing his reputation as a dramatist. The Authorised Version of the Bible had been in existence for only just over fifty years.

An interesting and amusing example of the two languages is provided by Joseph Glanvill, the author of *The Vanity of Dogmatizing*, from which Arnold took the story of the Scholar Gypsy. This book was first published in 1661 and was then recast by its author in the scientific style, being republished under a different title in 1676. The changes made by Glanvill are highly significant.[3] He goes to immense pains to cut out all adjectives which make a direct appeal to feeling ('the frigid air' becomes simply 'air' and 'pretty images' become 'images'). Any descriptions which betray imagination or enthusiasm are ruthlessly pruned: 'loosely wandering up and down in the water' in the revised edition has been substituted for 'playing up and down within their liquid prison', while 'a truth . . . that to go about industriously to prove it, were to light a candle to seek the sun' of the first edition becomes in the second 'that I need not stay to prove it'. Another interesting feature is the attempt to standardize words so that the author can restrict himself to a limited vocabulary which is more accurate and better able to express what can be measured and classified ('midnight compositions' become 'dreams', and 'praeter-lapsed ages' become 'past ages').

The new plain style is, however, not able entirely to exclude

---

[1] Thomas Sprat, *History of the Royal Society* (1667; second edition, 1702), pp. 111–13.

[2] Sprat, p. 340.

[3] I have made this comparative analysis from extracts published by R. F. Jones in '17th century scientific prose' (*Publications of the Modern Language Association of America*, xlv, 992 ff.).

subtlety, and it possessed a greater ability to convey over-tones and under-tones than its practitioners cared to admit. Hobbes is himself a great master of the calculated insinuation, and his appeal to our emotions is the more effective because it lurks unsuspected beneath the bluff and apparently matter-of-fact development of his argument. Although his intention was to 'bring about a marriage of words and things', he is not above slipping in the unnecessary word in order to recommend an attitude, as when, for example, in speaking of the meaningless and 'insignificant sounds' of medieval theology he says 'though many think they understand . . . when they do but repeat the words *softly*, or con them in their mind' (my italics).[1]

Hobbes is, however, officially suspicious of metaphor, which is to use words 'in other sense than that they are ordained for',[2] and he uses it solely in the manner of Bacon to illustrate what has already been clarified by more general argument.

No major English dictionary occurs before Dr. Johnson's work of 1755, because the meaning of words cannot be stabilized and codified until the Cartesian view of language is generally acceptable. It is not coincidence, therefore, that our greatest poetry is written in the seventeenth century before, in this sense, our language is formed; and it is no wonder that Rousseau accused Descartes of having cut poetry's throat. A distinction which now develops between thought and feeling, reflection and action, is radical enough to have been described by T. S. Eliot as a dissociation of sensibility. Something of its consequences for religion can be seen in the changing attitude to the sermon between Donne (1571–1631) and Tillotson (1630–94). Donne saw his task as a preacher 'to convey and usher the true word of life into your understandings and affections (for both these must necessarily be wrought upon) . . . for the word of God to enter and triumph in you'.[3] Tillotson's aim, as expressed by Burnet in his sermon at Tillotson's funeral in 1694, shows the degree to which the climate of opinion has changed: 'He said what was just necessary to give clear ideas of things and no more. Thoughts of such gravity and

[1] Thomas Hobbes, *Leviathan*, ed. Michael Oakeshott (Oxford, 1946), I. 5, p. 24.
[2] *Leviathan*, I. 4, p. 19.
[3] Donne, *Fifty Sermons* (1649), Sermon XXIV.

use that he generally dismissed his hearers with somewhat that stuck to them.'[1]

Behind this transformation stand the rational theologians. William Chillingworth, for example, believed that since 'the true meaning of scripture' could be known to us exactly as it was to those who heard Christ preach, we may be 'well assured that we understand sufficiently what we conceive *plain* in their writings' (my italics). The Deist, Anthony Collins, who much admired Tillotson, took it as self-evident that all analogies and prophecies must yield a single, literal meaning; 'any other method' he finds 'very extraordinary and difficult to understand'. 'Poetick' and 'Mystick' are for him purely terms of abuse.

It was Bentham's characteristic to push this revolution in philosophy, as Mill termed it, to its limits. For him, as for Hobbes, 'the understanding is by the flame of the passions never enlightened, but dazzled'[2]; and Bentham is determined to deny even lip-service to what he calls 'sacramental expressions', by which an appeal is made to the authority of some general or traditional maxim. Error lurks in generalities, since we cannot know complex unities. Knowledge is by analysis and of details; and words are perverted if they are used to convey anything but precise logical truth—'all poetry is mis-representation'.

Mill's criticisms of this point of view are perceptive. 'A man of clear ideas errs grievously,' he says, 'if he imagines that whatever is seen confusedly does not exist'; and he ascribes this limitation of view to a shallow or under-developed power of feeling. Bentham, he says, 'was a boy to the last', and his philosophical analysis takes for granted foundations which it is unable to elucidate. All it can do is to teach us how to organize and regulate the merely business part of society. If we want to know what mankind knew before the logicians taught it to them, we must look elsewhere—to Coleridge. 'Nobody's synthesis can be more complete than his analysis.'[3]

Coleridge takes profound exception to this dry and empiric climate and to the lean and barren men by whom Bentham had been formed. Standing, as he does, within the received usages of

---

[1] Quoted in W. F. Mitchell, *English Pulpit Oratory from Andrewes to Tillotson* (1932), pp. 192, 335. Coleridge also noticed this distinction: see below, chapter 3, p. 43 and note.

[2] *Leviathan*, II, 19, p. 123.

[3] Mill, *Bentham and Coleridge*, pp. 49–50, 58–9, 61–2, 73, 95.

language and within the beliefs and institutions which have produced them, Coleridge accepts the width and diversity of expressive forms as evidence of what cannot be reduced to one form only: 'and as every passion has its proper pulse, so will it likewise have its characteristic modes of expression'.[1] The extent of his world is revealed by the extent of his language; a richer analysis has yielded a richer synthesis. Coleridge regards the Benthamite appeal to common sense as being merely to 'the moveable index of its average judgement and information'.[2] He is concerned with what sustains the index; and he looks for it in a subtle response to language in all its forms and diversity.

'I have known,' he wrote to Thomas Poole on 16 October 1797,

some who have been *rationally* educated, as it is styled. They were marked by a microscopic acuteness; but when they looked at great things, all became a blank and they saw nothing—and denied (very illogically) that any thing could be seen, and uniformly put the negation of a power for the possession of a power—and called the want of imagination Judgment, and the never being moved to Rapture Philosophy.[3]

The aspect of Coleridge's work which remains acceptable to succeeding generations is his analysis of language and especially the language of great literature. For Coleridge poetry is not misrepresentation but the most accurate and profound use of language possible; and he does not regard it as a mere coincidence that many religious assertions are linguistically similar to poetic assertions in their formal structure.[4] If we take the descriptions of Christ as both Shepherd and *agnus*, or as the Shepherd who knows and is known by His sheep in St. John 10, we are required to make a response to the language which has first to be learned in terms of a response to the metaphors and symbols of poetry. A special kind of linguistic attention is required—to the inter-relationship of the images and to the order of words.

Wittgenstein comes to make the same kind of discoveries about language and the diversities of its legitimate employment in his

[1] S. T. Coleridge, *Biographia Literaria* (Everyman, 1952), p. 184. (*BL.*)
[2] S. T. Coleridge, *Aids to Reflection* and *The Confessions of an Inquiring Spirit* (Bohn ed., 1904), p. 172. (*AR*) cp. Coleridge's *Philosophical Lectures* (1818–19), ed. Kathleen Coburn (1949), p. 200. (*Phil. Lect.*)
[3] S. T. Coleridge, *Collected Letters*, ed. E. L. Griggs (1956), vol. I, pp. 354–5.
[4] *Shakespearean Criticism*, ed. T. M. Raysor (Everyman, 1960), vol. 2, Lecture VIII, p. 111.

Philosophical Investigations (1929–49). He distinguishes between
our saying that we understand a sentence because it can be replaced by another which says the same; and our saying that we
understand a sentence because it cannot be replaced by any other.
'In the one case,' he says, 'the thought in the sentence is something
common to different sentences; in the other, something that is
expressed only by these words in these positions (Understanding a
poem).'[1] This last point is exactly Coleridge's when he defines
poetry as the best words in the best order[2]; and it is a truism of
literary criticism that one of the marks of great poetry is its opacity
to paraphrase: it cannot without loss be translated (as a proposition can be translated) into another order of words. Poetry is
language which insists on its syntax, prose does not.

But there is more than this to a poetic response which is
fundamentally to that facility in metaphor which Aristotle held
to be the hall-mark of the true poet. At his best, in Coleridge's
phrase, the poet 'hovers between images'[3]; and to settle into a
mere image and to produce a straightforward picture which would
prompt us to say, 'Oh, that is really what he means', might be a
philosophical triumph, but it would be a poetical disaster. This is
because the poet confronts us with a use of language in which
words do not stand for terms possessing a constant meaning but
are to be seen as components in a field of force that take their
value from the charge of the field *as a whole*. And it is in order to
define this particular kind of unity that the great Shakespearean
tragedies are referred to as 'extended metaphors', since we do not
really know what they signify until their expression has been
completed, for this use of metaphor is itself evidence of a mind
that has possessed in a unified apprehension all that it wants to
express before composition—poets and composers as various as
Wordsworth and Mozart have testified to this characteristic of
composition as the act of realizing, even transcribing an antecedent
unity. Yet, as Coleridge frequently emphasizes,[4] a poem succeeds
only when our appreciation of it as a whole is compatible with an
appreciation of its component parts. He further emphasizes the

[1] *Philosophical Investigations* (Oxford, 1953), para. 531.
[2] *Table Talk* (Oxford, 1917), pp. 73, 255.
[3] *Shakespearean Criticism*, vol. 2, p. 103.
[4] *BL*, p. 150. But see also *Shakespearean Criticism*, vol. 1, p. 148; vol. 2,
p. 42.

extent to which this method of apprehension is not confined to poetry, but has a more general application:

In order to obtain adequate notions of any truth, we must intellectually separate its distinguishable parts; and this is the technical process of philosophy. But having so done, we must then restore them in our conceptions to the unity, in which they actually co-exist; and this is the result of philosophy.[1]

This view of language presupposes that words and things cannot be simply equivalated, and that there are aspects of experience which cannot be committed to one precise image, since we start by experiencing unities rather than things in isolation. Thus those linguistic forms which express wholeness and unity of apprehension may be even more fundamental than those which permit analysis into separate and distinguishable words and things. The sacramental expressions anathematized by Bentham may stand for what cannot be expressed in any better way. Faced by such experiences the mind has frequently to describe 'what it cannot satisfy itself with the description of, to reconcile opposites and qualify contradictions'. It 'hovers between images', the result of which—if successful—is 'the substitution of a sublime feeling of the unimaginable for a mere image'.[2] Many of the greatest phrases in Wordsworth seem nonsense statements as they stand; and it is not until we relate them to their context that we discover whether they make sense or not.

When Wordsworth speaks of 'the light that never was, on sea or land', or Milton describes Death as

the other shape,
If shape it might be call'd, that shape had none,

we do not take these examples of simple self-contradiction, since the contradiction is not in the facts, but is a recurring characteristic of language when it is used for a particular purpose. This is a failure of language in one respect—to pin the words down to exact and determinate meanings—but it is also a success—the diverse and apparently contradictory aspects of a complex experience are being held in the unity which is its essential character, and in terms of which it can alone be adequately communicated to us. This use of language is 'fiduciary'—we are taking the words, as it were, on trust—and it is what is recommended by Berkeley in his

[1] BL, p. 149.   [2] Shakespearean Criticism, vol. 2, pp. 103-4.

Introduction to the *Principles of Human Knowledge*. '. . . it is not necessary (even in the strictest reasonings) significant names which stand for ideas should, every time they are used, excite in the understanding the ideas they are made to stand for.'[1]

Which, then, is primary—the fiduciary or the analytic use of language? Can it be that a language is rendered fit for science or logical analysis only at the expense of an essential expressiveness or range? It is not only in prescientific or primitive usage that words first require an active as distinct from a reflective response. Religious truths and mysteries also require us to act in accordance with them before we can effectively reflect upon them. In *Alciphron*, Berkeley speaks of terms, such as the Trinity, which, although they are significant signs, need not suggest ideas represented by them, 'provided they serve to regulate and influence our wills, passions, or conduct'.[2] Berkeley reminds us that one of the ends of language is not only 'the imparting or acquiring of ideas, but rather something of an active operative nature, tending to a conceived good'. It is possible to find difficulties with words used in religious and moral discourse, such as duty, grace, or salvation, because they can only be understood as 'operative principles'[3] which we must first use before we can satisfactorily understand. To linger over such words as if they stood for substantive 'things' is to fail to see that this is not to purify language but to risk its degeneration into arbitrary abstraction. It is easy to raise a dust and then complain we cannot see.

If this use of language which I have called 'fiduciary' is not only legitimate but primary, then the attempts to rationalize or purify language which I have been describing would have to be subject to the warning that words are meaningful within the idiom in which they occur (within what Coleridge calls the *lingua communis*), since if language cannot explain itself, nothing else can explain it.[4]

[1] *The Works of George Berkeley*, ed. Sampson (1898), vol. I, para. 19, p. 173.

[2] 'Whence it seems to follow that a man may believe the doctrine of the Trinity, if he finds it revealed in Holy Scripture that the Father, the Son, and the Holy Ghost, are God, and that there is but one God, although he doth not frame in his mind any abstract or distinct ideas of trinity, substance, or personality.' Berkeley, *Works*, vol. II, *Alciphron*, Dialogue VII. 8, p. 445.

[3] ibid., Dialogue VII. 14. pp. 456, 446. Some four years later (1736), Joseph Butler writes: 'For we experience, that *what we were to be*, was to be the effect of *what we would do*.' (*The Analogy of Religion*, I. 6.)

[4] 'A technical term, in so far as it calls for explanation, is to that extent not

When George Eliot wished that life might stand still until she had solved the problems of belief that never ceased to trouble her, she was imprisoned within the tradition of Bentham. Coleridge, by standing within the older tradition of Hooker, Donne, and Berkeley, holds to an alternative principle—that a language is for action as well as reflection: it must be responded to in all its richness and diversity before we can know what some of its words mean. If meanings elude us it may be because the experiences for which they stand are not easily or fully available to us. To explore the vocabulary and idiom of a language is to find guides to experiences of which we may not yet be capable; but to tamper with or abrogate the language we find is to risk narrowing the mind:

> But still the heart doth need a language, still
> Doth the old instinct bring back the old names.[1]

---

language but something else which . . . pre-supposes language, for the terms of which it consists are intelligible only when defined.' R. G. Collingwood, *Philosophical Method* (Oxford, 1933), p. 204.

[1] Coleridge, *Wallenstein*.

II

THE LANGUAGE OF ULTIMATE
CONCERN

(i) *The linguistic community*

THE difficulties of Coleridge's style are well known and have been the frequent subject of adverse comment from Carlyle onwards. To a great extent they are the inevitable result of his intellectual isolation, and it is hard for a prophet not to adopt a hierophantic manner when he is so often obliged to be in dialogue only with himself. A modern philosopher is under no such disability. The contrast in Wittgenstein's attitudes to language, for example, between the *Tractatus* and the *Philosophical Investigations* is closely akin to that between the two traditions—analytic and fiduciary—which I have been describing. And his consequently more rigorous and detailed treatment of common themes and pre-suppositions not only helps us to grasp the continuing importance of the issues raised by Coleridge, but it elucidates and deepens their understanding. It also helps us to assemble those implications and connections which lie beneath the random nature of Coleridge's account of language, since it is part of my purpose to argue that this account—still so acceptable to literary critics—derives from theological presuppositions which Coleridge does not so much conceal as take for granted as self-evident.

At the period of the *Tractatus* (1922), Wittgenstein sees the task of philosophy as confined to separating the thinkable from the unthinkable, on the supposition that 'everything that can be thought at all can be thought clearly'. Logic is not a theory but a reflection of the world, and its form sets a limit to what language can do. The limits set by language are, therefore, limits set to experience, since 'the limits of my language mean the limits of my world'.[1] What cannot be expressed in the propositions of logic has no meaning, since meaning and logic are aspects of the same fact; and although there may be an aspect of experience which cannot

---

[1] Ludwig Wittgenstein, *Tractatus Logico-Philosophicus* (1922) (London, 1955), 4.116; 6.13; 5.6.

be expressed in this way (Wittgenstein called it 'the mystical', intending by this term to include ethical and aesthetic judgements) we must be silent, because we can say nothing to which any meaning can be attached; and if we try we shall talk nonsense. We cannot claim to have had an experience, unless we are able to describe it satisfactorily; and the logical criteria for meaningful descriptions limit what we may claim to describe—'certainty is a character of propositions'.[1] This is that strong and recurring objection to the truth and certainty of religious claims to which, of the writers covered by this study, Newman alone attaches sufficient importance.

Wittgenstein closes the *Tractatus* with a famous warning— 'Wovon man nicht sprechen kann, darüber muss man schweigen' —which has been perceptively paraphrased as 'what we can't say we can't say, and we can't whistle it either'. But whistling in the more sophisticated form of music-making is exactly what we obstinately insist upon continuing to do. And we thereby testify to the claim that some things can only be said in particular ways and in the characteristic forms of poetry, painting, and music, because these are the only ways by which what has to be said can be said.

By the time he had come to write *Philosophical Investigations* (1929–49), Wittgenstein had moved from the uncompromising position which Bentham would have found so congenial to an acceptance of the full range and diversity of discourse. He now advocates 'a radical break with the idea that language always functions in one way, always serves the same purpose: to convey thoughts . . .'. He now seems prepared to accept the view that to say something is senseless is not to say that it is non-sense, but only that it does not make a particular kind of sense: 'it is not as it were its sense that is senseless'. A more 'fiduciary' conception of language is evident in his perception of the dangers of separating sentences from their context, and of endeavouring to attach constant meanings to particular words. No single meaning can be attached to a word,[2] which seems to depend for its meaning upon the way in which it is used,[3] or even in the case of poetry, as we have already seen, upon its position in the context: 'these words in these positions'.[4]

[1] cp. A. J. Ayer, *The Problem of Knowledge* (1956), p. 52.
[2] *Philosophical Investigations*, paras. 304, 500, 561, 595.
[3] ibid., 563 'its role in the game'.   [4] ibid., 527, 531.

Wittgenstein repudiates the presuppositions which animated, for example, Bacon, Hobbes, and Bentham: language is not able to be purified and made more satisfactory by means of reductive analyses, or a 'digging-down' beneath the deceptions of ordinary language to clearer and more constant meanings. Instead, he has become suspicious of those who talk of seeking for what is hidden, since he now attributes our failing to find what we were looking for to its being 'already open to view'. Expecting something 'queer' and 'out of the ordinary', we have pursued 'chimeras'; 'dazzled by the ideal' we have failed to attend to 'the actual use' of words.[1] 'Philosophy', he says, 'is a battle against the bewitchment of our intelligence by means of language';[2] but he no longer means by language which bewitches, the language of everyday life. He has come to see that 'philosophy may in no way interfere with the actual use of language', and he declares that 'what *we* do in philosophy is to bring words back from their metaphysical to their everyday usage'.[3] Why we frequently misunderstand words when we analyse them is because words analysed are in a different position from words used. In the latter case, they are working as parts of a team, in the former they are taken out of their context and looked at as though the context and usage did not affect their meaning. This is what gives rise to confusion about meaning and to the demands (mistakenly conceived) that language needs to be 'reformed'. In such conditions language is in the untypical condition of 'an engine idling'.[4]

The most illuminating parallels between Wittgenstein and Coleridge are to be found in their presuppositions about the nature of language itself. Wittgenstein compares it to a city, and goes on to say that 'to imagine a language means to imagine a form of life'.[5] In the quotation from St. Augustine which Wittgenstein places at the head of his work, Augustine speaks of the way in which, as a boy, he learned his language from his elders, who revealed their intentions 'by their bodily movements, as it were the natural language of all peoples'. The understanding that words are invitations to action as well as to reflection which is so fundamental to Coleridge is frequently adverted to by Wittgenstein. It needs to be borne in mind against too mechanistic and superficial an interpretation of his remark that 'to understand a

---

[1] ibid., 92, 94, 98, 100.   [2] ibid., 109.   [3] ibid., 116, 124.
[4] ibid., 132.   [5] ibid., 18, 19.

language means to be master of a technique'. His statement that
'words are deeds' needs to be related to his account of their
functioning in a manner which recalls Berkeley's 'operative
principles': we claim to be able to grasp the whole use of a word in
a flash; and what is queer about this is that 'we are led to think
that the future development must in some way already be present
in the act of grasping the use and yet isn't present'.[1]

This remark in particular brings us to the very heart of Coleridge's
position and helps us to elucidate it. Words which have for a long
time been operative parts of a language, such as love, mercy, or
duty, may frequently point to meanings which we can only understand by performing the kind of actions which have *traditionally*
been associated with such words; and this is what Bentham means
when he speaks of 'sacramental expressions'. A language also
contains words, such as evil, free-will, grace, or providence, which
the tradition of the language requires us to examine in a special
way—that we should persist in seeking examples of behaviour
which make sense of such expressions before accepting substitute
explanations in terms of simple, determinative cause and effect.

It is, as Coleridge remarks, a merely negative account of language
to see it 'as a Chaos grinding itself into compatibility'.[2] It must
also be seen as a process of what Coleridge calls 'de-synonymization': meanings tend under pressure (especially from univocal and
scientific usage) to coalesce; whereas they should be kept distinct.
Thus Bacon's attempt to restrict metaphor to illustration, Hobbes's
treatment of duty and inclination as synonyms, and Bentham's
identification of poetry with mis-representation are all attempts to
close language up, and are examples of linguistic degeneration.
Instead, the words we inherit should be regarded as 'ready-made
materials of future appropriation, when in the progress of intellectual development new distinctions are brought into consciousness'.
They constitute, therefore, 'the reversionary wealth of a language'.[3]

To speak of this diversity of linguistic use exclusively in terms of
games and rules has its dangers, as Coleridge points out:

The science of criticism dates its restoration from the time when it
was seen that an examination and appreciation of the end was neces-

---

[1] ibid., 19, 197, 199, 546.
[2] *Coleridge on Logic and Learning*, ed. A. D. Snyder (Yale, 1929), p. 138. (*Log.*)
[3] *Log.*, p. 132; cp. *BL*, pp. 42–4.

sarily antecedent to the formation of the rules, supplying at once the principle of the rules themselves, and of their application to the given subject.[1]

For Coleridge a language is a living organism produced by a people (or in his time a nation) which is able to transmit their past as well as their present experiences. 'What a magnificent History of acts of individual minds, sanctioned by the Collective Mind of the Country a Language is', he writes.[2] And this living quality of a language is further exemplified in its power to develop our responses to the future by giving us the means of making intelligible what we have not yet experienced: 'For language is the armoury of the human mind; and at once contains the trophies of its past, and the weapons of its future conquests'.[3]

The Benthamite or post-Cartesian approach to language is defective because unhistorical; to adopt it is to narrow our response by ignoring that part of the present which derives from the past. And Coleridge's celebrated criticism of Wordsworth's theory of poetic language—that it should be the speech of simple countrymen—is making the same point. The best language for poetry is not that spoken by a particular class, unless that class had been so successfully educated as to preserve the *lingua communis* in its richest purity: 'education, or original sensibility, or both, must pre-exist, if the changes, forms, and incidents of nature are to prove a sufficient stimulant'. A satisfactory theory of poetic language must be deduced from 'considerations of grammar, logic, and the truth and nature of things, confirmed by the authority of works, whose fame is not of one country nor of one age'.[4]

Coleridge is at one with Wittgenstein in believing that language must be reclaimed from false usage; and it is the function of poets to guard this depth and living quality of the *lingua communis* or public language which, 'anterior to cultivation . . . exists everywhere in parts, and no where as a whole'.[5] Here Coleridge is quoting from Dante; and he also cites Dante for his remark that poets are the 'guardians of the vast armory of language, which is the intermediate something between matter and spirit';[6] and the characteristic of Shakespeare's achievement is his ability to ex-

[1] *Log.*, p. 110.   [2] *Log.*, p. 138.   [3] *BL*, p. 159.
[4] *BL*, pp. 166, 193.   [5] ibid., 173.
[6] *Literary Remains* (1836), vol. i, p. 159. (*Lit. Rem.*)

ercise 'a perfect dominion, often domination, over the whole world of language'.[1]

But Coleridge makes a further claim—it is slipped in, as it were, when he speaks of language as 'intermediate between matter and spirit'.[2] It is that language reveals not only the traditions and living principles of a people, but the world of ideas by which all men live. This is to claim that language is hermeneutic or world-revealing. 'Words are not THINGS,' he writes in the Preface to *Aids to Reflection*,[3] but 'LIVING POWERS, by which the things of most importance to mankind are actuated, combined, and humanized'. And the proper response to language of this kind must be such that, 'the focal word has acquired a *feeling* of *reality*—it heats and burns, makes itself be felt. If we do not grasp it, it seems to grasp us, as with a hand of flesh and blood, and completely counterfeits an immediate presence, an intuitive knowledge'. And once more Coleridge slides the argument a stage further than the circumstances strictly require by concluding with the rhetorical question, 'And who can reason against an intuition?'[4]

Behind these descriptions of how the language of poetry acts upon us and of how we respond to it is the claim that such a response is of the nature of 'a realizing intuition'.[5] The poet's success is in his ability to bring into activity and more fully into existence what can only be grasped in this particular form: 'it exists by and in the act that affirms its existence'.[6] In his *Treatise on Method* Coleridge lays down the conditions for the successful artist: he must be 'impelled by a mighty, inward power', and he will succeed only when 'the obscure impulse' gradually becomes 'a bright, and clear, and living Idea'.[7] A successful poem mediates a particular kind of knowledge, which Coleridge terms an *Idea*: and, since 'truth is correlative to being', such knowledge implies a

---

[1] *BL*, p. 157. Cp. L. C. Knights, 'Poetry, Politics and the English Tradition', in *Further Explorations* (1965), p. 57: 'Shakespeare, in other words, is a poet engaged in the poet's task of retrieving words from the realm of abstraction and bringing them back to human experience in its fullness, whence they draw their life.'

[2] A Notebook entry (*CN*4233) speaks of language being the medium of all thoughts; and nothing can be 'a medium in the living continuity of nature but by essentially partaking of the two things mediated'.

[3] *AR*, p. xix.   [4] *Inquiring Spirit*, ed. K. Coburn (1951), p. 101.
[5] *BL*, p. 124.   [6] ibid.
[7] *Treatise on Method*, ed. A. D. Snyder (1934), III, 21, p. 63. (*TM*)

reality to correspond: 'To know is in its very essence a verb active'.[1]

There are, however, two objections which Coleridge fails to anticipate. The first is that he seems to be claiming that the poet is somehow able to have a knowledge by virtue of his being a poet which is not possessed by others. In his Shakespeare Lectures, for example, he says: 'The poet is not only the man made to solve the riddle of the universe, but he is also the man who feels where it is not solved.'[2] Such an account may be true of Dante or Wordsworth, but is it true of Dryden and Pope? And if not, is this not because what determines the difference is in the subject matter rather than in the ability which all poets possess of being able to realize their matter into a living unity? What Coleridge is chiefly concerned to describe is the work of the philosophic poet (as he so describes Wordsworth, for example), or the poet whose task is to communicate what Tillich calls the language of ultimate concern.

This brings me to the second and more fundamental objection. Coleridge moves from describing *how* we respond to the language of ultimate concern to *what* that language is about without appearing to think it necessary to notice a distinction which, at least today, would have to be pressed. Is what the language of ultimate concern is about true or false; and does a reality exist to correspond? Why not account for the unifying and realizing power of poetic language entirely in instrumentalist terms—that *if* there were a reality to correspond, *then* what the poem is would be its character? Poetry could be, in Wittgenstein's deliberately more tentative terminology, a technique or language-game which the community has taught us to use. What we cannot be taught is whether what the game is about is true or false, world-revealing or world-concealing. Coleridge himself does not seem to see how much he concedes when he speaks of poetry's power to procure for 'these shadows of imagination that willing suspension of disbelief for the moment, which constitutes poetic faith'.[3]

The imagination is like Ariel—it is not at ease when it is harnessed to a particular view-point or made to bear messages—it must have the air at freedom; and artists are most creative when they are most able to express a 'negative capability'. The very capacity to paraphrase which is the hall-mark of the successful use

[1] *BL*, p. 129.   [2] *Shakespearean Criticism*, vol. 2, p. 112.
[3] *BL*, p. 147.

of metaphor reminds us that a characteristic of any successful work of art is that it does not have to lean on anything outside itself for its validity; it does not demand interpretation, but brings powerfully alive a sense of order, unity, or organism in terms purely of what it is—a visual pattern as in a painting by Picasso, or an expanded metaphor as in *Macbeth*.

Metaphors and symbols act by 'diffusing, dissipating, and recreating' parts and diversities into a unity; and since they relate us to a situation in its totality, their statements are assertions and not interpretations. We must take or leave such assertions as 'I am the way, the truth and the life', as we take or leave Edgar's strictures upon the bastard Edmund:

> The gods are just, and of our pleasant vices
> Make instruments to plague us:
> The dark and vicious place where thee he got
> Cost him his eyes.[1]

In claiming that this is what *Lear* is about I cannot go behind the text: whether life is like that or not is another question. Here is the difference between poetic and religious assertions. The metaphors and symbols of Scripture claim to be *a priori*, metaphysical assertions which can be paraphrased into *true* statements of what is the case, and verified in action—in the lives of those successful practitioners we call saints, or within that community we call the Church, whose language they are.

Thus, although we can see how the metaphors and symbols which compose the language of ultimate concern or religion come to be identified with the practice of poetry in general, we must press the distinction. The former reach beyond themselves (it is their function) to a reality which they stand for: they are either true or false, adequate or inadequate. It can be argued that all the latter have as their function is pleasure—the production of a 'willing suspension of disbelief'; that they need not be true or false provided, whilst our pleasure lasts, we suspend our scepticism of what is asserted; but that when the pleasure ceases, and we close the book, or watch the curtain fall, the effect vanishes and leaves not a wrack behind.

Whether or not these distinctions and objections are conclusive, Coleridge did not consider them; and I wish to argue that this was

[1] Shakespeare, *King Lear*, V. iii, 170 f.

because his original concern was with religious language, and that his account of poetic language must always be interpreted as a derivative from a more fundamental enquiry. In the *Biographia Literaria* he speaks of the time *before* his active collaboration with Wordsworth as a period in which 'I retired to a cottage in Somersetshire at the foot of Quantock, and devoted my thoughts and studies to the foundations of religion and morals'.[1] And we notice that the vocabulary Coleridge uses when he attempts to explain *what* the poetic use of language is concerned to communicate is insufficiently clear and determinate until we apply it to religion. Religion provides us with the objects to correspond to the terms which Coleridge uses when he is trying to explain the effect and function of the language of poetry. Coleridge has been condemned for being obscure on the grounds that such terms as 'idea' and 'realizing intuition' should be explanatory solely in terms of literary appreciation and response. I wish to argue that they are only clearly explanatory in terms of Coleridge's account of religious assent, since it is from this prior concern that they originate. Obscurity arises because Coleridge fails to keep his literary and religious categories sufficiently separate, or to preserve a firm enough distinction between philosophy and theology; and he frequently weakens his theological arguments by grounding them on a particular form of idealist epistemology.

On the other hand, if we see Coleridge's account of poetic language as being ultimately an account of religious language, and in particular of our response to the Christian claim as mediated through the Scriptures, the Church, and the sacraments, then a number of his cloudier terms become useful and even clarifying.

This brings us to Coleridge's use of a key term—*idea*; since it is in terms of ideas that he describes what poetry discloses. His usage is confusing because he makes the term serve at least three distinguishable purposes; and he gives us no clear guide as to which is primary. As I have already suggested, his claim for what poetry discloses goes beyond a purely formal or instrumentalist description of the action of such language upon us, since it implies that we can know more than our separate senses can disclose or sense experience generally can verify, and that this knowledge can be

---

[1] *BL*, p. 95. Coleridge moved into his cottage at Nether Stowey on 31 December 1796. Wordsworth did not move into the neighbourhood until the following July.

had only as we are 'activated and harmonised in a living response to living form'.[1] Such a claim may well be right, even essential for literary appreciation; but to make it implies a prior conviction of what the human personality is for, and that a part of ourselves— and that the best part—can only be known in this way.

This is the claim that Coleridge is making when he speaks of an *idea* as the 'form in which the Absolute distinctly . . . is realized and revealed',[2] and as 'a something which the mind can know but which it cannot understand, of which understanding can be no more than the symbol'.[3] Ideas are what the man of genius— 'whether a statesman, a poet, a painter, a statuary, or a man of science' devotes himself to producing; and their successful realiza- tion enables us to feel 'that our being is nobler than its senses'.

Of the three distinguishable uses of the term *idea* in Coleridge, the least satisfactory is that in which they are spoken of as self- evident truths which guarantee their own reality or as self-evident *a priori* conceptual principles which are yet 'the most real of all realities'.[4] This usage derives from Coleridge's frequently ex- pressed desire to reach a view of the world from which it could be grasped as the manifestation of a single principle.[5] It is what Newman, in criticizing Kant, refers to as 'the obstinate assump- tion that all things must be reduced to *one* principle'[6]; and in Coleridge it encourages that confusion of fact with speculative principle which leads him, for example, to speak of the idea of the Church, of the State, even of the British Constitution, whilst holding that an idea is, by virtue of what it is, undefinable.[7]

Coleridge also uses *idea* to describe functional (as distinct from speculative) principles. This is the sense which is given to the term in his *Treatise on Method* (1817). This work, one of Coleridge's most lucid and coherent expositions, deals with the principles on which knowledge is organized; and it was one of the works New- man consulted and summarized when he was preparing his Lectures on University Education (probably in 1851). Here an *idea* is described as 'the INITIATIVE of all method', the 'leading thought,

---

[1] L. C. Knights, 'Theology and Poetry' in *Theology and the University*, ed. J. Coulson (1964), p. 217.

[2] *Log.*, p. 136.   [3] *Phil. Lect.*, p. 168.

[4] Coleridge, *On the Constitution of Church and State* (1830), ed. H. N. Coleridge (1839), p. 18 (note). (*C & S*)

[5] J. H. Muirhead, *Coleridge as Philosopher* (1930), p. 60.

[6] D.E.M.S., p. 43.   [7] *Log.*, p. 135.

3—N.C.T.

this keynote of the harmony, this "subtile, cementing, subter-
raneous power"'. Nowadays we might use 'model' in this sense
(rather than hypothesis),[1] especially as Coleridge is at pains to
distinguish idea from mere hypothesis, equating it to the expression of a law which, in its developed form, is clear and distinct, but
which may also exist in the undeveloped form of an instinct.[2] It
was this part of Coleridge's exposition which Newman summarized;
and he notes that Coleridge's use of instinct is equivalent to his
own use of implicit.[3]

To apply this usage of idea to education not only elucidates it,
but shows how much it determined Newman's own exposition.
Coleridge cites the example of the 'poor Indian', whose 'learned
and systematic ignorance' is 'mere orderliness without method'
because it is guided by 'no leading idea'. When a 'friendly missionary' arrives, he supplies such leading ideas by explaining the
nature of written words, translating them into native sounds, and
thence into 'the thoughts of his heart'. 'Henceforward the book is
unsealed'; and the native 'communes with its spirit as with a
living oracle. The words become transparent and he sees them as
though he saw them not'.[4]

---

[1] *TM*, I (3). Coleridge speaks of an *idea* as a *model* in *C & S*, p. 21.
[2] *Treatise on Method:*
III (17) (*Friend* VII, p. 314–5) 'True Theory is always in the first and purest
sense a *locum tenens* of Law; when it is not, it degenerates into hypothesis.'
I (10) 'and as by Law we mean the laying down the rule, so the rule laid down
we call, in the ancient and proper sense of the word, an *Idea*; and consequently
the words Idea and Law are correlative terms, differing only as object and
subject, as Being and Truth.'
I (11) 'In the Infancy of the Human Mind all our ideas are instincts; and
Language is happily contrived to lead us from the vague to the distinct, from
the imperfect to the full and finished form.'
[3] Newman, Oratory Archives. Paper watermarked 1851. The transcription
reads: 'Idea, when clear, is proper—but when not known but suspected, is
instinct. (I should say implicit.)'
Newman treats of this distinction between implicit and explicit in the
University Sermon *On Implicit and Explicit Reason* preached in 1840 (*O.U.S.*,
pp. 251–77). He cites St. Peter as an example of implicit faith—he acted
spontaneously and then contemplated his acts. The grounds for so acting or
concluding are not, however, irrational but 'latent and implicit'. All men have a
reason but not all men can give a reason—Faith can be complete without its
grounds having been explicitly demonstrated—and clearness in argument is not
indispensable to reasoning well, since 'words are incomplete exponents of ideas'.
[4] Coleridge, *The Friend*, a series of essays (1809–10, collected in 1818)
(London, 1866), p. 339. (cp. *TM* III (6).) The argument of the *Treatise on
Method* is partially reproduced and developed in section III of *The Friend* (op.
cit., pp. 296–345).

Newman has a similar example—that of the sailor [1] who sees
great cities and wild regions but without drift or relation, since
nothing in what he sees carries him forward or backwards 'to any
idea beyond itself'. Until a 'formative idea' [2] is provided, everything stands by itself, since it is the characteristic of 'a form or
idea' [3] to collect together into one, and to provide the centres of
thought around which our knowledge grows and is located [4]: only
thus can we make the objects of our knowledge subjectively our
own.

Such principles of growth, even as they become clear and
distinct, are arrived at by a process far more complex than the
simple reductive analysis advocated by Bentham. Definition comes
at the end of a period of trial and error, in which part of the effort
is to resist or hold off the development and imposition of explanations which are too easily 'clear and distinct'—a conflict which is
brilliantly depicted in the opening chapters of Dickens's *Hard
Times*. In this sense to seek an idea is comparable to trying to
define a personal identity. It is difficult but not impossible; and
the successful poet or novelist does succeed in providing answers
to the question: 'Who is Sylvia, what is she?'

The functional use of idea to denote the organizing principles of
knowledge has led us to the third and, as I shall try to establish,
primary use of the term as equivalent to what might be called a
realizing principle. This is the sense in which it is used by Coleridge
in his *On the Constitution of the Church and State according to the
Idea of Each* (1830). Here he speaks of an idea as 'a principle existing in the only way in which a principle can exist—in the minds and
consciences of the persons whose duties it prescribes, and whose
rights it determines'. [5] In this sense it is being used as a way of
describing a claim made upon us to which we must first respond
totally, before we can fully understand what we have committed
ourselves to. Such a claim would be that Christ was God, and that
we must live our lives according to his principles, that the Church

---

[1] Newman, *Idea of a University* (1925), pp. 133–6. (*Idea*.)

[2] In the *Grammar of Assent* Newman speaks of our instincts being developed
by 'formative ideas' (p. 49); and his *Essay on the Development of Doctrine* is
conceived in terms of the development of ideas. See below, chapters 5, p. 74,
and 6, pp. 87 ff.

[3] Newman: from the subsequently suppressed Discourse V of *Discourses on
the scope and nature of University Education* (Dublin, 1852), p. 148. (*S & N.*)

[4] Newman, *Idea*, p. 502.   [5] *C & S*, p. 19.

and its sacraments are the forms by which his Grace is mediated to us, or that we must love one another irrespective of the consequences. These are akin to Berkeley's 'operative principles'; they must first be acted upon before they can be fully understood. Thus Coleridge speaks of an idea as 'an experiment proposed', and an experiment 'as an idea realized'.[1] It is in this sense that we might interpret his reference to *ideas* as *models*.[2]

Thus when Coleridge talks of our response to language as active, and as a 'realizing intuition', he is more properly speaking of our assent to moral and religious claims. Faith, he says, is an anticipation of knowledge.[3] We must first believe in order to acquire a reason for our belief, since 'to believe and to understand are not diverse things, but the same thing in different periods of its growth'.[4]

(ii) *Realizing principles*

My argument thus far has been to show that the fiduciary (as distinct from the analytic) use of language to be found in certain kinds of poetry and in much of Scripture is evidence of a claim to communicate and realize a 'complex act both of inference and of assent'.[5] When it is successful, this fiduciary use of language describes both the process of disclosure and what is being disclosed. What is known is known as a whole and in terms of those factors which unify it. These unifying factors are what Coleridge calls 'realizing intuitions'; and his primary use of the term *idea* is to denote such unifying and realizing principles, which although communicated to us through the senses give us knowledge of what lies beyond them.

Ideas, therefore, are more than speculative principles; they can be understood only as they are used or realized: they are the principles we require for the organization of our knowledge, and for our own self-realization. Their action is comparable to that of symbols and sacraments, as Coleridge himself was to point out, since they partake of the reality they render intelligible. They both realize or disclose our commitment and identify it.

Further elucidation as well as confirmation of this argument is

---

[1] *Friend*, p. 323.   [2] *C & S*, p. 21. See above, p. 24 and note.
[3] *Phil. Lect.*, p. 280.   [4] *AR*, p. 128.
[5] I have deliberately used Newman's words at the conclusion of the *Grammar of Assent* (p. 374), for reasons which I hope the rest of the work will make clear.

to be found most clearly and simply expressed, not in Coleridge, but in Wordsworth's *The Prelude* and in his *Letter to Mathetes* (1809–10), which Coleridge republished in the Introduction to that third volume of the *Friend* in which he also recapitulated the argument of the *Treatise on Method*.

The Prelude, which is specifically addressed to 'a dear friend'— Coleridge—has for its theme the growth of the poet's mind towards the certitude that not only are we 'inmates of this active universe',[1] but we are in an intelligible and purposive relationship to it. Wordsworth writes from the standpoint of one who has survived a period in which he had been unwilling to commit himself to what he could not initially verify, and in which, therefore, he had 'zealously laboured to cut off my heart/From all the sources of her former strength'. From this temporary state of Benthamite rationalism, in which he had 'murdered to dissect', and had been close to unsouling 'by syllogistic words/Those mysteries of being',[2] he had been saved by Coleridge.

Wordsworth had learned that the way to recovery was, 'to measure back the path of life he has trod',[3] and by a deliberate effort to recollect in tranquillity, and recall those events or, as he calls them, 'spots of time', which had been formative of his moral understanding. His greatness is shown in what he does not attempt to do: he sets strict limits to what he can explain:

> . . . the soul
> Remembering how she felt, but what she felt
> Remembering not, retains an obscure sense
> Of possible sublimity. . . .[4]

Yet, as Whitehead remarks in commenting on Wordsworth's achievement in the *Prelude*, 'the sheer statement, of what things are, may contain elements explanatory of why things are. Such elements may be expected to refer to depths beyond anything which we can grasp with a clear apprehension.'[5]

In the early books Wordsworth's theme is that of 'Nature teaching seriously and sweetly through the affections'.[6] Thus the

---

[1] *The Prelude* (1850), bk. ii, line 254.   [2] ibid., xii. 80, 83–4.
[3] 'Letter to Mathetes', *Friend*, pp. 266–7. (*LM*)
[4] *Prelude*, ii. 315–8.
[5] A. N. Whitehead, *Science and the Modern World* (Cambridge, 1927), p. 115.
[6] *LM*, *Friend*, p. 266.

formative effect of his parents' love upon him is that, on being
orphaned at the age of thirteen,

> ... I was left alone
> Seeking the visible world, nor knowing why.
> The props of my affections were removed,
> And yet the building stood, as if sustained
> By its own spirit! [1]

This, one of Wordsworth's earliest experiences, characterizes all
the others of which the *Prelude* is composed: they can be recognized
only in retrospect, never at the time, for what they are; and they
can be interpreted not by means of an analysis of their details, but
only in terms of the whole which the details accumulate to disclose.
This is what justifies, by necessitating, a fiduciary use of language:
the language succeeds to the extent that it is translucent to what it
has evoked—the emergence into actuality of a 'realizing intuition'
that we depend upon a living, purposive, and intelligible reality
which is never plainly and only intermittently revealed to our
senses. We grasp it only by avoiding the wrong kind of clarity and
distinctness: we can clarify how, not what, we experience; but to
succeed in stating how is to trigger off our understanding of what
we have come to know. Thus to avoid 'trite reflections of morality'[2]
by keeping language successfully hovering between images is to
understand that what we tritely call the awakening of conscience,
for example, can only be convincingly *realized* when it is spoken of
in terms of 'steps almost as silent as the turf they trod',[3] or as

> ... growing still in stature the grim shape
> Towered up between me and the stars, and still,
> For so it seemed, with purpose of its own
> And measured motion like a living thing,
> Strode after me.[4]

The accounts which Wordsworth gives of such spots of time
and of our commitments to moral and religious beliefs are not in
terms of a standing back from such an experience, of viewing it in
a spirit of detachment, and then by some kind of introspective
gamble deciding to jump. Instead—if we live, we are already
committed; and our recollection of spots of time is a recognition of

[1] *Prelude*, ii, 277 f.   [2] ibid., xii. 314.   [3] ibid., i. 324.
[4] ibid., i. 381.

decisions already made. The question is not shall I assent, but
how have I come thus to commit myself. One doesn't decide to
jump but—if the sensibility is in healthy working order—one lives,
and in living jumps. Recognition is *retrospective*, not *prospective*.
Thus, when the man recognizes the candle which he first noticed
when a boy as 'a visible type of his own perishing spirit', 'a world
of fresh sensations will gradually open upon him as his mind puts
off its infirmities . . . [and] . . . he makes it his prime business to
understand himself'.[1] We grow into our values and certitudes, and
this is the only way by which they can be recognized for what they
are.

This is Coleridge's position when he speaks of faith as an
anticipation of knowledge, and of belief and understanding as the
same thing in different periods of its growth. But it is Newman's
also, when in the *Grammar of Assent* he speaks of that 'complex
act both of inference and of assent', which is elicited 'by arguments
too various for direct enumeration, too personal and deep for
words, too powerful and concurrent for refutation'.[2]

We should not be side-tracked into thinking that the insights of
which Wordsworth speaks depend uniquely upon natural sur-
roundings. These were his chief source, it is true, but he associates
his spots of time not with the pleasingly picturesque but with a
'visionary dreariness', and with

> The single sheep, and the one blasted tree,
> And the bleak music from that old stone wall.

Nevertheless, it was to these which Wordsworth returned to
drink 'as at a fountain'. They retained, for him, 'a renovating
virtue',[3] since they are the means by which we realize ourselves;
and each successive spot of time recognized for what it is is the
foundation for the next:

> So feeling comes in aid
> Of feeling, and diversity of strength
> Attends us, if but once we have been strong.

This is because they are evidence of our ability to stand forth
'a *creative* soul'—to create the conditions by which we can alone

---

[1] *LM, Friend*, pp. 266–7.   [2] *GA*, p. 374.
[3] *Prelude*, xii. 210, 256, 319, 325.

come to a knowledge of the values and destiny to which we are
committed. In 'such passages of life', we gain,

> Profoundest knowledge to what point, and how,
> The mind is lord and master—outward sense
> The obedient servant of her will.[1]

But how do we know that such insights are true? How can we
distinguish self-realization from self-deception? What is the source
of the guarantee that there is a reality to correspond to such dim
imaginings?

It would, however, be rash to brush aside too quickly what
amounts to Wordsworth's answer—that verification is in terms of
what we have become, as when in the last lines of the *Prelude* he
asks Coleridge to remember the events of the *Annus Mirabilis* of
1797–8:

> When thou dost to that summer turn thy thoughts,
> And hast before thee all which then we were.[2]

Mill himself came to realize the limitation imposed upon a
philosopher who has but the heart of a boy, and is the product of
the leanest and barrenest minds his country has yet produced. It
provoked him to remark, in criticism of Bentham, that no man's
synthesis could be more complete than his analysis. And in the
famous passage in his *Autobiography*[3] Mill relates how he came to
learn the value of Wordsworth's protest against restricting reflection and sensibility to what can be analysed into clear and distinct
conceptions. But this is to ask, as it were, for a breathing space
merely: the claims of clarification and verification are postponed
not denied; and the questions remain—how, when we let the
fiduciary use of language trigger off our response to a spot of time,
do we know that there exists a reality to correspond to the pattern
of our response? How much of a language game is it? And if a
reality exists to correspond does it help to explain it in terms of the
ideas it discloses?

Of the three writers with whom I am concerned Newman alone
sees the need to pose these questions specifically; and he answers
them in terms of the prior authority of the truths revealed and
committed to the Catholic Church, whose *lingua communis* they

---

[1] ibid., 269 f., 207, 221.   [2] ibid., xiv. 408.
[3] J. S. Mill, *Autobiography* (1873) (Oxford, 1949), Chapter V, pp. 113, 125.

are. The importance of Coleridge for this study is that this, too, is his position, which—in point of time—he is the first to advance or revive; but he does so in terms of self-evident connections. It is for us to provide the argument.

For him, the use of language he discovers and describes in Shakespeare and Wordsworth is without question world-revealing or hermeneutic; and all the arts, including poetry, have as their 'parent and fosterer' religion.[1] In his *Aids to Reflection* he is at pains to cite the early Wordsworth of *Tintern Abbey* in order to deny that the realizations and disclosures of which he speaks are merely of 'a sense sublime'. They are, he says, of a living God, and of the God, moreover, who is the subject of Scripture,[2] whose language—'the poetry of all human nature'[3]—is fundamentally one of 'events and symbolical persons'. By this language we are *found*; 'and in short whatever *finds* me, bears witness for itself that it has proceeded from a Holy Spirit'.[4]

The general *ideas* of Providence, love, duty, and compassion which are realized or disclosed within the Wordsworthian spots of time are not abstractions but instinctive (or implicit) and developable perceptions of the attributes of that living God whom Christianity reveals: He is the 'sole ground' of the reality of such ideas, which, since they are intended to be starting points for moral actions 'may not, like theoretical or speculative Positions, be pressed onward into all their possible *logical* consequences.' The ideas or doctrines of Christianity are more profitably discussed in relation to men than metaphysically as they relate to God, since 'Christianity is not a Theory, or a speculation; but a *Life*'; and to the question how may it be proved the only answer, says Coleridge, is 'TRY IT'.[5]

It is passages such as these which help to establish the conviction that, for Coleridge, the primary meaning of *idea*, is that of a principle claiming a response in terms of action—we must first perform, express, or embody it before we can clarify our understanding of it sufficiently to be certain of its truth. But the value of Wordsworth's description of such processes of commitment in the *Prelude* lies not only in the power successfully to realize such acts, but in the further questions provoked by the nature of Wordsworth's achievement.

[1] *C & S*, p. 260.   [2] *AR*, pp. 270-1.   [3] *C & S*, p. 267.
[4] *AR*, p. 295.   [5] ibid., pp. 108, 110, 114, 134.

The way in which Wordsworth is successfully able to bring alive those moments in time when, at last, we know what to believe, what to do, or how to choose between equally weighted claims and explanations, obliges us to ask if we can go beyond their description in terms of spots of time; and, if we can, whether an explanation of them in terms of self-evident general principles or ideas is not too ambiguous to be useful. On the one hand we ought to be prepared to distinguish more radically between the event and its explanation; yet, on the other hand, if we are obliged to speak of an act or event as being its own explanation, then it would be better to use a term with a more restricted meaning, like symbol, than one like idea, which is by tradition committed to a more systematic and generalized account than circumstances may warrant.[1]

To see, with Wordsworth, into the heart of things is to understand that what characterizes a deep and rich sensibility is its success in holding and unifying the diversities and conflicts of experience in equilibrium; and that it is from this equilibrium that our subsequent acts and decisions derive their certainty and authority. As Wittgenstein says of St. Augustine, the fact that such a man could hold certain beliefs is what authorizes our consideration of them: can we usefully go behind personal integrity or the successfully unified sensibility? Once again it is the descriptions of what such an integrity feels like and how it works that best provide 'elements explanatory of why things are'; and once again it is important to notice how explicitly Christian is the terminology of Coleridge's descriptions.

Coleridge's descriptions of such a unified sensibility in 'man fully developed' is in terms of an equilibrium or 'tri-unity' of functions, whose coincidence is 'neither a sensation nor a sense; but a testifying state'.[2] Such a condition we call conscience; and it bears the same relationship to God 'as an accurate time-piece bears to the sun'.[3] Coleridge defines the three functions as reason, religion, and will; and says that each of the three, though functionally distinct, 'implies and demands the other two, and loses its

---

[1] With a splendid disregard for his principle of de-synonymization Coleridge seems to use idea, symbol, sacrament, and mystery as synonyms: e.g. his discussion of marriage in *AR*, p. 251.

[2] *Statesman's Manual*, in *C & S*, p. 263.

[3] *Friend*, p. 92.

6

THE LANGUAGE OF ULTIMATE CONCERN   33

own nature at the moment that from distinction it passes into division or separation'.[1] This explanation in terms of an equilibrium of functions can also be applied to society.[2]

Reason, by itself, allows us to see clearly, but without depth, and to achieve at the best no more than a far-sighted prudence. Such rationalism is corrected by religion—'the executive of our nature'—which acts by contracting universal rights into individual duties, 'such contraction being the only form in which those truths can attain life and reality'. Without the check provided by the generalizing power of reason, religion can degenerate into superstition, and go wandering off with its pack of 'amulets, bead-rolls, periapts, fetisches and the like pedlary ... arm in arm with sensuality on one side and self-torture on the other'.[3] Both reason and religion depend for their existence upon that 'sustaining, coercive and ministerial power'—the will—which Coleridge identifies with the Platonic *thumos* and with the officers of war and police in *The Republic*. This, in the Old Testament, is the power of wisdom; and in the New, the power of love. It is the quality of the man of commanding genius; but it, too, degenerates when it finds 'in itself alone the one absolute motive for action'. Then it becomes dark and savage; and it promotes hope without cheerfulness, violence with guile, temerity with cunning. It is the character of Satan.[4]

Coleridge has already spoken of the constitution of the State as its *lex equilibrii*[5]; but he does not appear to think it necessary to try to produce one here, yet it is the crucial question. What is the *lex equilibrii* which enables conscience to function as a testifying state, or the sensibility to be so balanced that it may be 'found' by the language of Scripture?

---

[1] *C & S*, pp. 260 ff.
[2] The account which now follows is remarkably similar to Newman's prescription for the healthy functioning of the Church by means of a deduction from the three offices (or functions) of Christ in the Preface to the *Via Media* of 1877. The copy of *Church and State* in the Library of the Birmingham Oratory is inscribed 'Ambrose St John, 1839'; and among the passages marked are those on pp. 263–7, which deal with the effects of functional imbalance. Not only do they call to mind Newman's description of the Church's functions as likely to degenerate, when in dis-equilibrium, into rationalism, superstition, or tyranny; but they also recall Newman's distinction between intellectual and religious excellence in the *Idea of a University*.
[3] *C & S*, p. 261, 264, 266.   [4] ibid., p. 262.   [5] ibid., p. 23.

(iii) *Idea, Sacrament, and Symbol*

It is when we come to the general question of verification that we see how much Coleridge's account of what constitutes a unified sensibility or of what the fiduciary use of language discloses or realizes is dependent upon the prior acceptance not only of Christian revelation, but of the Church as its essential vehicle. He deliberately restricts the power of the individual private judgement or reason to the negative function of demonstrating that 'a doctrine is cogitable', but not that it is logically necessary.[1] Man's development is a social process: 'his faculties cannot be developed in himself alone, and only by himself. Therefore the human race not by a bold metaphor but in a sublime reality, approach to, and might become, one body, whose Head is Christ (the Logos).'[2] A use of language which claimed to be world-revealing would, therefore, be seen as deriving from a community which claimed to possess the knowledge which the language has been developed to express. Coleridge specifically claims that the language of Scripture must be 'taken in connection with the institution and perpetuity of a visible Church'[3]; and this is what we should expect from his account of poetic language as requiring and reflecting a community. Similarly the realizing intuitions, performative utterances, and symbols of religion are a *lingua communis* and imply a people, a tradition, and a community in which they have developed and through which they live. All living languages imply existing communities; and we must first identify the community whose language of belief this is. Otherwise our response is merely to metaphors and figures of speech and not to the realities they are used to reveal.

'My fixed principle', says Coleridge (and he prints it in capital letters), 'is that a Christianity without a Church exercising spiritual authority is vanity and dissolution.' Dissolution will show itself by divorcing religious language from the realities it expresses: 'in the mystery of Redemption metaphors will be obtruded for the reality; and in the mysterious appurtenants and symbols of Redemption (Regeneration, Grace, the Eucharist, and Spiritual Communion) the realities will be evaporated into metaphors'.[4]

---

[1] *AR*, p. 122.   [2] *Letters* II, p. 1197 (13 Oct. 1806).
[3] *AR*, p. 322.
[4] *AR*, p. 200. It is interesting to note that Pusey sounds exactly the same warning in his Lectures on *Types and Prophecies* to the extent of using the very

The process of verification is both philosophical and historical: we are dealing with what, historically, claim to be facts, yet with facts as they are 'symbols of ideas'. Thus religion is distinguished from philosophy and history 'by being both at once'.[1] Elsewhere Coleridge speaks of the Church itself as an *idea*, by which he means not 'a chimera or a fancy, but a real being and a most powerful reality'.[2] On this view the Church is a community of historic origin which possesses the ability to verify its own insights; it acts, in other words, as a self-verifying language system; and if we recall Coleridge's frequent use of idea, symbol, and sacrament as synonyms, then it makes better and more exact sense to equate this description of the Church to Coleridge's definition of a symbol as 'partaking of the reality it has rendered intelligible'. It is this conception of the Church which is presupposed in Maurice, the Tractarians, and Newman; and in his history of the Oxford Movement, R. W. Church instances Coleridge's contribution to a better understanding of the 'idea, history, and relations to society of the Christian Church', and to his having lifted the subject 'to a very high level'.[3]

The conception of the Church which derives from Coleridge— that of symbol or idea—is of an 'organismus'[4] which requires from us a similar organic and unified response: its function is to bring all the aspects of religion, all aspects of the believer into a unifying focus. We can understand this conception more exactly if we see how Coleridge talks of the sacrament of marriage: 'it is an outward sign co-essential with that which it signifies'[5]: it is a part of the whole in the sense of being an intensification of what we already experience, and not something different or separate. 'Thus the husband and wife exercise the duties of their marriage contract of love . . . all the year long, and yet solemnize it by a more deliberate and reflecting act of the same love on the anniversary of their marriage.'[6]

same expression of evaporation into metaphors (*RN*, p. 70; see below, chapter 5, p. 67), and that von Hügel spoke of Newman as having taught him to glory in his 'appurtenance' to the Catholic Church (*The Mystical Element of Religion*, i. xxxi).

[1] Notebook 26 as quoted in John D. Boulger, *Coleridge as Religious Thinker* (Yale, 1961), p. 229. See also *Table Talk*, 3 Dec. 1831, p. 162.
[2] *Lit. Rem.*, iii, p. 270.
[3] R. W. Church, *The Oxford Movement* (1891), pp. 128–9.
[4] *Lit. Rem.*, vol. iii, p. 366.   [5] *AR*, p. 25[1].
[6] *Lit. Rem.*, iii, p. 344.

For Coleridge, sacrament and symbol are the particular forms for the realizing of religious assent. When we marry, are baptized, or go to Communion, we are performing the act necessary for the further and more complete understanding of our assent. We might say that the sacrament or symbol was the model for a performative utterance which, on performance, discloses a more complete understanding of the model—the model (or symbol) and our understanding of it being, therefore, 'the same thing but in different periods of its growth'.[1] We must believe in order to act, and act in order to understand our belief.

Thus, when in a celebrated passage in the *Statesman's Manual* Coleridge speaks of its being 'among the miseries of the present age that it recognises no medium between literal and metaphorical', the argument he then advances for the necessity for symbolic disclosure is most fully understood if it is interpreted as a plea for a particular way of seeing the Church and its sacraments. My contention is that this is the source of Coleridge's more generalized account of our experience in terms of ideas and symbols. In the passage I have cited, Coleridge goes on to speak of the symbol, as distinct from the dead letter or the mere allegory, as the means by which faith is disclosed: 'a symbol is characterised . . . by the translucence of the eternal through and in the temporal. It always partakes of the reality which it renders intelligible; and while it enunciates the whole, abides itself as a living part in that unity, of which it is the representative.'[2]

To see the Church as the archetypal form of this description is to understand more fully what Coleridge means when he speaks, for example, of the Absolute as being revealed and realized through an *idea*, or of our being *found* by the language of Scripture: he is referring to that dual function of the symbol—that it points not only to the transcendent, but it is the means by which the transcendent or absolute claims or finds us. In one sense we discover symbols; but in another they discover us, as we express, embody, or perform the actions they enjoin.

This sense of symbol has been retained particularly in our description of the actions of the sacraments; and Coleridge's account of ideas and symbols is, I have tried to argue, most clearly understood when it is seen as originating in an understanding of

<hr />

[1] *AR*, p. 128, see above, p. 26.   [2] *C & S*, p. 230.

the Church as sacramentally—in act and explanation—the presence
of Christ in the world; since it is, in Coleridge's own words, the
function of Christ to be the supreme 'Realizer . . . who was the
fountain of all and who in the substance superseded the shadow'.[1]

[1] *Phil. Lect.*, p. 169.

III

'CHURCH AND STATE, ACCORDING TO THE IDEA OF EACH'

THE state of the question would appear to be thus: The Benthamite dismissal of religious belief is grounded on the presupposition that only what is clearly and distinctly perceived is true. Religious statements are meaningless, because meaning and truth cannot be conceded to uses of language which are inconsistent with this presupposition. Coleridge opposes this view by providing an alternative account of language—that what it has been evolved to express is most fully realized and most truly communicated in the language of poetry (and, therefore, of Scripture). It follows that what is thus communicated cannot be regarded as mere unified sensations producing transient pleasure—explanations in such behaviourist or instrumentalist terms do not occur to Coleridge—nor is it *merely* a language game determined by a fallible human community. Coleridge's concern is theological rather than philosophical; and if we are seeking for a contemporary parallel it may perhaps be found in the writings of Paul Tillich. Coleridge's own view could not be more exactly expressed than it is when, in speaking of the function of the arts, Tillich says that not only do they reveal 'a level of reality which cannot be reached in any other way', but they also 'unlock dimensions and elements of our soul which correspond to the dimensions and elements of reality'.[1]

I have argued that the terminology Coleridge uses in his account of poetic language implies a prior explanation in terms of Christian revelation, and that the closer we relate his terminology of idea and symbol to its origins in Christian teaching the clearer and more helpful it becomes: his ideas and symbols function in the manner of sacraments—they are 'realizing principles' in the sense that they help to bring about the reality they explain, and their usage presupposes a community whose beliefs have come to be expressed in these terms. And although this community is the Church, con-

[1] Paul Tillich, *Dynamics of Faith* (1957), p. 42.

ceived as 'essentially a religious society of divine institution',[1] it is, for Coleridge, the Church as embodied in the nation—an important development which we must now pursue. Nevertheless, it is, I suggest, this sacramental conception of the Church, which is at the heart of Coleridge's writing on language, metaphor, symbol, and idea; and it is to this community that they point for their fuller comprehension and verification. They state the conditions which our response must fulfil, in order that this sacramental or symbolic 'medium between literal and metaphorical' may *find* us, and be able in thus finding us to fulfil the work of redemption it was founded to perform: 'Revelation is first of all the experience in which an ultimate concern grasps the human mind and creates a community in which this concern expresses itself in symbols of action, imagination and thought.'[2]

Such a sacramental conception of the Church is at the heart not only of the Oxford Movement and of Newman's idea of the Church, but also of that other movement which derives even more directly from Coleridge and is associated with F. D. Maurice. It is a solution to the problem of religious verification; but it appears at first sight to produce more difficulties than it resolves, the chief of which is—how can such an account of the Church be squared with its empirical reality? Coleridge had to face the Church-Establishment; and R. W. Church speaks of the dilemma of the Oxford Reformers as they contemplated on the one hand 'the Church of England with its "smug parsons", and pony carriages for their wives and daughters', and, on the other, 'the great unreformed Roman Church, with its strange, unscriptural doctrines and its undeniable crimes, and its alliance, wherever it could, with the world'.[3]

[1] Church, *Oxford Movement*, p. 129: 'Coleridge's theories of the Church were his own. . . . But Coleridge had lifted the subject to a very high level. He had taken the simple but all-important step of viewing the Church in its spiritual character as first and foremost and above all things essentially a religious society of divine institution, not dependent on the creation or will of man, or on the privileges or honours which man might think fit to assign to it; and he had undoubtedly familiarised the minds of many with this way of regarding it. . . .'

[2] Tillich, op. cit., p. 78. It is interesting to note that Tillich defines a symbol as 'participating in the reality of that to which it points' (pp. 42, 45), and that he speaks of the character of a sacramental religion as that 'of being grasped by the holy through a special medium' (p. 58).

[3] R. W. Church, *Occasional Papers*, ed. Mary Church (1897), vol. II, pp. 472–8: the obituary notice of Cardinal Newman published in the *Guardian*, 13 Aug. 1890.

Coleridge's account of the Church seems to imply that we do not meet it in the sacramental sense directly, but as it is embodied in the nation, which is not merely the context of the Church, but its external form, and in which it is realized. Our encounter with the Church is, therefore, in a kind of overlap between Church and society; and this condition arises from the successful development of Christianity. This state of overlap is what Coleridge means by Christendom. It has grown out of that earlier Christian world in which there were the Many who did not think, and the Few who did nothing but think [1] by a unique but inevitable process of development in which the

Mysteries of Faith are brought within the *hold* of the people at large, not by being explained away in the vain hope of accommodating them to the average of their understanding, but by being made the objects of love by their combination with events and epochs of history, with national traditions, with the monuments and dedications of ancestral faith and zeal, with memorial and symbolical observances, with the realizing influences of social devotion. . . . *There*, however obscured by the hay and straw of human Will-work, the foundation is safe. [2]

Christianity is the power or *idea*, Christendom is the 'wide and still widening' fact. [3] Thus Coleridge's account of the Church is in terms of a dialectical relationship between its idea and its context or embodiment, between its sacramental origin and aspiration, and its empirical reality as it is encountered in daily life and, for Coleridge, in the fact of its relation to the State. By conceiving the Church in this way, Coleridge draws attention to that question which came to be Newman's chief preoccupation—how to account for its double aspect, how to square its superstitions and tyrannies with its function as the visible part of the Body of Christ. But Coleridge's emphasis falls not upon the opposition of these two faces, but upon their mutuality: the relationship between Church, Nation, and State—even the terms of its definition—is a fact which Coleridge is still able to take for granted; although Mill believed that his account of the relationship of Church and society was more prescriptive than descriptive, and that it amounted to 'the severest satire upon what in fact it is'. [4]

Such a criticism, however true, does not invalidate the importance of Coleridge's conception of the Church as being both the

[1] *AR*, p. 126.   [2] ibid., p. 196.   [3] ibid., pp. 125, 319.
[4] Mill, *Bentham and Coleridge*, p. 147.

ACTON TO THE IDEA OF EACH'   41

means to the Kingdom, and an end in itself, and of his way of
seeing these two aspects as existing, not in opposition, but in
mutuality. It was this insight which Mill so particularly commends
Coleridge for propounding [1]; and it is the one which F. D.
Maurice develops in the *Kingdom of Christ*—it is that to conceive of either
face of the Church in separation from the other is to risk dealing in
dangerous abstractions, since we may come either to require the
Church to be constituted as a temporal power, or to acquiesce in
the divorce of the civilization of a society from the principles of its
cultivation.

For Coleridge, as for Tillich, culture is the form of religion, and
religion is the substance of culture [2]; and his conception of our
encounter with the Church in terms of a kind of overlap between
Church and society has to be seen in relation to that more general
theory of social and cultural development which is expressed in the
two *Lay Sermons*, and in the *Church and State*. It has remained
one of Coleridge's most influential contributions to the continuing
debate on the relation of culture and society.

Coleridge distinguishes between civilization—which represents
a particular material standard of life and amenity—and cultivation
—which is 'the harmonious development of those qualities and
faculties that characterise our humanity'. A nation which is
civilized without being cultivated is merely polished or varnished;
but the development of cultivation (or as we should now call it—
culture) is a social process requiring an appropriate social form or
'estate'. This Coleridge terms the 'Nationalty'. It is a social order
whose function is not only to guard tradition—'and thus to bind
the present with the past'—but 'to perfect and add to the same, and
thus to connect the present with the future.' This is the function
of the National Church or Church-Establishment, which Coleridge
terms the *Enclesia*, in order to distinguish it from the Church
universal (in its sacramental character) or *Ecclesia*: it is a distinction between men as they are in the world, and as they are called
out of it. [3]

The *Ecclesia* is 'the sustaining, correcting and befriending
opposite of the World'; but its relation to the *Enclesia* is a 'blessed
accident',[4] in that the relationship of Christian belief with the
culture of the English people is an accident of history. What is

[1] ibid., p. 124.   [2] Tillich, *The Protestant Era* (1951), p. xvii.
[3] *C & S*, pp. 46–8.   [4] ibid., pp. 59, 124.

essential and not accidental to cultural development is a learned class, or (as Coleridge now calls it) a clerisy, to provide the dynamic or 'theological' element of society, since 'not without celestial observations can even terrestrial charts be accurately constructed'.[1] This was the function of the Church in medieval society: it ought also to be its function now.

In 1817, in his second *Lay Sermon*, Coleridge diagnosed the immediate ills of society as deriving from an over-balance of the commercial spirit. It had arisen in the absence of counter-weights and in particular of that afforded by a 'learned and philosophic' class. Hence the present excessive attachment to 'temporal and personal objects', which could only be counteracted 'by a pre-occupation of the intellect and the affections with permanent, universal and eternal truths' or, as he expressed it in his *Table Talk*, 'this accursed practice of ever considering *only* what seems *expedient* for the occasion, disjoined from all principles or enlarged systems of action'.[2] Under such influences, religion becomes narrowed into a 'thirst for righteousness alone', and theological scholarship is disregarded in favour of appeals to instant common sense. The understanding of the devout is thereby left 'vacant and at leisure for a thorough insight into present and temporal interests, which, doubtless, is the true reason why its followers are in general such shrewd, knowing, wary, well-informed, thrifty and thriving men of business'.

The revival of a learned class would not only provide the desired counter-balance to looking at all things 'through the medium of the market', but enable Christianity to sprinkle 'its holy damps on the passion of accumulation'.[3]

It is from within the context of this social and political analysis that Coleridge speaks in the first *Lay Sermon* of the need of this 'hunger-bitten and idea-less philosophy' and of the age and religion it has engendered for that 'medium between literal and metaphorical' which, in its pre-eminent form, is represented by the Church.[4] It was his achievement to rediscover and to gauge anew the extent to which our language and institutions have been

---

[1] *C & S*, p. 52.
[2] *TT*, p. 433.
[3] *Second Lay Sermon* (1817), in *C & S*, pp. 359–61, 378–82, 390.
[4] *First Lay Sermon* (1816), or *The Statesman's Manual*, in *C & S*, p. 230; see above, p. 36.

formed by the Church.[1] It was, as I have suggested, the nerve of his criticism of Wordsworth's account of poetic language and of his own descriptions of what is involved in a full response to the range of our language: 'it is to the Church assuredly that we owe all the origins, all the groundworks of our present state of civilization'. The principal and unique means by which the Church achieved this influence was by its power of symbolic enactment: 'great truths were connected with all its ceremonies', and 'the pernicious distinction between truth and reality was thereby destroyed'.[2]

For this reason Coleridge felt unable to view the theological disputations of the Middle Ages with 'the contempt it is customary to do':

I see something awful in the fact that three or four thousand men could collect together in a single place to hear one great teacher—men barely able to read, begging on the road and submitting to every species of privation and yet crowding to hear—what? An amusing tale, or to see a splendid tragedy.... No! To listen with greedy ears to the forms of their own minds.... It certainly does not degrade the men themselves in my mind; but most assuredly it greatly elevates our nature.[3]

It is passages like this which make us understand why Newman spoke of Coleridge as preparing the mind of the nation for the reception of Catholic truth. Even so, the relationship of the *Ecclesia* to the *Enclesia* is as the olive to the vine; and however much the olive may fertilize the soil in which the vine grows and improve the strength and flavour of the wine, 'the olive is not the same plant with the vine, or with the elm or poplar (that is, the State) with which the vine is wedded'.[4] It follows that the national Church is not necessarily to be identified either with any particular scheme of Christian theology or even with Christianity itself: what is essential is the function performed by the national Church and especially by its learned members—the clerisy.

[1] John Tulloch, *Movements of Religious Thought in the Nineteenth Century*, chapter 1: 'This idea of the Church as the mother of philosophy, and arts and learning, as well as the nurse of faith and piety was unknown (in Coleridge's day)' [cited in *Phil. Lect.*, p. 431].
[2] *Phil. Lect.*, pp. 201, 259, 261.
[3] *Phil. Lect.*, pp. 262-3. A similar point is made in the second *Lay Sermon*, when Coleridge compares the attention paid to preaching and theology in the age of Donne with 'the transfer of interest' since 1680 (in *C & S*, pp. 394-6), see above, chapter 1, pp. 7-8.
[4] *C & S*, p. 60.

The clerisy operates in that area of society where theological principles are realized, viz., in the universities, schools, and parish pulpits; and it is comprised of the learned—lay and priests—of all classes. Some will be members both of the nationalty and of the Church universal, or *Ecclesia*, and as such will perform a double function: this is not a handicap, but a positive advantage, since 'the perfection of each [function] may require the union of both in the same person'.[1] Thus the purpose of the clerisy is primarily educative; their purpose is comparable to that of a university as it is defined by Newman—to be 'a great ordinary means to a great but ordinary end',[2] which is to form and train up the people of the country to be good citizens and to provide a culture for civilization.

This conception of the dual function of the clerisy shows that Coleridge is no mere medievalist. In earlier times the relation of Church to Nation may have been so exact and explicit that Christian doctrines, symbols, and observances were completely assimilated to the national way of life, and 'every craftsman had, as it were, two versions of his Bible, one in the common language of the country, another in the acts, objects and products of his own particular craft'.[3] Neither the interests of Christianity nor those of the State require this integral relationship, however; and it may give rise to a confusion of functions, since the paramount aim and object of the Church of Christ is 'another world, not a world to come exclusively, but likewise another world that now is'.[4]

Although the Church is set over against the world, it exists not in a hostile relationship but as 'the sustaining, correcting, befriending opposite of the World'.[5] It acts rather like the sun in relation to the planets,[6] by collecting into itself 'as in a focus' all the beneficent and humanizing tendencies in the State 'to radiate them back in a higher quality'.[7]

This is far from a merely Erastian conception of the relation of Church and State since, although the Church will have an interest in the welfare of the State, it can discharge this interest only if it is constituted into a visible, public body. It is not a secret society; and its members should claim no peculiar rights in the State but

[1] *C & S*, p. 61.   [2] *Idea*, p. 177.   [3] *Friend*, p. 279.
[4] *C & S*, p. 127.   [5] *C & S*, p. 124.   [6] *C & S*, p. 125.
[7] *Lit. Rem.* iii, p. 27.

should make themselves known 'only by the more scrupulous and exemplary performance of their duties as citizens and subjects'.[1]

Coleridge's use of the olive/vine analogy to describe the relationship of the Church of Christ to the Church as embodied in the nation, of the *Ecclesia* to the *Enclesia*, seems deliberately to be confined to a one-way working. In Scripture the Church is itself referred to as the vine; and there is a sense in which the nation could be said to act as an olive by helping the vine to fructify and bear fruit. And it was Maurice's particular contribution to have seen this point, and to develop its implications. But Coleridge seems unwilling to allow the analogy to be used in a double or reversible sense; and the reasons are clearly revealed in his writings, and especially in the second volume of his *Notebooks*[2] which deals with the period of his residence in Malta.

In a phrase frequently repeated Coleridge speaks of the first and fundamental apostasy of the Church as being its, 'gradual concentration . . . into a priesthood, and the consequent rendering of the reciprocal functions of love and redemption and counsel between Christian and Christian exclusively official, and between disparates, namely, the priest and the layman'. A further consequence was the conversion of 'ethical ideas' which promote moral growth into a system of 'fixed practical laws and rules' which was imposed on all Christians, irrespective of age and circumstances.[3] A Church thus constituted becomes 'a negative totality',[4] a clerical system imposing itself upon a laity whom it encourages to remain uneducated and consequently subservient. Such a Church will increasingly alienate itself from its local roots and from the nation, and prefer to owe allegiance to a foreign power—to the potentate at Rome, as Coleridge calls the Pope.

To concede the Roman claim—that the Church must have a residual power of self-determination—was, Coleridge believed, to commit the Church to becoming a temporal power, to deny the principle that religion is *realized* through local and national attachment,[5] and to substitute for the scriptural opposition of the Church

---

[1] *C & S*, pp. 126, 133. In his correspondence, Coleridge frequently cites as his exemplar the man who made it possible for him to settle in the Quantocks, Thomas Poole of Nether Stowey. See *C & S*, p. 98 and note, in which Coleridge speaks of 'the integrity or entireness of his being'.

[2] *The Notebooks*, ed. Kathleen Coburn, vols. 1, 2,—in progress (1957-). (*CN*)

[3] *Lit. Rem.* iii, pp. 377-8, 386.

[4] *AR*, p. 141.   [5] *Friend*, p. 193.

to the world a false opposition of the Church to the nation. This was to accept a permanent principle of social disharmony and unsettlement, since, as Mill pointed out in commendation of Coleridge's argument, one of the essential conditions of political stability is a principle of sympathy, not of hostility, 'so that one part of the community do not regard themselves as foreigners with regard to another part'.[1]

Furthermore, and as a consequence of its structural principles, such a Church could not tolerate an educated laity, as the experience of Roman Catholic countries showed. It would remain 'the religion of the crowd'[2]; and, as Dean Church himself observed, this was a question the Tractarians were never really obliged to take sufficiently seriously, until those of them who had become Roman Catholic laymen had to suffer the consequences of the change. It is on these grounds that Coleridge speaks of the Romish Anti-Catholic Church[3]; but what clinched the argument was his experience of the Church in Malta which is revealed in the *Notebooks*. He certainly based his opposition to Roman Catholicism in later life on what he then observed[4] of what he calls 'the indefatigable ubiquitarian intrusia of the Catholic superstition'.

He objects to the noise of religious festivals, and to the moral ambivalence of those who, as he puts it, carry the rosary in one pocket and the stiletto in the other, and judge of the morality of their actions purely in terms of an Epicurean calculation of pain and pleasure ('so that thinking of murder they think instantly of Hell'). But what is of special interest is that it is in the middle of such reflections and experiences that Coleridge produces the first record of what is one of the central arguments of *Church and State* —the necessity for and double function of the clerisy. It comes to him in terms of the need for a class of learned men to be interposed between the priesthood and the people: 'Prelacy combined with Episcopacy the better/the C. of E. clergy are utterly removed from the Laity, the Laity from Religion, by the want of *Elders*.'[5]

Coleridge is far from denying that the Church of Christ should be visible and should possess a determinate form. He speaks of it as

---

[1] Mill, *Bentham and Coleridge*, p. 124.
[2] *Life and Letters of Dean Church*, ed. Mary C. Church (1895), p. 73.
[3] *Lit. Rem.* iii, p. 81.
[4] See the long note in *Church and State* (pp. 130 f.; and p. 47); and *Notebooks*, CN 2481 and note; 2420; 2717 f. 98; 2983; 2440 f. 6; 2481; 2664; 2812.
[5] *CN* 2649 and note (*c.* August 1805).

'a body spiritual, yet outward and historical', and as acting 'not as an aggregate or sum total, like a corn sheaf, but [as] a unity'.[1] But the Church must be, as it were, what finds us, not what we create; and he finds the Church of England as then existing the least corrupt and therefore 'the most Apostolic Church'.[2] His position is very akin to that taken by Maurice—Christendom, or Christianity as embodied in the nation, is the fact; and the Church is the eschatological and dynamic principle which exists within Christendom or the nation as a 'walled Academy, a pleasure garden' in which each member seeks 'private audience of the invisible teacher'.[3] He also speaks of the Church as that city set on a hill whose members, by their baptism, are to be known to all men by the intensity of their universal charity, but especially by their love for each other.[4] Yet what happens when the surrounding countryside has given up love for genocide, or has decided that the language of religion is meaningless? How is the olive when the vine has withered?

In his Preface to the 1839 edition of *Church and State*, Coleridge's nephew, H. N. Coleridge, felt obliged to raise such questions. He anticipated a time when the nation would repudiate its corporate existence and character and, although the Church *of* England would thereupon have an end, the Church of Christ *in* England would stand erect and become a more conspicuous opposite to the darkening world.[5] Coleridge's mind was too seminal not to be unaware of such questions; but he does not press them. He seems, for example, to have anticipated the necessity for some kind of doctrinal development, when he asks—'What is Christianity at any one period? The Ideal of the Human Soul at that period.'[6] And one of his most interesting notes anticipates the questions which provoked the Oxford Movement and the publication of *Tract XC*, when he criticizes certain of the Thirty-nine Articles and

---

[1] *Lit. Rem.*, iii, p. 366.
[2] *AR*, p. 257.
[3] *Lit. Rem.*, iii, p. 275.
[4] *AR*, pp. 249–50.
[5] *C & S*, pp. xxvii–xxix.
[6] *Unpublished Letters*, ed. E. L. Griggs (1932), II, 6 Feb. 1826: 'It does seem to me a very mean and false view of Christianity to suppose that even the Apostles themselves had the degree of clearness and enlargement which a philosophic Believer of the present day may enjoy. . . . What is Christianity at any one period? The Ideal of the Human Soul at that period.'

for failing to make clear 'on what or whom is the practical authority [of their interpretation] built'.[1]

[1] *CN* 2888. An examination of Articles 3, 6, 8, 13, 18–21, and 23, in the course of which Coleridge notes that an appeal to Tradition is presupposed yet precluded, that arts. 19 and 20 are 'objectionable from the extreme looseness and nugatoriness of the definition of the word, Church. . . . Who is to decide? And which of these are to possess "authority in controversies of Faith"? . . .' (f. 51). 'On what or whom is the practical authority finally built? This may be considered as one of the two or three main vantage grounds of the R. Catholics, from which their Fire commands the Eng. Church.' (f. 50.)

IV

CONCLUSION

COLERIDGE'S pioneering achievement is considerable. His commentaries on such writers as Dante, Shakespeare, and Wordsworth are not only of lasting critical importance, but are elaborate justifications of the metaphorical and symbolic use of language in religion, as well as in poetry. By such means and from within such concerns Coleridge revives an understanding of the Church as a visible society of divine origin and maintenance; and his theory of language helps us to understand how the Church functions, symbolically and sacramentally, as this continuing presence of Christ in the world. Furthermore, by demonstrating how the living power of a language is determined by the character of the community from which it is derived, Coleridge shows that we cannot arbitrarily separate the Church, and especially its sacramental and explicative functions, from its context within society, since the ability of the Church to verify its insights depends upon their fructification within the life of a nation. Yet, in order to keep this symbolic or sacramental function free from that species of corruption termed by Coleridge 'Romish' and by Maurice and Newman 'Romanism', Coleridge limits his discussion of the Church as embodied in the nation to the analogy of olive to vine, which operates only in one way.

He does not, therefore, discuss the further question—in what manner does the Church of Christ depend for the fulfilment of its sacramental function upon its social context; and what, for example, ought to be its constitution in an age in which the Church and Nation cease to be at one, as was the case before the establishment of Christendom? The value of his analysis for an age 'rushing headlong into unbelief' is his emphasis that the Church's relation to the world can be seen as a befriending, mutual relationship, and not necessarily one of inevitable collision between two rival powers. And it is this account, in terms of a nation and clerisy exercising a double function and membership of both society and Church, which provides a common element in the conceptions of the Church subsequently developed by Maurice and Newman respectively.

The need for an educated laity—this element common to Church and society—to perform an essential function in the realizing and communication of Christian truth, and yet to be the creative centre or ethos of their society, and thus the form which Christian social and political commitment takes in particular circumstances—this need is at the heart of Coleridge's and Maurice's conception of the Church. It is now to be found expressed in the documents of the Second Vatican Council, particularly in *Lumen Gentium* (On the Church) and *Gaudium et Spes* (The Church and the Modern World); and it was Newman's achievement not only to anticipate but to explain how such views constituted important but neglected Catholic principles.

From Coleridge spring two lines of inquiry which have, as their common ground, the same conception of the Church (or *Ecclesia*) as the sacramental presence of Christ; but because of the intensities of denominational difference in the nineteenth century they are pursued separately and in seeming opposition to each other.

Maurice faces the practical issues raised by an age of rapid and revolutionary social change; and he tries to determine to what extent the Church of Christ (or *Ecclesia*) depends upon the nation and laity (or *Enclesia*) to *realize* its sacramental function, which he interprets as the redemption of the whole world by the bringing about of the Kingdom of Christ upon earth.

Newman and the Tractarians face the theological issues raised by such an age, which they at first conceive as rushing headlong into infidelity and consummating its apostasy from the Church. Their question is to what extent the *Ecclesia* has to become a visible polity, with powers of self-determination independent of the civil power, for it to perform its sacramental or 'disclosing' function. Although their answer eliminates Coleridge's distinction between the *Ecclesia* and the *Enclesia* as separate states of the Church, it does not invalidate it as one between functions within the visible Church.

Newman alone saw the importance of this point; but, to begin with at least, he was more concerned with the fundamental question raised by Bentham—that of verification. Even if the Church were to be successfully re-established within the forms of a new society, the question still remains: how are we certain that Christianity is true? And, if it is by means of the authority of the Church, what are the conditions to which the Church on earth must conform for it to be able to fulfil this function?

PART TWO

NEWMAN'S IDEA OF THE CHURCH

V

ORIGINS IN ENGLISH TRADITION

(i) *The development of an idea*

NEWMAN begins by taking his stand within existing religious institutions and by asking the same kind of question as Coleridge—what is the truth which their continued existence implies. Where he differs from Coleridge is in the inevitable and irresistible movement of his mind to a position where he comes to see that it is Bentham's question which is the one to ask: how do we know that Christianity is true? And it is the priority which Newman gives to this question and to his way of answering it that leads him ultimately to become a Roman Catholic. Yet the way he sets up the question shows to what extent he is within what might be called a common English tradition: the conclusions to which he arrives may seem at odds with that tradition, but the methods by which he arrives at them are formed within the tradition.

By the adoption of certain criteria, as I shall hope to show, Newman made his move to Rome inevitable; but as he himself argues in the *Apologia*, this did not imply a wholesale repudiation of the tradition in which he had been formed, but rather its affirmation in what Newman now came to regard as its legitimate setting. In the important letter of 2 June 1860, in which he said that 'Catholics did not make us Catholics; Oxford made us Catholics', Newman specifically states that he did not oppose 'the Anglican Church, but National Protestantism, and Anglicans only so far as they belong to it'.[1]

From the start it was Newman's willingness to move and to grow, to face the consequence of his conclusions that stamped him as the odd man out of the Oxford Movement; and his life may be

[1] *W.* ii, p. 57.

seen as a series of acts (provoked by circumstances and occasions) in which his conception of the Catholic Church was put to the test empirically. The method he adopted as an Anglican he continued as a Roman Catholic; and because he saw his own movement to Rome as a theological growth, he conceded nothing of his past, if he were convinced of its orthodoxy by the standards he had come to adopt. It was for this reason that Pusey spoke of him as the bridge between the two Churches in a letter of remarkable prescience published only a fortnight after Newman's reception:

Yet, since God is with us still, He can bring us even through this loss. We ought not indeed to disguise the greatness of it. It is the intensest loss we could have had. They who have won him know his value. It may be a comfort to us that they do. In my deepest sorrow at the distant anticipation of our loss, I was told of the saying of one of their most eminent historians, who owned that they were entirely unequal to meet the evils with which they were beset, that nothing could meet them but some movement which should infuse new life into their Church, and that for this he looked to one man, and that one was N. I cannot say what a ray of comfort darted into my mind. It made me at once realise more, both that what I dreaded might be, and its end. With us, he was laid aside. Engaged in great works, especially with that bulwark against heresy and misbelief, S. Athanasius, he was yet scarcely doing more for us than he would if he were not with us. Our Church has not known how to employ him. And, since this was so, it seemed as if a sharp sword were lying in its scabbard, or hung up in the sanctuary because there was no one to wield it. Here was one marked out as a great instrument of God, fitted through his whole training, of which, through a friendship of twenty-two years, I have seen at least some glimpses, to carry out some great design for the restoration of the Church; and now after he had begun that work among ourselves, in retirement—his work taken out of his hands, and not directly acting upon our Church. I do not mean of course, that he felt this, or that it influenced him. I speak of it only as a fact. He is gone unconscious (as all great instruments of God are), what he himself is. He has gone as a simple act of duty with no view for himself, placing himself entirely in God's hands. And such are they whom God employs. He seems then to me not so much gone from us, as transplanted into another part of the Vineyard, where the full energies of his powerful mind can be employed, which here they were not. And who knows what in the mysterious purposes of God's good providence may be the effect of such a person among them? You too have felt that it is what is unholy on both sides which keeps us apart. It is not what is true in the Roman system, against which the strong feeling of ordinary religious persons among us is directed, but against what is unholy in her practice. It is not anything in our Church which keeps them from acknowledging us, but heresy existing more or less within us. As each, by God's grace, grows in holiness, each Church will recognise, more and more, the presence of God's Holy Spirit in the other; and what now hinders the union of the Western Church will fall off. As the contest with unbelief increases, the Churches which have received and transmitted the substance of the Faith, as deposited in our common Creeds, must be on the same side with it. 'If one member suffer, the other members suffer with it', and so in the increasing health of one, others too will benefit. It is not as we would have it, but God's will be done! He brings about his own ends, as, in his sovereign wisdom, he sees to be best. One can see great ends to be brought about by this present sorrow; and the more so, because he, the chosen instrument of them, sees them not for himself. It is perhaps the greatest event which has happened since the communion of the Churches has been interrupted, that such a one, so formed in our Church, and the work of God's Spirit as dwelling within her, should be transplanted to theirs. If anything could open their eyes to what is good in us, or soften in us wrong prejudices against them, it would be the presence of such an one, nurtured and grown to such ripeness in our Church, and now removed to theirs. If we have by our misdeeds, (personal or other) 'sold our brother', God, we may trust, willeth thereby to 'preserve life'.[1]

It is possible to trace in the incidents of Newman's life before and after 1845 a developing theology of the Church, and especially of the policies and opinions required if the Church is to fulfil its nature and to express itself in all its traditional fullness. But what is especially interesting is how much of the ecclesiology of Coleridge and Maurice, and of other parts of English tradition, are to be found re-expressed within an unfamiliar and at times uncongenial setting.

In the *Apologia* Newman quite explicitly acknowledges the influences within the Church of England which had formed him. He gained his understanding of 'a visible Church' and of 'the historical nature of Revelation' from Butler,[2] of 'the doctrine of Tradition' from Hawkins,[3] and of 'the idea of the Church' as independent of the State from Whatley.[4] It was from Keble, 'my new master', that he gained his understanding of the sacramental

[1] H. P. Liddon, *The Life of E. B. Pusey* (1893), vol. 2, pp. 460–1.
[2] *Apo.*, p. 113.   [3] *Apo.*, p. 112.
[4] In 1825 (*K. Corr.*, p. 351); *Apo.*, p. 115; *A. W.*, p. 69.

nature of the Church (viz., 'the doctrine that material phenomena are both the types and the instruments of real things unseen').[1] This symbolic understanding of the Church was enriched by Newman's Evangelical grasp of the indwelling presence of Christ to the believer. It accounts for a certain rigour in his spiritual attitudes, which was not always to the taste of his fellow Roman Catholics, for his insistence that religion is realized in personal morality, and above all for his understanding of the Church as the ground of a *personal* encounter with Christ by means of its ordinances and sacraments. For Newman, as for Coleridge, the Church 'partakes of the reality it renders intelligible'; and it is not surprising that Newman should speak of the Romantic Movement as preparing the imagination of the nation for the reception of Catholic truth, and of the contribution of Coleridge in particular.[2]

As we have already seen, what Coleridge recovered and reintroduced into English religious thinking was the notion of the Church as the living symbol of Christ's presence, and that to speak of the Church as the Body of Christ was to do something more than to use metaphor, employ a figure of speech, or refer to a mere institution of the State; it was to see the Church as a medium between literal and metaphorical, and, in Coleridge's words, as 'partaking of the reality which it renders intelligible'.[3]

Newman read Coleridge for the first time in the spring of 1835, and was 'surprised how much I thought mine, is to be found there'.[4] The evidence does not so much establish that Coleridge had a direct influence on the formation of Newman's ideas as the existence of a common way of seeing the Church and of setting up the problem. It amounts more to a shared tradition and common vocabulary than to the influence directly of one mind upon the other.

What is immediately remarkable is the similarity between Newman's understanding of the term *idea* and its employment by Coleridge; although there is an important distinction, which I wish to discuss later.

Faced by the question: 'Assuming a Divine Revelation to have been given, how do we come to know it?' Newman frames his

---

[1] *Apo.*, p. 120.   [2] *Apo.*, p. 195.   [3] *C & S*, p. 230.
[4] At the instigation of T. D. Acland (1809–98), members of whose family had known Coleridge in Somerset (*Moz.*, ii. p. 39). See the Appendix: 'How much of Coleridge had Newman read?' (pp. 254–5, below).

answer in terms of images and ideas. These are the inevitable partial accounts of the Divine objects for which they stand.[1] This is what might be called Newman's principle of limitation: not only does it form the basis for the argument of the *Essay on Development*, but it is the foundation on which his *Idea of a University* and its structure rest. Here it is possible to detect the influence of Butler, that since our knowledge is always probable and therefore corrigible, certitude is not what we start from but what we grow into; but there is also the enduring influence of empiricist epistemology[2]—that our knowledge of the external world is in terms of the images formed by the senses.

The theory of language implicit in the *Essay on Development* is most explicitly stated in two unpublished letters—one to Dr. Charles Meynell of Oscott on Mansel's *Limits of Religious Thought* (20 December 1859), the other, entitled 'Letter on Matter and Spirit', is incomplete and is addressed to an unknown correspondent.[3]

Newman holds that the senses convey truth and reality but only up to a certain point—they betoken the unknown, they do not reveal it; and, acting as they do like figures of speech,[4] they can be pushed too far.

Accuracy is achieved, however, not by means of a reductive analysis to what is clearest and freest from ambiguity, but by

---

[1] 'If Christianity is a fact, and impresses an idea of itself on our minds and is a subject-matter of exercises of the reason, that idea will in course of time expand into a multitude of ideas, and aspects of ideas, connected and harmonious with one another, and in themselves determinate and immutable, as is the objective fact itself which is thus represented. It is a characteristic of our minds, that they cannot take an object in, which is submitted to them simply and integrally. We conceive by means of definition or description; whole objects do not create in the intellect whole ideas, but are, to use a mathematical phrase, thrown into series, into a number of statements, strengthening, interpreting, correcting each other, and with more or less exactness approximating, as they accumulate, to a perfect image. There is no other way of learning or of teaching. We cannot teach except by aspects or views, which are not identical with the thing itself which we are teaching.' (*Dev.*, p. 51.)
[2] See J. M. Cameron, 'Newman and the Empiricist Tradition', in J. Coulson and A. M. Allchin (eds.), *The Rediscovery of Newman* (1967) (*RN*), pp. 81–2: 'Revelation, then, is of an object that is given, known in us by an impression which is self-authenticating in the way the impressions of normal sense perception authenticate the reality of the objects to which they correspond.'
[3] 1 Sept. 1861 (L.M.S.)
[4] Newman quotes Milton 'darkness visible' as an example. L.M.S. (MSS.), pp. 15, 19, 28.

accepting the reciprocal action of the senses. Instead of a process of reductive abstraction therefore (of the kind recommended by Descartes and Bentham) we must adopt one of addition, allowing each sense to correct the range of the other. This is achieved by attending to all the rich complexity, ambiguity, and apparent breakdown of language, and by regarding this kind of 'hovering between images', as Coleridge calls it, as the essential condition for the communication of transcendent truth: 'Transcendent truths may admit of but partial communication to us and that under the images of earthly things . . . , [which] are not true representations in the fullness of their meaning. . .', yet there is a gradual approximation to the truth 'by the various images correcting each other'.

They do not complete an exhibition of the divine fact, but they do suggest certain portions of the whole. Though we speak of the Son & Word we have not thereby a clear and perfect picture of the second person of the Divine Trinity, but a broken outline and a faintly tinted picture.

Thus the various images we have about unseen things in theology modify each other as our Lord is both Pastor and agnus, priest and sacrifice.[1]

The connection between images and ideas is never systematically treated, but the illative sense to which Newman refers in the *Grammar of Assent* may perhaps be interpreted within this context as acting as a sixth or additional sense, which unifies the contradictory and separated images, and acts thereby as a power which realizes or forms ideas. Both Newman and Coleridge belong to a tradition which can still refer to general truths or ideas as if they were self-evident facts[2]; and in distinguishing images, concepts, or

[1] Summary of Newman on Mansel in the letter to Meynell, 20 Dec. 59.

[2] F. D. Maurice noticed this in 1838, as did Hort; and spoke of it as a kind of Platonism. But it was a Platonism derived ultimately from the Fathers and, in Coleridge's case, as they were mediated by the 17th cent. Anglican Divines, to whom Coleridge (so Hort considered) owed his understanding of the nature of the Church.

'Coleridge belonged to another generation than ours—one of which the business was to indicate the preciousness of truths as distinct from facts. . . . But I believe also that we are come upon an age in which truth without facts will be as impossible as facts without truth; and that the attempt to set up either exclusively must be conducted in quite a different spirit from that which animated either Coleridge or the good men of the preceding age. . . .' (Maurice, *Life* i. p. 251; Hort, *Coleridge*, Cambridge, 1856.)

propositions from ideas, for example, they will be found to be presupposing a more fundamental distinction between distinguishable parts and the antecedent unity in which those parts co-exist. As Newman remarks, the characteristic of what has life (as distinct from an object) is that 'it is a whole or nothing' [1]; and the argument of the *Grammar of Assent* is that although we respond to religious truths or ideas as a whole, our certitude of their truth is acquired gradually, step by step, and is not an immediate certainty. Such insight as we gain is the reward of virtue: as we grow into certitude, so the objects of devotion become as objects of sight.[2] In the words of Blake: 'the fool sees not the same tree as the wise man sees'.

In speaking of the Christian *idea*, of the *idea* of the Church, or of the Trinity, Newman is using the term in a way which is strikingly similar to Coleridge's use of it as a realizing principle to which we must first make a fiduciary response as a whole before we can fully understand its implications. We must, as it were, grow into an understanding of what an idea stands for [3]; and this language of ideas is intelligible only in terms of the community whose language it is and within which it has been formed and developed.

Thus in the *University Sermons* Newman speaks of 'how the great idea takes hold of a thousand minds by its living force', and of how 'centuries might pass without the formal expression of a truth, which had been all along the secret life of millions of faithful souls'.[4] And part of the foundation of the argument in the *Essay on Development* is that ideas have the power to live in the minds of men and require to be developed socially: 'the germination and maturation of some truth or apparent truth on a large mental field ... is carried on through and by means of communities of men ...; and it employs their minds as its instruments, and depends upon them, while it uses them'.

Newman, also, speaks of the distinguishing mark of an *idea* as being its ability to bring contrary and opposite aspects into

[1] *L.M.S.*, p. 36.
[2] *GA*, p. 43; *Diff.* i, pp. 237, 240. In a copy of the *Essay on Development* which Newman used for the revision of 1877, he wrote a note headed 'Development equals translation into a new language', and goes on to say, 'Revelation is not of *words*—from the derivation of the term it is addressed to the *sight*'.
[3] *AR*, p. 128. See above, chapter 2, p. 26.
[4] *O.U.S.*, pp. 316, 323.

harmony, so that 'no one term or proposition will serve to define it', since 'whole objects do not create in the intellect whole ideas, but are, to use a mathematical phrase, thrown into series, into a number of statements . . . approximating, as they accumulate, to a perfect image.'[1]

To Coleridge as to Newman it was in this sense that the Church was an idea, and our acquaintance with it was not with a simple series of concepts or propositions, but with an object[2] as indefinable, complex, and concrete as a living thing, and thus easily misrepresented by impatient demands for clear definition and simple recognition. Since, therefore, our response is both to a whole and to its component parts, the Church cannot be confined to one mode of presence: it will be both as diverse as the human personality, but as unified.

Yet for Newman as for Coleridge the problem is the same: it is to identify the society in which this language of ideas has been formed and developed: it is a *lingua communis*; and it is the community alone who can determine between true and false interpretations of ideas. For Newman as for Coleridge the way to certitude in matters of belief is not only linguistic (and therefore theological), but social (and therefore ecclesial).

Newman in common with Coleridge assumes that this verifying community is that of which Scripture speaks when it refers to the Church, that its existence is therefore implied in Revelation, and that it reveals the presence of Christ, or, in Pusey's words—'for Christ dwelleth in the Church, and it visibly exhibits Him'.[3] Christ is present to his Church, and His is the verifying power.

Where Newman and Coleridge differ is over the extent to which this Church of Christ is a tangible, visible, and identifiable empirical entity or, to use Newman's term, polity. When Coleridge speaks of the idea of the Church he seems to do so in order to distinguish the Church of Christ from its empirical polity as the Church-Establishment, or *Enclesia*; and his general discussion of *ideas* is often as if *ideas* were self-subsistent entities which were most effectively discussed in terms of themselves and without references to the realities for which they stood. Newman is, in this

---

[1] *Dev.*, pp. 32, 33, 36, 51.
[2] *O.U.S.*, pp. 330–1. cp. Coleridge, *Lit. Rem.* iii, p. 270.
[3] Pusey, MSS. Lectures on 'Types and Prophecies' (1836), cited by A. M. Allchin, *The Rediscovery of Newman* (1967), p. 73.

sense, a 'simpler' thinker. And although he admits that at an earlier stage when he was composing his *Lectures on the Prophetical Office* the Church was still for him 'a generalised idea',[1] the whole course of his development is towards a relating of ideas to their objects: the distinction between idea and object is made necessary by the limits of our language; and the contradictory qualities of ideas are purely linguistic in origin.[2]

This distinction between Newman and Coleridge was itself perceived by Newman and referred to in one of his University Sermons; and it is particularly revealed in their differing attitudes to conscience. For Coleridge conscience is a principle—it is Kant's practical reason. For Newman such a view is but natural religion: it is inadequate to the fact of Revelation. And it is in the very University Sermon in which Newman acknowledges a similarity between his views and Coleridge's that the difference is most clearly given between a philosophical and theological view of conscience: 'The philosopher aspires towards a divine *principle*; the Christian towards a Divine *Agent*.' And in the next paragraph Newman defines this as a 'method of personation' which is 'carried throughout the revealed system'.[3]

In 1836, Newman himself spoke of Coleridge as 'looking at the Church, sacraments, doctrines, etc., rather as symbols of a philosophy than as *truths*—as the mere accidental types of principles'.[4] In the early nineteenth century such an appeal to self-evidence was less likely to be questioned than it would be today; and Coleridge tended, as we have seen, to speak of ideas as 'of all realities the most real'. But, as Newman could see, this was to overlook the double function of religious language—that its formulations function both as theological definitions and as descriptions of religious facts: 'the notion and the reality assented to are represented by one and the same proposition, but serve as distinct interpretations of it'.[5] Otherwise we fail to distinguish theology

---

[1] *V.M.*, i. p. 260.
[2] 'The very word "contradiction" has reference to *language*, not to *fact*' (Newman, Letter to Meynell).
[3] *O.U.S.*, pp. 28–9.   [4] *Moz.*, ii. 156.
[5] *GA*, p. 91. Language performs a similar function in poetry. In speaking of the period which came to an end with Donne, T. S. Eliot says, 'the intellect was immediately at the tips of the senses. Sensation became word and word was sensation.' (*Selected Essays*, 1934, p. 210). And Dylan Thomas remarked: 'When I experience anything, I experience it as a thing and a word at the same time'.

from religion, explanation from what seeks explanation in order to survive and adapt itself to changing human needs. The facts of religion, because of their living and developing nature, require for their expression this essentially ambiguous language of metaphor and symbol: otherwise 'the intellect runs wild; but with the aid of symbols, as in algebra, it advances with precision and effect'.[1]

Simply to identify the Church, as Coleridge seems content to do, with an idea or symbol gives no means of verifying our religious descriptions; and it evades the question: 'On what grounds do we hold that there exists a reality to correspond to this language of ultimate concern?'[2] Although Newman accepts Coleridge's assumption that the mind embraces more than it can grasp, and that what it thus embraces can be identified in terms of ideas, an *idea* is not reality at its most real but an image of what acts upon us in the manner of objects of sense-perception.[3] Thus to speak of the Church as an *idea* and to leave it at that is to have nothing more substantial than a paper Church; since to start from an idea is—as it were—to start in mid-air; we must begin and end with what the *idea* or symbol is *of*: 'As God is one, so the impression which He gives us of Himself is one; it is not a thing of parts; it is not a system. . . . It is the vision of an object.'[4]

For Newman the starting point must be the objectified presence or 'Body' of Christ existing in the world. It is to be identified by what Newman calls his 'method of personation'—a method which would be as arbitrary as Coleridge's reliance on self-evident ideas if it were grounded on introspection. But although Newman always conceives our encounter with Christ as a 'personal visitation' and 'a personal Presence'[5]—an emphasis which undoubtedly derives from his Evangelical origins—the difference consists in his claim that Christ is not encountered directly or introspectively as an *alter ego*, but always through the Church as a public body.

In a sermon preached in 1826 which he regarded as 'one of the first, if not the first, declarations I made of High Church

[1] *GA*, p. 200.

[2] See above, chapter 2, pp. 20 ff.

[3] *O.U.S.*, p. 330: 'the ideas which we are granted of Divine Objects under the Gospel . . . answer to the Originals so far as this, that they are whole, indivisible, substantial, and may be called real, as being images of what is real.'

[4] ibid.; see also p. 340. Newman seems to be specifically refuting Coleridge's doctrine of symbolism in his University Sermon XV, para. 31, p. 338.

[5] *P.S.* II, pp. 221–2.

principles',[1] he said: 'Had it so pleased God, each Xtian mt [might] have been a Xtian to himself: alone—each Xtian might have been required to look only after his own personal salvation, without concerning himself in the welfare of others.'

Instead, we were formed by Christ into one body, which was 'to be an open public union ... [and] compacted with the visible Church as the human body is with the soul'.

Christ is therefore encountered primarily through outward and sacrament forms; and his grace is of its nature social and ecclesial. He is uniquely present to each Christian in that 'special mode of approaching Him'[2]—the Eucharistic assembly:

> He has shown us, that to come to Him for life is a literal bodily action; not a mere figure, not a mere movement of the heart towards Him, but an action of the visible limbs; not a mere secret faith, but a coming to church, a passing on along the aisle to His holy table. . . . If then a man does not seek Him where He is, there is no profit in seeking Him where He is not. What is the good of sitting at home seeking Him, when His Presence is in the Holy Eucharist?[3]

Newman returns to develop this point in an important sermon on 'The Duty of Public Worship':

> It has been the great design of Christ to connect all His followers into one, and to secure this, He has lodged His blessings in the body collectively to oblige them to meet *together* if they would gain grace each for himself. *The body is the first thing and each member in particular the second* [my italics]. The body is not made up of individual Christians, but each Christian has been made such in his turn by being taken into the body.

We must pray *with* others, and not like the Pharisees, *among* others, and it is among the dangers of the age to forget that 'public confession as well as secret faith is a Christian's duty'.[4]

If the precondition for Christ's indwelling is the bodily act of placing ourselves within the people of God as they offer the Eucharist, then worship becomes as fundamental a note of the

[1] 'On the One Catholic and Apostolic Church', 19 Nov. 1826. (MS. Sermon 157.) Newman associates this declaration with a reference to an earlier sermon, 'On the use of the Visible Church', 4 Dec. 1825 (MS. Sermon 121.)
[2] *P.S.* II, p. 144.
[3] *P.S.* VII, p. 149 (see also MS. Sermon 213, p. 1).
[4] MS. Sermon 213, pp. 7, 16, 17, 22. This MS. has been very thoroughly worked over, and the sermon was preached in 1829, 1834 (twice), 1836; and at Littlemore 15 May 1842.

Church as its prophetical and episcopal tradition[1]; and the Church's establishment as a visible polity becomes essential for its effective acts of worship. Thus it is the Church which is visible, not Christ, 'whose more perfect and powerful presence which we now enjoy, being invisible, can be discerned and used by faith only'; but 'what is seen, is not the whole of the Church, but the visible part of it'.[2]

Newman, therefore, will only accept a distinction, not a dichotomy, between the visible and invisible Church; and Coleridge's analogy of the olive and the vine is unacceptable because it deliberately denies the possibility of that reciprocal relationship which presupposes the invisible Church to be hidden within the visible Church in the same way as Revelation is 'a doctrine lying hid in language'.[3] What the Church is now, so was Christ's material body when he was on earth: 'it is that which we must approach to gain good from him'; but it is also 'a body of humiliation, almost provoking insult and profaneness'; since Christ himself 'was a hidden Saviour' who might be approached 'without due reverence and fear'.[4] Yet this does not make of outward ordinances, 'mere forms', since 'the *inward* principle' which is 'the only true fruit of religion . . . is only gained by *outward* observances; certain outward acts are the *means* by which we become inwardly pure'.[5] The root is Evangelical, but is an Evangelicalism modified and developed by Butler—as Newman himself admits in the *Apologia*. Butler accepts the same relation between internal and external religion,[6] and speaks of the visible government, 'which God exercises over the world', as being 'by the instrumentality and mediation of others'.[7] Thus the visible Church is 'the condition of the existence of the Invisible Church',[8] which it gradually moulds and matures.[9]

It is the emphasis upon the reciprocal interdependence of the visible and invisible Church that is not only an outstanding early feature in Newman's theology of the Church, but it is the explanation for Newman's indifference to Coleridge's distinction between

---

[1] By worship 'we realize the invisible' (*P.S.* III, p. 250).
[2] *Jfc.*, p. 214, *S.V.O.*, p. 57.   [3] *Tract* 73, p. 8.   [4] *P.S.* IV, pp. 249–50.
[5] *MS. Sermon* 156, p. 4.
[6] 'In what external manner this internal worship is to be expressed, is a matter of pure revealed command'. Joseph Butler, *The Analogy of Religion* (1834), pp. 173–4.
[7] ibid., p. 208.   [8] *Tract* 11, p. 2.   [9] *P.S.* III, p. 240.

the idea of the Church Catholic and its visible manifestation in the Established Church. To Newman the invisible and visible Church are like the unilluminated and illuminated sides of the same object [1]; and he would have objected to Coleridge's distinction on two grounds. Epistemologically, he would have been unable to accept a distinction between an idea and its corresponding object of so elaborate a kind as to make for a radical dichotomy between the idea of the Church and its reality, here and now, warts and all. [2]

But a further factor reinforced his unwillingness to accept Coleridge's dichotomy; and that was the influence of his Patristic studies. Evidence has recently been published that Newman attended the *Lectures on Types and Prophecies* of the Old Testament given by Pusey in 1836. [3] In these lectures Pusey speaks in commendation of the practice of the Fathers who 'fearlessly blend the sign and the thing signified, and speak of the reality under the terms under which it was set forth'. [4] Pusey is describing the nature of the sacramental form by which God is revealed in scripture and tradition; and his discussion of the relationship of type to archetype not only reminds us of a similar and later discussion by Newman in his University Sermon XV, but bears upon the distinction between the idea (or archetype) of the Church and its local empirical reality (or type). Pusey asserts that God has created 'a sort of sacramental union between the type and the archetype', such that the type is meaningful only to the extent that it expresses the archetype, and the archetype can be grasped only by means of its embodiment within the type. [5]

Pusey applies this principle to 'the figurative language of Holy Scripture', which cannot therefore without loss, or what Pusey calls 'evaporation', [6] be translated into clearer or more abstract

[1] See his distinction between Revelation and Mystery in *Tract* 73, p. 9.

[2] cp. his treatment of Coleridge's celebrated distinction between Reason and Understanding. In a letter to Blachford (11 March 1886) Newman speaks of the distinction as 'words which (Then as now) I could not understand'; and he refers to his dismissal of the distinction in *Stray Essays*, 1890, pp. 94–5, 102, where he speaks of the fallacy of arguing with two contrary views of reason and using 'one of them to refute the other'. It is more than probable that Newman would have used Ockham's razor in similar fashion on the distinction between the *Ecclesia* and the *Enclesia*.

[3] Allchin, 'The Theological Vision of the Oxford Movement,' in *The Rediscovery of Newman*, p. 52, note 2.

[4] ibid., p. 72.   [5] ibid., p. 69.

[6] ibid., p. 70. 'evaporation' is the term used by Coleridge (*AR*, p. 200). See above, chapter 2, p. 34.

terms: 'Men think they gain in clearness; but they lose in depth; they would employ definite terms, in order to comprehend that which is infinite!'[1] The effect is to 'strip the type of that whereby it resembled the archetype—that in it which was divine'.[2]

In spite of reservations about the interpretation of Scripture, which might have prevented him from accepting this account of religious language without important modifications, what Newman would certainly have accepted was the symbolic functioning of the Church which is implied. In the *Apologia* he speaks of his studies in the Fathers as being responsible for his first becoming acquainted with the view that 'Holy Church in her sacraments and her hierarchical appointments will remain, even to the end of the world, only a symbol of those heavenly facts which fill eternity'.[3] And by symbol Newman means what Coleridge had meant when he spoke of the symbol's function as to partake of the reality it had rendered intelligible, or what Pusey means when he speaks of the fearless blending by the Fathers of the sign and the thing signified.

In essentials Newman's understanding of the symbolic function of the Church is closely akin to Coleridge's. She has 'to act out what she says she is'[4]; and for us to partake of the reality the Church renders intelligible, we must be prepared to act out the functions she prescribes in order to advance our understanding.[5] The sacraments are 'promises on our part to perform' by which 'we make an engagement to serve God'[6]: we must offer the Eucharist to understand what it signifies.

From Newman's distinctively empirical conception of the Church in its given form, here and now, as a symbolic function or performative utterance of the presence of Christ arises that problem to which he devoted the rest of his life—how to reconcile the abuses of the external forms to the inward principles. But the circumstances in which the conception originated provided him with the criterion for its solution—to what extent was he standing within the continuing tradition of the Church of the Fathers? Having rejected Coleridge's convenient dichotomy between the

---

[1] ibid., p. 71.   [2] ibid., the unpublished MS. p. 24.
[3] *Apo.*, p. 128.   [4] *Diff.* i. p. 190.
[5] In speaking of the rites and ceremonies of the Church, Newman defines them as 'usages [which] are symbols of common, not individual opinions, and more or less involve the doctrines they symbolise'. ('Holy Scripture in its relation to the Catholic Creed', September, 1838, in *D.A.*, pp. 241–2.)
[6] MS. Lecture 4 'On the Sacraments' Oratory (156) A.50.3.

idea of the Catholic Church and the empirical reality of the Church-Establishment (with their reciprocal relationship grounded on nothing firmer than the claim that it was self-evident) Newman and the chief members of the Oxford Movement sought within the Church-Establishment for the signs which would establish the evidence for a living link with the Apostolic Church.

Newman's Evangelical origins had prepared him to be rightly sensitive to what he called this double aspect of the Church—to the personal disclosure of Christ to his people, and yet to the superstitions and tyrannies by which this disclosure was obscured. The existence of the life-giving Christian idea was to be sought for within existing communities of Christians; and the problem was to establish the criteria whose present acceptance established not only the conformity of the present with the past, but the guarantee that those promises which Christ had made to the Church he founded were actively continued within the Church of England.

As R. W. Church pointed out, the choice in fact would become one between the Church of England with its 'smug parsons', and the Church of Rome 'with its strange unscriptural doctrines'. But this is to anticipate, since the criterion which Newman adopted— the argument from Tradition as expressed in the canon of Vincent of Lérins—at first seemed to rule out Rome as an alternative to the Church of England. Rome, by adding to the faith, had failed to fulfil the prescriptions of the canon—that its teachings should be what was believed everywhere, always, and by all (*quod ubique, quod semper, quod ab omnibus creditum est*).

Newman begins by applying the Vincentian canon to the doctrine and practice of the Church of England in a purely historical and unmodified sense; and the history of the Oxford Movement to 1841 is the history of putting this claim to the test. What at this stage was being sought for was evidence of a sufficient degree of self-determination within the Church of England for it to be clearly apparent that these were the conditions which its teaching claimed to fulfil, and which its members were required to conform to.

Newman's purpose in publishing *Tract XC* was to put the Vincentian canon to the test; and the collision between the Tractarians and the main body of the Church of England occurred when the issues between them became focussed into a single question, the answer to which clearly disclosed the basic theological implications at issue. This was what the publication of *Tract XC* achieved, and the question it put was—are the Thirty-nine Articles 'patient but not ambitious of a Catholic interpretation'?[1]

The Tract was welcomed by men like Palmer of Worcester, who saw it as shaking people out of their reception 'of *traditionary interpretations* which impose human opinions as little less than articles of faith'; and Palmer hoped that it would lead to a 'really *critical* system of interpreting the Articles'.[2]

Here in germ is the very principle of the *Essay on the Development of Doctrine*: its reception and rejection by the majority of the bishops was seen by Newman as an empirical testing of the claims of the Church of England to be Catholic. His position was opposed by those, of whom Maurice is a characteristic spokesman, who clung 'even more tenaciously than ever to the *words* of our creeds and prayers', and wished to see 'nothing changed in our liturgical statements'.[3] This standpoint is particularly well caught by R. W. Church in his obituary notice of Maurice, whom he speaks of as 'ever striving, not so much to find new truths as to find the heart and core of old ones, the truth of the truth, the inner life and significance of the *letter*, of which he [Maurice] was always loth to refuse the traditional form'.[4]

I have italicized *words* and *letter* in order to emphasize how radically opposite to this point of view is Newman's argument in *Tract XC*, implying as it does the necessity to separate doctrine from its expressions, which are conditioned by particular circumstances. These, as in the case of the Thirty-nine Articles, may be of a polemical nature; and the Church must have the authority at all times to be able to interpret its formularies. Furthermore, Newman held that, since the Church of England claimed to be Catholic, its interpretations of its formularies should conform to the requirements of the Vincentian canon and show themselves to be universalizable.

In the circumstances of the time Newman's formulation of the question made his move to Rome inevitable, since he was to find that directly he proposed the Vincentian canon in *Tract XC* as the *type* of verification, he was met by 'a present, living, and energetic heterodoxy' which 'impelled' him to Rome,[5] by refusing 'the

[1] *K. Corr.*, p. 72.   [2] ibid., p. 77.
[3] *Life*, ii, pp. 367–8 (my italics).   [4] *Occasional Papers*, II, p. 323.
[5] *S.S.D.*, p. 341.

liberty of teaching in the Church of England the *semper, ubique, et ab omnibus* of the Catholic Religion'.[1] The difficulty was made critical when 'the Bishops and the people of my Church' not only 'rejected primitive Catholic doctrine', but 'tried to eject from their communion all who held it'.[2]

The rejection by his Church of the Vincentian canon obliged Newman to consider three further questions: was the Church of England a Church or merely the expression of national sentiment[3]; was it sufficient to apply the Vincentian canon in a purely historical sense, and was there not perhaps a deeper issue than that of 'Apostolicity versus Catholicity'[4]; and was it right to persist in claiming that Rome had perverted the faith by adding to it?

To take the first question. It was implicit in a sacramental conception of the Church that it should be self-determining—even Coleridge in his use of the analogy of the olive and vine implies that the *Ecclesia* (or olive) is 'not the same plant as the vine' (or Church-Establishment) and must preserve an essential integrity. And some ten years after the events of *Tract XC* we find Newman arguing in *Difficulties of Anglicans* along the following lines: Since the sacramental character of the Church obliges it to function as a person[5] and to manifest the unity of its divine personality, then it must be kept distinct from the State, since both Church and State are distinguished in form from each other by virtue of their each having a different purpose.[6]

The purpose of the Church is 'the propagation of the truth'; that of the State to secure the well-being of its citizens.[7]

The Church must be sovereign, self-sustaining, self-governing in order that it may secure its truth to Christ,[8] and where the Church and State are identified and improperly distinguished the Church falls under the power of the State, and truth and well-being become identified. The purpose of the Church then becomes to promote a 'unity of sentiment'[9]—this was Constantine's

---

[1] This statement is taken from Newman's Preface of 1877 to the republication of *Tract XC* in *V.M.* ii, p. 265.

[2] *Apo.*, p. 250.   [3] *Diff.* i, p. 17.   [4] *Apo.*, p. 204.

[5] *Diff.* i, p. 6.   [6] ibid., p. 177.

[7] ibid., pp. 166-7. cp. his argument in 'Primitive Christianity' that too close a union of Church and State involves a preference for social peace at the expense of truth. (*H.S.* i, pp. 375-6.)

[8] ibid., pp. 151, 158, 173. 'He lodged the security of His truth in the very fact of its Catholicity' (p. 158).

[9] ibid., p. 335.

expressed aim, and it was only prevented by the power of the Church at the time to determine itself and its teachings. Otherwise the Church exists solely to express national sentiment[1] and becomes, as we should now say, an ideology rather than the expression or 'oracle'[2] of the truths of Divine revelation.

The question thus arises can a national Church be in possession of the sacraments?[3] Is it not impeded from being their channel?[4]

Newman interprets the Oxford Movement as an attempt to develop the Establishment towards a due separation of powers. Its 'idea or first principle' was therefore 'ecclesiastical liberty'[5]— it aimed at making the Church of England a Church in the sense already defined, and it relied for this achievement not upon the Establishment but upon the people,[6] and upon restoring 'the connection, at present broken, between bishops and people', since it is in this union that the 'great idea of the Church' consists.[7]

This last part of the argument is of great importance for an understanding of Newman's idea of the Church as being what, nowadays, we should call the whole people of God. It was a conception which was not only from the Anglican point of view politically 'radical',[8] as Newman himself confessed but from the current Roman point of view almost heretical, and in practice wholly unacceptable.

In a later summary of these arguments in the *Apologia* Newman admitted that they counted against the Church of England as then constituted, but it would be a gross error to see them as implying the rejection of the traditions which I have been describing. Newman himself saw them as being duly fulfilled. What he does reject is the claim that there can be a *via media* between Catholicism and Protestantism, and that the Church of England is that *via media*. He does so on the grounds that the *via media* stands for no verifiable institution. But, as he ruefully admits, 'it is not at all easy (humanly speaking) to wind up an Englishman to a dogmatic level'. Newman proceeds to show how it was done by, in his own words, bringing us continually back from doctrine to history, and from speculation to fact. To the question, was the Church of

---

[1] ibid., p. 17.
[2] cp. *Apo.*, p. 395, and the discussion below in chapter 9 (i), *Context of a Common Culture.*
[3] *Diff.* i, 68–9, 144, 188.   [4] ibid., 114.   [5] ibid., 89.
[6] ibid., 52–3.   [7] ibid., 91.   [8] *Moz.* i, p. 450.

England what it claimed to be—the *via media*?—Newman opposed the facts. It did not stand the test of events. It did not work. And he instanced the principles conceded by the establishment of the Jerusalem Bishopric in 1841. The *via media* was a paper religion; it had 'slept in libraries' and was 'the substitution of infancy for manhood'. What the behaviour of the Church of England testified to instead was 'a present, living and energetic heterodoxy'.[1]

It was in the light of this rejection that Newman came to see the issue as whether the Church of England had divided itself 'from the consent of the universality and antiquity of the Catholic Church'.[2] The issue was not, as he had originally thought, that of 'Apostolicity versus Catholicity', but whether a local Church was acting in conformity not only with antiquity but also with the whole Church throughout the world. Thus the correct application of the Vincentian canon is both terrestrial and chronological.[3] And this is how Newman came to be haunted by the phrase from St. Augustine—'securus judicat orbis terrarum'.[4]

This additional requirement placed even greater stress upon the need of the Church to have a power of self-determination; but it also raised a further and more alarming question. It seemed that Rome was the only Church which accepted the application of the Vincentian canon to its teachings and practice—but that Rome permitted the canon to be applied only in terms of its development, or what Newman had called its corruptions or additions.

This obliges Newman to take a second look at Rome, and to ask himself if he has mistaken additions and corruptions for developments of doctrine which were not only inevitable but were implied in Revelation. Had the difference between the Church of the Fathers and the Roman Church of today to be accounted for in terms of a development of doctrine?

Here is the question which led Newman to propound 'the hypothesis to account for a difficulty',[5] which is the starting point

---

[1] *Apo.*, p. 241.
[2] Vincent of Lérins, *Tract on Heresy*, chapters 27–34, cited in *H.S.* i, p. 390.
[3] Newman cites Vincent on what is meant by the *depositum fidei* as follows: '[It is] a thing not of wit, but of learning; not of private assumption, but of public tradition; a thing brought to thee, not brought forth of thee; wherein thou must not be an author, but a keeper; not a beginner, but a follower; not a leader, but an observer' (op. cit., p. 388).
[4] *Apo.*, p. 212.
[5] *Dev.*, p. 28.

of his *Essay on the Development of Christian Doctrine.*[1] Further-more, if the development of doctrine is inevitable and intended in Revelation, then there must also be intended an authority competent to distinguish true from false development.[2]

These are the assumptions upon which the *Essay on Development* is based. What is especially interesting for our purposes is how the theory of religious language which Newman shares with English tradition provides him with the vocabulary for his investigation. Christian doctrine is, as it were, the *lingua communis* of the Church; its language of ideas is verified by its placing within the community which was formed by Christ to receive his teaching and to develop its consequences. Our first acquaintance with this community is with the ideas associated with it; and our closer acquaintance comes as we become concerned to understand the fuller implications, and to distinguish true from false interpretations. Our growth in understanding the implications of Christ's Revelation is theological (because linguistic) and ecclesial (because we have to relate our ideas of Christ's truth to the community within whose traditions these ideas continue to live and fructify).

Newman's concern with authority is therefore theological; and his conception of that authority is deeply and widely social.[3] By definition, it cannot be merely authoritarian, since it is 'an undeniable fact that the Church, when purest and when most powerful, *has* depended for its influence on its consideration with the many'. Thus the question he has to resolve is how the Church may be 'in favour with all the people without any subserviency to them'.[4]

(ii) *The crucial criticism*

The crucial criticism which Newman's idea of the Church has to face is that the degree of self-determination it requires is in fact

---

[1] 'that the increase and expansion of the Christian Creed and Ritual, and the variations which have attended the process in the case of individual writers and Churches, are the necessary attendants on any philosophy or polity which takes possession of the intellect and heart, and has had any wide or extended dominion; that, from the nature of the human mind, time is necessary for the full comprehension and perfection of great ideas; and that the highest and most wonderful truths, though communicated to the world once for all by inspired teachers, could not be comprehended all at once by the recipients, but, as being received and transmitted by minds not inspired and through media which were human, have required only the longer time and deeper thought for their full elucidation. This may be called the *Theory of Development of Doctrine.*' (ibid.)

[2] *Dev.*, pp. 81–2.   [3] *Dev.*, pp. 90, 229.   [4] *H.S.* i, 342, 348.

gained at the expense of more fundamental qualities, since it makes inevitable the Church's degeneration into an imposed system.

This is what Coleridge had anticipated, when he spoke of the first and fundamental apostasy of the Church as occurring when its powers of self-determination were entrusted to a clerical caste of professional theologians and Church rulers. And the disease consisted in divorcing the verifying or sacramental function of the Church from its context within what alone could give it life and reality—the particular circumstances and culture of the nation. Was not Newman's idea of the Church—with its apparently exclusive concern for verification—a disembodied truth and a dangerous abstraction? And how is what appears inevitably to produce a theological system imposed by a priestly caste able to mediate the *personal* presence of Christ to the believer?

This particular charge of what was in general termed 'Romanism' is returned to, time and time again, by Newman's critics. It is to be found specifically expressed by F. D. Maurice, by Kingsley in his attack upon Newman's integrity which provoked the *Apologia*, and by Gladstone in his examination of the political consequences of the First Vatican Council. And nothing more exactly demonstrates Newman's capacity to function as the bridge between the Church he left and the Church he joined than the importance he attached to the substance of these criticisms; it is a concern which grows rather than diminishes.

I propose to begin with Maurice's criticisms of Newman's idea of the Church as expressed in the *Essay on Development*. These were published in the form of a lengthy Preface to Maurice's Lectures on the Epistle to the Hebrews in 1846.[1]

Both Maurice and Newman agree that 'the very idea of revelation implies a present informant and guide, and that an infallible one'.[2] Maurice agrees with Newman that 'we need an authority the same in kind with that which the first ages had', and 'I admit that this personal authority must be infallible—that it must be One'. For Maurice this 'unseen God is actually ruling over men', and we gain our leading ideas of him from the Bible: 'He whom the Bible proclaims as the true King is actually reigning over us'.[3]

Newman's objection is to be found in these words: 'We are told

[1] F. D. Maurice, *Lectures on the Epistle to the Hebrews* (1846). (*H.*)
[2] *Dev.*, p. 81.
[3] *H.*, pp. xxxiii, xxxvi, cxxv.

that God has spoken. Where? In a book? We have tried it and it disappoints.'[1]

Maurice's reply is to pose the counter-assertion; and he asks whether

there be not an antecedent probability that [the Scriptures] would unfold that primary idea which he [Newman] needs and yet denounces men for venturing to seek; that it would explain that law, or method of development, which, he says, it exhibits so remarkably; and so that it would save us from the monstrous contradiction of looking into the history itself for that with which it is to be compared, and by which it is to be judged.[2]

The text of the first edition of the *Essay on Development* which Maurice used confirms the claim I have already made that it is Newman's empiricist epistemology as much as any more theological cause that prevents him from accepting this view of Scripture:

It may be objected that inspired documents, such as the Holy Scriptures, at once determine its doctrine without further trouble. But they were intended to create an idea, and that idea is not in the sacred text, but in the mind of the reader.

Although this is modified in later editions, Newman stands by the consequences:

and the question is whether those ideas which the letter conveys from writer to reader, reach the reader at once in their completeness and accuracy on his first perception of them, or whether they open out in his intellect and grow to perfection in the course of time.[3]

Hence Newman's conclusion that the Scriptures were never intended to teach doctrine, only to prove it[4] and that it is the formularies of the Church which teach us what to believe: 'A revelation is not given, if there be no authority to decide what it is that is given.'[5] But to appeal to the authority of the Church is to be confronted by a difficulty—'the want of accord between the early and the late aspects of Christianity'. And the theory of

[1] *Dev.*, p. 81.   [2] *H.*, p. xxvi.
[3] Chapter II, sect. 2 (*Dev.*, p. 52).
[4] *Apo.*, p. 112.   [5] *Dev.*, p. 82.

development was Newman's hypothesis, as we have seen, to account for this difficulty.[1]

Arguments and proofs based upon the evaluation of a historical development must accept the logical possibility of empirical refutation—an objection Newman never denied; and although Maurice felt that the *Essay on Development* should be welcomed as repudiating the more extreme scepticism of the *Lectures on the Prophetical Office*, which 'identified faith with the willing endurance of doubt and confusion',[2] in a letter written whilst he was preparing his analysis, he was not so hopeful: Such a solution as Newman proposed could only be propounded by one for whom the truth meant 'probable security as to the notions we have upon certain subjects'; and in despair of finding truth, such people are 'willing to put up with a plausible substitute for it. . . . They want the living God, and they fly to the fiction of ecclesiastical authority.'[3]

'Once adopt Mr. Newman's hypothesis,' he says in the Preface to his Lectures, 'and the belief of this living Divine Government is at an end. He finds an established system, not indeed a dead system, but a living one.' Romanism substitutes a system for the living presence of God, and its members work 'as parts of a system' rather than 'as the servants of the living God'.[4]

The essential Christian idea is 'distinctly and precisely set forth' in the Epistle to the Hebrews. It rests upon the assertion that 'God hath spoken to us by a Son'. And if we read the Bible as a whole, we shall discover that 'the text seems . . . brighter and clearer than the comment'; and instead of the Fathers and the Schoolmen helping us to understand the Bible, the Bible will help us to understand them. We must follow Luther, who cut through the questions of the Schoolmen, 'by calling upon men to believe in a Person'. Can Newman seriously suggest that when our Lord said 'I came to bear witness of the Truth', He meant 'I came to bear witness of certain opinions'?[5]

---

[1] In seeking to account for the complex and often contradictory history of the doctrine and worship of Christianity in terms of the development of the Christian idea, Newman holds that no aspect is deep enough to exhaust the contents of such an idea, 'no one term or proposition will serve to define it' (*Dev.*, p. 33). 'The maintenance of the original type' must be discerned, therefore, amidst the process of development (*Dev.*, p. 192).

[2] *H.*, p. xxxii.   [3] *Life* i, pp. 423–4.   [4] *H.*, p. xlii, xxxvii.

[5] *H.*, pp. lvii, lxxx, lxxxiii, xc.

For Maurice, therefore, Newman substituted belief in opinions for faith in a Person; and he was obliged to argue accordingly for 'a human Developing Authority to whom He [Christ] has committed his government'.[1] This is to give the Church a false Centre.[2] This view of the Church Maurice ascribes to the influence of 'practical, business-like Latin minds' who find it difficult to conceive 'the idea of Christianity apart from a society'. Such minds can only grasp an idea if it is 'embodied'.[3] Under such influences the mistake is made of supposing that we must seek for the Church rather than accept its presence already in our midst, 'to be content, if we can, to dwell in a house not made with hands, without caring to raise one'.[4] And to Newman's celebrated passage in which he compares the Roman Church of his day to the Christianity of the fifth and sixth centuries, Maurice replies with a brilliant parody:

If then there be any society now existing in the world which has substituted another centre for this living invisible Centre by which Christians were livingly bound together in the fourth century; if the effect of that substitution has been that the body is no longer one for all nations and languages; that it has become a Latin Church, ruled over by a Latin Sovereign; if the further effect has been to make all who join this society feel that they belong to a Catholic system, rather than that they are parts of a living body under the governance of a living Head; then . . . such corruptions would have long ago extinguished the body in which they dwell, if it had not pleased God to raise up a protest against the pseudo Catholic centre, for the real one. . . .[5]

In Maurice's *Theological Essays*, we again find the Church described as 'a house not made with hands, eternal in the heavens',[6] and it is a key-note of Maurice's writings that the Church cannot be 'formed', in the Tractarian sense, or sought for, in the sense attributed to Newman. As long as we think we can form or select Churches, 'we cannot believe that we do not choose Him, but that he chooses us and sends us to bear witness'.[7] The Church is an organism, because it is the In-Dwelling of Christ;[8] and the disease

[1] *H.*, p. xcviii.
[2] F. D. Maurice, *Theological Essays* (1871), p. 404. (*TE*.)
[3] *H.*, p. xcv.   [4] *H.*, p. cxxii.
[5] *H.*, p. lxi. Cp. Newman, *Dev.*, pp. 299–300.
[6] *TE*, p. 283.   [7] *Life* ii, p. 300.
[8] The Church as the Divine In-Dwelling is spoken of as such in *Theological Essays* (pp. 243, 386, 398), *Kingdom of Christ* (*KC* II, p. 146), and in *Religions of the World* (pp. 233, 241–2).

of Romanism is to substitute a system of divinity and of international rule for what must be localized and, therefore, national in order to be effective; because, although the principle of the Catholic Church is that of a 'direct, real and practical union between men and their Lord', it is a relationship 'yet imperfectly understood'; and it requires for its realization the mutual interaction of Church and Nation.[1] Romanism arises from the undervaluing of the supernatural In-Dwelling of Christ within his Church, and 'every pretension of the Church, which has been felt as tyrannical and intolerable by the inward conscience and reason of mankind, has arisen from this low and imperfect view of its own position!'[2] The consequent paradox is that in magnifying the claims of the Church to rule, Romanists have undervalued it; and in glorifying these claims, they have disparaged the State and civil order. This is because they have not believed that 'Christ came into the world to regenerate all human society'. Regeneration is social as well as individual.[3]

It is from this standpoint that Maurice's criticism of Newman's theory of development is most telling. God reveals himself not merely in the Church, but in history: 'Oftentimes it would not be so much by the agency of men as by fearful historical crises, that He would make His purposes evident and confound the counterfeits of them.'[4] Here is exemplified not only Maurice's value as a critic of Newman's idea of the Church, but his continuing relevance as a theologian, viz., his insistence that Christ is the Lord of both Church and World, and that they are both aspects of the one in-dwelling presence. Thus to be exclusively preoccupied with the Church—as he thought the Tractarians advocated and the Romans practised—was to turn men's minds back from the present to the past, back from the realities of the human problems of industrial England to the unrealities of the Schoolmen and other old half-forgotten things. Such preoccupations turned the Church into a world, and abandoned the everyday world to the rule of the devil. Thus when Newman speaks of the doctrine of Purgatory as being necessary to provide a sufficient motive for the gaining of members required for effective work in the missions in China, Africa, or 'our great towns', Maurice's biting comment is: 'There is too

---

[1] *KC* II, pp. 308; 146; 306.   [2] *TE*, p. 243.
[3] *TE*, pp. 245, 248.   [4] *H.*, p. xl.

much truth left in our English character, soiled as it is, for such advice as this.'[1]

The structure of Newman's theory of the development of doctrine within the Church is complex and subtle, and Maurice dealt with it more justly than did most of his contemporaries. But when Newman spoke of the development of ideas he meant neither syllogistic inference nor arbitrary papal imposition. Maurice feared that the theory 'would identify development and accumulation'. Were this the case, then the result would be an elaborate deductive system for which a computer rather than a human spirit would seem to be the appropriate theological tool. For Newman, however, ideas are developed *socially*.[2] Thus his question is not where is the appropriate *system*, but where is the appropriate *community* of ideas. And the passage parodied by Maurice is an attempt to prescribe the characteristics of that community which fulfils the Vincentian canon, *quod ubique, quod semper, quod ab omnibus*.[3]

In 1845 Newman's view is still at the level of a hypothesis; it required many more years for him to deal successfully with the questions it raised. How, for example, before a doctrine is defined, is the mind of the Church to be discovered? This question Newman attempted to answer in his essay *On Consulting the Faithful in Matters of Doctrine* in 1859.

The heart of Newman's contention is that the Church's existence as a living and developing polity is essential to the intelligible transmission of Christian truth; and the Christian idea must be thus embodied not, as Maurice suggested, because Latin minds are too material, but because all effective religious teaching is by means of such embodiments, that is, within communities. This argument Newman was to develop in the *Idea of a University*; and it is interesting that it was this aspect of his theory of development which most appealed to Matthew Arnold, when he discussed it in *St. Paul and Protestantism*.[4]

'It is not an idea, or abstract notion, or quality, but a being only, which is capable of life and action, of happiness and misery', wrote Bishop Joseph Butler;[5] and both Maurice and Newman are united

---

[1] *Dev.*, p. 368; *H.*, p. cxix.
[2] 'on a large mental field ... and through and by means of communities of men and their leaders and guides'. (*Dev.*, p. 36.)
[3] *Dev.*, p. 10.
[4] M. Arnold, *St. Paul and Protestantism* (1870), pp. 144 f.
[5] Joseph Butler, *Dissertations*, I, 'Of Personal Identity', op. cit., p. 302.

in recognizing this as the starting point. I wish to argue that, with the passage of years and in the light of his experience as a Roman Catholic, Newman expressed his idea of the Church and the conception of doctrinal development it involved less in terms of *ideas* and increasingly in terms of persons and communities, and of their functions.[1] The problem of how papal authority might be reconciled with *personal* freedom and to the very nature of the Church as the *personal* In-Dwelling of Christ was one that occupied Newman for the rest of his life. Far from denying that the Church was that in-dwelling presence, he expressed it in memorable terms in the Parochial Sermons; and it is this understanding that he shares so fully with Maurice. A further question remained, however: how ought we to describe that presence of Christ to his Church; and what is the principle by which the Church, as transmitting that presence, is duly ordered and regulated? It was not until 1877 that Newman felt able to publish his answer.

Maurice ends his analysis of Newman's theory with a tribute which testifies not only to Maurice's integrity as a man, but to his ability to respond intuitively to something to which his arguments may not have done sufficient justice:

I think we shall miss the lesson, the humbling and therefore the useful lesson, which Mr. Newman may teach us, if we busy ourselves in seeking excuses for condemning him. *He finds the barriers he thought would preserve us from Rationalism insufficient.* [My italics.] Will a mere belief in the Fathers, or in Succession, avail to answer the question, 'Is GOD really among us or no?' Will Sacraments avail, if we look at them apart from Him, if they do not testify of His presence? The Rationalist has gone beneath all visible things, and has asked what is at the ground of them. If we can ... give the answer, ... our own ground will be what it has ever been, but we shall *know* that we are standing on the Rock of Ages.[2]

Maurice is with Coleridge—content to stand within received opinions and institutions, and to respond to the truth they safeguard. Newman moves closer to Bentham by asking of what we accept why it is true, and how we become certain of its truth.

[1] When he came to revise the first edition of the *Essay on Development* for republication in 1877, Newman adds to the passage (*Dev.*, p. 36) 'it is carried on through individuals and bodies of men; it employs their minds as instruments' the strengthening phrase 'through and by means of communities of men'; and the phrase 'on a large mental field' is also added. (Annotated copy in the Oratory library.)
[2] *H.*, p. cxxviii.

Maurice conceived the difference between them to be one in religion and about what is revelation—these are the grounds of his controversy with Mansel in 1859 and of his continuing criticism of Newman. But it is possible to argue that such differences are more properly philosophical and about how we respond to religious language; and I shall return to this point in a concluding section.[1]

[1] See below, Part Three, Chapter 15, 'What is Revelation?'

VI

THE FORMATION OF THE CHRISTIAN COMMUNITY

(i) *The Idea*

WHEN Newman became a Roman Catholic it might appear that his idea of the Church—to the extent that the principle of self-authenticating verification was over-riding—was too simple. As he says, he knew no Catholics; and his grasp of the context within which the sacramental action of the Church verified or authenticated the presence of Christ must have, as yet, been notional. But there is a risk of overlooking certain important and explicit pre-suppositions. From the start, Newman's conception of the context which the Church's verifying power required for its due exercise had been a social vision of great breadth and unity. In the '30s when he had been writing his study of the Arians, he had spoken of the Church as being based upon popular power, of the people as its fulcrum, and of the past union of Church and State enjoyed by the nation as 'a happy anomaly'—an accidental relationship not normally to be expected.[1]

His conception of the intimate and organic relationship of bishop to people was not only, as he put it, far more 'radical' than the Anglican view,[2] it was bound to collide with that even narrower conception of the Church then possessed by most Catholics. And the problem which Newman found himself confronted by when he became a Catholic was an apparent acquiescence in precisely those conditions which he, together with Maurice and Coleridge, had condemned as Romanism—viz., the dissociation of the Church's function to verify from its context within a society which was itself rapidly changing and as rapidly separating itself from its traditional union with Christian principles.

---

[1] *Moz.*, i, pp. 450, 454, 458.
[2] *Diff.* i, pp. 52–3, 91; *H.S.* i, pp. 340–2, 348; see above pp. 72 ff. In April 1836, Newman is proposing that, in order to free the Church from its dependence upon an aristocratic social order, it should be 'made to dwell in the affections of the people at large' (*Moz.* ii, p. 186).

The dissociation—dichotomy would not be too hard a word—could be expressed in various ways as that between religion and culture, an authoritarian Church and a liberal State, or between Grace and Nature; but it is fundamentally one between truth and relevance, between the verifying function of the Church and the context in which such a function can alone be meaningfully realized and understood.

This was at once apparent to Newman. In Rome he noticed the Italians' capacity to disjoin religion from morality[1]; but the principal symptom of this state of dissociation was the cleavage between clergy and laity which, by threatening the internal unity of the Church, prevented it from expressing love for those whom it was founded to teach. At a deeper level he regarded this cleavage, aggravated as it was by so many distinguished but unemployed converts now 'lay-men', as evidence of a defective theology of the Church, which was itself derived from too radical a disjunction between Nature and Grace. This it was which was responsible for the disjunction of religion from morality he had noticed in the Italians; but it also produced that suspicion, even resentment, of education from Catholics of all classes. A further consequence was that the converts who had joined the Roman Church with Newman could not be fitted into its present character. They were like the early monks of Fountains, 'living under trees till their house was built'.[2]

The current circumstances of the Church, particularly in Italy, obliged it to take an increasingly defensive posture; and it would be reasonable to expect it to assert its truth at the expense of a relevance which could still, on the surface, be taken for granted, and to emphasize the need for Grace rather than for the co-operation of Nature. But although, for theological purposes, these elements may be distinguished, it is a dangerous matter when, in practice, they become disjoined; and the remedy—a keeping of

---

[1] Thus, as early as January 1847, he is writing of the Romans, 'I observe *every where* a simple certainty in believing which to a Protestant or Anglican is quite astonishing—but though they have this, they show in a wonderful way how it is possible to disjoin religion and morality . . . the same people, who have a sort of instinctive conviction of the unseen world, which is strange to an Englishman, have not that *living* faith which leads to correctness or sanctity of character'. (*Letters* XII, p. 24.)

[2] A state of affairs anticipated by Newman in a letter to Keble in December 1844 (*K. Corr.*, p. 364).

them in due relationship—is pre-eminently the task of education. Thus Newman welcomed the invitation he received in 1851 to found a university for Catholics in Dublin. He threw himself into the undertaking with all his heart, since its success would accomplish what he had already seen to be necessary for the Catholic community. It would assist the integration of clergy and laity, and the assimilation to the Church not only of converts but of that educated laity who were becoming essential to the upkeep of a modern society.

When Newman undertook the formation of this university, which was not intended to be confined to the Irish, but to be the English-speaking equivalent of Louvain, he was still only a recent convert, having been received in 1845, ordained in Rome two years later, and returning to England to establish the Birmingham Oratory in February 1848. His prestige was untarnished, but his understanding of the empirical reality of the Church was notional.

His aim was simple: in his own words, it was 'to import Oxford into Ireland',[1] but he soon learned that to the average Dubliner he was 'a mere page of history . . . they have heard my name, but they have no associations with it'.[2] But the apathy by which he was confronted had deeper and more political origins: British injustice and Irish incapacity to remedy it had produced what one patriot called in the very year of Newman's arrival: 'a paralysis of national feeling'.[3]

Not only did this destroy the possibility of a class coming into existence for whom a university education was possible, but most people believed that what was wanted was not so much an educated Catholic laity as a politically united Ireland, and that, in the words of Frederick Lucas, the editor and founder of the *Tablet*, 'in this island where people are mixed, and society is mixed, education must be so'.[4]

Newman's other difficulty was the personality of his patron, Dr. Cullen, the Archbishop of Dublin, who until the age of forty-six had been Rector of the Irish College in Rome, was a determined opponent of mixed education, and saw the establishment of a

[1] Letter to Mrs. William Froude, 14 Oct. 1851 (*Letters* XIV, p. 389).
[2] *W.* i, p. 387.
[3] Cited in Fergal McGrath, *Newman's University—Idea and Reality* (1951), p. 265.
[4] Letter from F. Lucas, 9 Oct. 1851 (in McGrath, op. cit., p. 131).

Catholic university as a political move against his opponents within the Church; he seems to have been too long in Rome to have been able to adapt himself to local conditions; he judged Irish political aspirations by Roman standards; his narrow views were strictly adhered to; and in negotiations he preferred a system of clandestine manoeuvres punctuated, after the Roman fashion, by periods of unnerving silence and delay. Newman noticed that he treated him not as a colleague, but as a servant. [1]

It is important to see the argument of the *Discourses on the Scope and Nature of University Education*, delivered and published in 1852, against this background. Newman complained that all his greatest works, with the exception of *The Grammar of Assent*, arose as responses to particular problems and situations, and these lectures are not a series of messianic utterances at the highest and safest levels of generality, but attempts to resolve a set of awkward questions, each pointing in a different direction, and to produce a coherent argument which will operate and succeed on many fronts. There were Catholics who saw no real difference between a mixed education at Trinity College, Dublin, and what the Catholic university could provide; and for them Newman had to show the advantages of a religious education over that which was purely secular or religiously indifferent. But there were others for whom a liberal education as defined by Newman and practised in England was a schooling in intellectual pride and an invitation to dabble in heresy and infidelity. 'The prelates,' Newman said, 'regard any intellectual man as being on the road to perdition' [2]; and a seminary or convent type of education was far more in keeping with Catholic tradition as it was then understood, than an institution modelled on the lines of what one Irish Dominican called 'Oxford College' [3]—and run not merely by converts, but—what was worse—by convert laymen.

In preparing his Lectures Newman set himself a course of reading. It included Maurice's *Subscription no Bondage*, but it also included Coleridge's Preface to the *Encyclopaedia Metropolitana* (or *Treatise on Method*, as it is now usually referred to). This, as has already been noted, is one of Coleridge's major works; and New-

---

[1] *Letters* XVI, p. 538 (note).
[2] *W*. i, p. 355.
[3] McGrath, op. cit., p. 146.

man thought it important enough to produce an abstract of its argument.[1]

Newman's approach to his subject is remarkably akin to Coleridge. He conceives the education of the individual in terms of an equilibrium of functions; and, furthermore, an equilibrium which is applicable to the society in which he is to be educated—his university. Those functions—intellectual, theological, and religious—whose equilibrium in the individual constitutes a Catholic education, constitute—in his university—the circle of the sciences; and it is this social or academic equilibrium which constitutes the university an educating community.[2]

Newman is setting up a model which—in terms of functions and their equilibrium—extends the argument implicit in the *Essay on Development*; and it prepares us for his final and most explicit description of the Church in 1877, as an equilibrium of functions regulated by theology. It is noteworthy that the model is republican rather than monarchal in conception. Newman's lectures are an attempt to reconcile three factors—the autonomy required by the intellect to develop according to its proper nature, free from arbitrary and external constraints; the rights and functions of theology within the economy of a university; and the extent to which the Church has the right to exercise a pastoral authority within the university. By attempting to define the limits within which each of these functions may legitimately be exercised, the lectures also establish how they may be harmonized.

Newman presupposes that the branches of knowledge form one whole; and he specifically commends Coleridge for being almost alone among contemporary English writers in seeing the cardinal importance of 'comprehensiveness and harmony of view' before pursuing 'truth in detail'.[3] But Newman's analysis, while presupposing this antecedent unity, also assumes that principle of limitation or, as he calls it, abstraction which is to be found in his theory of religious language. The mind is incapable of grasping its world at once and as a whole; we abstract parts from that whole in the manner of a short-sighted reader; we progress by degrees and circuitous advances. These partial views or abstractions, as Newman calls them, are what constitute the various sciences or subjects of our knowledge; since they are the results of abstraction, they

---

[1] See above, chapter 2, pp. 24 ff., and 32 ff.
[2] Discourse V, *S & N*, p. 144.   [3] *S & N*, p. 387.

have to do with the relations of things rather than with the things in themselves.[1] This knowledge is probable, hypothetical, and partial, yet by its nature it seeks to explain the whole of which it is part, and continually to encroach upon the territory of some other subject matter and some other method of analysis.

'It seems,' says Newman, 'that the human mind is ever seeking to systematise its knowledge, to base it upon principle, and to find a science comprehensive of all sciences', and that sooner than forego this gratification, we prefer the completeness and precision of bigotry to 'a fluctuating and homeless scepticism',[2] and that we will always 'put up with an illusion when we cannot get a truth'.[3]

The point at issue, then, is not whether our knowledge should be unified, but how that inevitable process ought best to be undertaken; and the first shock Newman gave to some of the more narrowly pious members of his audience was his deliberate avoidance of the easy denominational way out of the difficulty. Knowledge is unified by an insight possessed by all men, irrespective of creed, the use of which constitutes 'a sort of science distinct from all of them, and in some sense a science of sciences'.[4] It is the purpose of a liberal education to develop this insight; but although the pursuit of this liberal (as distinct from useful or vocational) knowledge is its own justification and is, therefore, an end in itself, it is a dynamic and dangerous acquaintanceship, and not a passive reception of ideas. A successful liberal education, by developing that power which enables us to seize the strong point in any matter we are considering, accomplishes an 'enlargement of mind'; but an unsuccessful encounter enfeebles, dissipates, and destroys: 'you must be above your knowledge', Newman reminds his audience, 'or it will oppress you'.[5]

The academic man is exposed to a further danger. The roots of his judgment lie far deeper than in his chosen field of study, and he is, in this sense, only half a man, so that once he fails to be able to give an account of how the various aspects of himself are interrelated, that power of judgment and comprehensiveness, which it is the purpose of a liberal education to foster and impart, weakens, and what we dimly feel, we cannot resolutely communicate.

What can happen to the individual can happen in turn to his

---

[1] *Idea* III. 2, pp. 45–6.   [2] *S & N*, Discourse V, p. 140.
[3] *Idea* IV. 3, p. 76.   [4] *Idea* III. 4, p. 51.
[5] *Idea* VI. 4, pp. 131 f.; 140.

university, if it permits practices to develop which weaken it as a community, and if it allows the web of its teaching to become unravelled. Then it becomes, in Newman's phrase, 'a sort of bazaar, or pantechnicon, in which wares of all kinds are heaped together for sale in stalls independent of each other'.[1]

Newman makes it clear that what all successful education has in common is the ability to grasp the idea it is attempting to embody, to define its type, to establish its criteria, and to clarify its motives. If you cannot assume this degree of common agreement, then all you will produce is mere specialists or victims of mass communication: illiberal men and illiberal communities. 'Excellence,' says Newman, 'implies a centre.'[2]

Such an education produces 'the gentleman'; and Newman uses the term descriptively rather than evocatively, as much in order to show what a gentleman is not, as what he is. This man who, in a celebrated passage in the *Idea*,[3] is spoken of as being as simple as he is forcible, too clear-headed to be unjust, and as brief as he is decisive, is also spoken of as possessing that effeminacy of feeling which tolerates religion, not because it is true, but because it is venerable, beautiful, and useful. Somehow the type lacks a certain initiative, a certain moral drive. His qualities, says Newman, may look like virtues—at a distance; but when he is faced with the sombre permanent problems that emerge periodically from the dark recesses of our ape-like consciousness, the gentleman is unprepared, and—if one may use the phrase—uncommitted: he has discovered the limits of a liberal education: 'Quarry the granite rock with razors, or moor the vessel with a thread of silk; then may you hope with such keen and delicate instruments as human knowledge and human reason to contend against those giants, the passion and the pride of man.'[4]

This, the distinction between intellectual and moral excellence which enables us to grasp the difference between Nature and Grace, is the recurring note in all Newman's writing about education. It is this which enabled him to understand the Catholic objections to a university conceived on the liberal, alien, Oxford pattern, and to say: 'Philosophy, however enlightened, however profound, gives no command over the passions, no influential motives, no vivifying

---

[1] *S & N*, V, p. 139.   [2] *H.S.* iii, p. 16.
[3] *Idea* VIII. 10, pp. 208-11; cp. p. 139.   [4] *Idea* V. 9, p. 121.

principles. Liberal education makes not the Christian, not the Catholic, but the gentleman.'[1]

It is, of course, true that the philosophical insights that are sharpened by a liberal education, since they are innate, are religious in implication—this is the argument from the illative sense—but they can as easily lead to simple scepticism as to religious belief, and Newman's answer to the question—what, then, are the grounds for giving religion a place in the university?—requires a distinction to be made between theology as a subject of university study, and the pastoral authority of the Church as it bears upon individuals and upon the study of theology.

Theology has a legitimate place in the university, since throughout his history man has concerned himself with the problems of a supreme Being—God. A body of knowledge has grown up to which we give the name of theology, and any curriculum of liberal knowledge, or university professing to take all knowledge for its province, denies the significance of such an existing body of knowledge at its own risk. This, as far as the university is concerned, is what Newman means by theology: 'the science of God, or the truths we know about God put into system'.[2] Nor must theology be allowed to interfere with the freedom of the individual sciences in their own sphere, and the theologian must remember that not even theology can

be excluded from the law to which every mental exercise is subject, namely, from that imperfection which ever must attend the abstract, when it would determine the concrete. Nor do I speak only of Natural Religion, for even the teaching of the Catholic Church . . . is variously influenced by the other sciences.[3]

Thus theology must find its own way and exist on the university's terms and not its own. But by being thus enabled 'to meet the times', theology can be kept in growth, since 'an obsolete discipline may be a present heresy'.[4]

Yet the peculiarity of its subject matter has certain irresistible side effects, since theology, treating of things as they are related to their creator, is bound to impinge on other sciences, and individual subjects will have one character when viewed in the context of theology, and another viewed out of it. Without the presence of

[1] *Idea*, p. 120.   [2] *Idea* III. 7, p. 61.
[3] *Idea* III. 4, p. 52.   [4] *Idea* IV. 7, p. 83.

theology in the university, other subjects will tend to encroach upon the space left vacant—to their own detriment as academic disciplines. Does this mean then that theology is the regulating factor of the university? Is Newman re-stating the old claim that theology is the Queen of the sciences, the glue which sticks them together in a new synthesis? No—he is quite determined to make no such claim [1]; it is the university *qua* university which unifies the subjects studied. Theology regulates only to the extent that it provides a true and unique account of Revelation: its power to regulate stems from its truth and not from any external coercion. Its presence in the university, by completing the circle of the sciences, enables the university to attain its unity as a teaching community—it is the special function of a university to draw many things into one, not by rules reducible to writing but by sagacity, wisdom, and forbearance [2]—and it is this social unity which regulates rather than theology specifically and in isolation:

The assemblage of sciences . . . may be said to be *in equilibrio*, as long as all its portions are secured to it. Take away one of them, and that one so important in the catalogue as Theology, and disorder and ruin at once ensue. There is no middle state between an *equilibrium* and chaotic confusion; one science is ever pressing upon another, unless kept in check; and the only guarantee of truth is the cultivation of them all. And such is the office of a University.[3]

We now come to the place of the pastoral authority of the Church within the university. Its bearing upon the moral life of the individual is implicit in Newman's distinction between intellectual and moral excellence, and in his description of the moral limitations of the gentleman. But what is its bearing upon theology as a branch of study?

Theology in the university is exposed to the risk of degenerating into an inductive science by basing its authority upon appeals to

---

[1] *S & N*, p. 152.   [2] *Idea*, p. 458.
[3] *S & N*, Discourse V: 'General Knowledge viewed as one Philosophy', p. 136. It was to this discourse that Newman appended the references to Coleridge in the Appendix. This discourse was suppressed when the lectures were reprinted as being contrary to the current papal policy expressed in the Brief addressed to the Irish Bishops in 1854 (and subsequently confirmed by the stipulations made in the Munich Brief of 1864).
See Newman: *My Campaign in Ireland*, and *Memorandum* (*A.W.*, pp. 322–3), 'I wrote on a different idea my "Discourses on University Education" in 1852, vid especially the original 5th Discourse.'

the text of Scripture, 'the events and transactions of ecclesiastical history, and the phenomena of the external world'. But, for the Catholic, knowledge of the revealed truths is gained ultimately not from research into such facts but 'simply by appealing to the authoritative keepers of them'.[1]

In a university Catholic theology risks failing to see that its doctrines are *deductively* verified by the authority of the Church and not *inductively* by an appeal to Scripture, antiquity, and Nature. And it can be saved from this mistake if the Church is present separately to the university.[2]

To the further question—how ought the authority of the Church to be exercised in this respect? Newman answers by a long peroration on St. Philip Neri and his spirit[3]; but this must form the subject of the next chapter.

We can now see how Newman answered the great questions with which he started. Ought Catholics to support a Catholic university? Yes, says Newman, if the Catholic university really is a university, since 'if the Catholic Faith is true, a university cannot exist externally to the Catholic pale, for it cannot teach universal knowledge, if it does not teach Catholic theology'.[4] Thus, for Catholics, the study of religion is not a mere trimming, a mere matter of dispute between the bishops and the government, but a condition of their general knowledge; and to blot it out is 'to unravel' (for them) 'the web of university teaching'.[5] Newman also answers the question: what is the difference between the education appropriate to a gentleman and that appropriate to a Catholic layman? Both, in receiving a liberal education, will have learned to think for themselves; but the religious education of the Catholic will have reinforced those powers of judgement, where they are weak; and by helping him to understand how the various aspects of his knowledge and himself are interrelated, will save him from falling into a simple scepticism. His assent to the truths of religion passes over from the notional to the real. Thus a Catholic who has received a liberal but religious education is less narrow and is possessed of a vitality or moral earnestness greater than that of the mere gentleman; since by the aid of his theology he has come to see his world as a whole; it is no longer dull,

[1] *Idea*, p. 446.   [2] *Idea* IX. 4–5, pp. 222–7.
[3] ibid., sections 9–10.   [4] ibid. 1, p. 214.
[5] *Idea* III. 10, p. 70.

monotonous, and unprofitable, but—with the vision of the people
of the Middle Ages—it is seen as a various and complicated drama,
with parts and an object, and an aweful moral. To such a man
religion brings its own enlargement: 'an enlargement, not of
tumult, but of peace'.[1]

It is a mistake to assume that Newman's *Idea* was a mere speculative perfection. The meeting of liberal and moral values, of
philosophy and theology, which he desires is a vigorous collision of
mind with mind in the hard give and take of a university community; and theology gets on to terms with the other subjects of
the curriculum not by an intellectual act *in vacuo*, but by surviving
these collisions and interpenetrations. Newman's stress is upon the
university not as an ideal but as an embodied idea: the very title
Idea of a University is itself an indication of Newman's approach,
since the term 'idea', standing as it does in his theology for a
principle with a life of its own and a power to develop into as yet
non-existent forms and institutions, is the very germ of a dynamic
community, of that ability (as Whitehead puts it) to embody high
ideals in great organizations which was the achievement of the
Benedictine centuries.[2]

The *Idea of a University* continues Newman's articulation of his
theory of development by demonstrating how 'ideas' are developed
over 'a wide human field'[3]; and in doing so he shows that 'ideas'
can only be effectively understood in terms of their embodiments.
The very process of education, based as it is on an 'idea', is
nevertheless that of a whole man within a community of men which
has 'stood the trial and received the sanctions of ages', and is
administered by men who are supported 'by their consistency
with their predecessors and with each other'.[4] Not only is Newman
extending his 'method of personation' by assimilating 'ideas' to
their embodiment in communities of persons and institutions, he
is also anticipating those views on the nature and function of
Tradition which are to be found independently in Möhler and later
in Blondel; and I shall discuss this in the Conclusion to this section.

But we are also and inevitably brought up against the relationship
of the individual to the authority of the Church. Because of Newman's profound understanding of the integrity of the person as the

[1] *Idea* VI. 4, p. 133.
[2] A. N. Whitehead, *Aims of Education* (1932), p. 92.
[3] *Dev.*, p. 36.   [4] *Idea*, Preface, p. xxii.

'temple' of Christ,[1] he could not acquiesce in the authoritarian views, either of education or of the Church, which his fellow Catholics seem to take for granted. These were what Maurice had rightly stigmatized as the material counterfeits of spiritual principles, and what Newman himself had referred to as 'the substitution of something earthly' for the contemplation of our maker.[2] It was like trying to provide a prescription for a good school in terms of corporal punishment and compulsory chapel. To Newman as to Maurice this was Romanist error—the Catholic Church was a Church of persons, or it was anti-Christ.

Thus the *Idea of a University* is not only the prescription of the kind of personal development which the Church must require for each of its members, lay and clerical, but a statement of the institutional conditions which the Church must see fulfilled, in order that this personal development may be brought about. It is for this reason that Newman now became so preoccupied with the need to bring the laity back into the fullness of the Church. They are, he says, 'the *measure* of the Catholic spirit', or standard by which the effectiveness of the Church is to be judged. But they must be a laity able to relate their religion to their secular knowledge, or, as we should say nowadays, they must be theologically literate, even expert:

I want an intelligent, well-instructed laity. . . . I mean to be severe . . . exorbitant in my demands. I wish you to enlarge your knowledge, to cultivate your reason, to get an insight into the relation of truth to truth . . . to understand how faith and reason stand to each other, what are the bases and principles of Catholicism.[3]

Newman's case for the Catholic university is, therefore, at once deeply theological and firmly empirical; and its definitive expression is in his first sermon preached after the opening of the University Church in April 1856:

I want to destroy that diversity of centres, which puts everything into confusion by creating a contrariety of influences. I wish the same spots and the same individuals to be at once oracles of philosophy and shrines of devotion. It will not satisfy me, what satisfies so many, to have two independent systems, intellectual and religious, going at once side by side, by a sort of division of labour, and only accidentally brought together. . . . I want the same roof to contain both the intellectual and

[1] *P.S.* II, p. 220.   [2] *V.M.* i, p. 102.   [3] *Pres. Pos.*, p. 360.

moral discipline. Devotion is not a sort of finish given to the sciences; nor is science a sort of feather in the cap, if I may so express myself, an ornament and set-off to devotion. I want the intellectual layman to be religious, and the devout ecclesiastic to be intellectual.[1]

Newman's idea of a Catholic university is that of a community— taking all knowledge for its object, autonomous in its administration—and constituting thereby a middle station in which priests and laity can meet, a point of equilibrium between clerical and lay education, where these partners in the Church 'may learn to understand and yield to each other', in order that they may 'act in union upon an age which is running headlong into infidelity'.[2] This is the institutional realization of that vision of the Church of the Fathers which first broke upon Newman in the '30s and then, ten years later, drove him to put the Church of England to the test. He was now to discover that the conditions within the Church he had joined were the reverse of that equilibrium of clergy and laity which was necessary both for the establishment of a Catholic university and for the realization of his idea of the Church.

(ii) *The Reality*

We have already seen something of the unpromising setting for Newman's great experiment, but there were even more fundamental objections. His fellow Catholics were unable to distinguish between a university (which had been asked for) and a college (which was really intended): in Newman's words, 'the office of a Catholic University is to teach *faith*, and of Colleges to protect *morals*'.[3] The clergy, however, if they were interested in intellectual studies at all saw them as a means of enforcing moral discipline; they could understand an education that had to be beaten into minds vitiated by original sin or they could enter into alliance with the useful knowledge places[4]; but their separation of intellectual from moral values was so radical that they seemed committed to the contradiction that where intellectual effort is not subversive of faith, it is indifferent to it. Thus either they had to deny the principle that all knowledge is influenced by faith, or assert that the process of intellectual development can be safely reduced to a mere technique, a something passive and neutral (which it never is)

[1] *S.V.O.*, p. 13.   [2] *W.* ii, pp. 397–8.
[3] Draft Introduction to Discourse VI (*Letters* XV, p. 134).
[4] Ornsby to Newman, 16 April 1852 in McGrath, op. cit., p. 147.

rather than dynamic and challenging (which it always has been). Behind these wrong-headed views was an assumption that made their adoption perfectly intelligible: it was that the realms of faith and reason are discontinuous, and that we must educate, therefore, upon the principle of an opposition, deep and unbridgeable between the verifying function of the Church and its context, between —in other words—religion and culture, Grace and Nature. Within the Roman Church such an education has always been narrowly denominational and entirely clerical in scope and control; under the regime it produces, the laity are indeed to be regarded as boys eternal, or—in the words of one of Newman's friends—'as a mass of suspects, supposed to be brooding on nothing but revolution, and only kept together by motives of fear and by the external pressure of a clerical organization'.[1]

These tendencies were reinforced by the continuous hardening of papal policies initiated by Pius IX after he had been obliged to flee from Rome in November 1848. And no matter how effectively Newman argued his case, he was bound—holding the views he did —to be on the losing side. His method of dealing with objections characterizes his method as a theologian. First, he answers them on their own terms at the empirical level, and then relates them to the theological principles which are being denied or disregarded— in this case the necessary function of an educated laity within the Church. Thus, if a university is turned into a convent, it will not work: great minds need elbow room, but so do lesser minds. If a university fails to reflect the world into which the layman must go, he will be driven to seek for his university in that world[2]; yet to educate the clergy and laity on a separate system of principles will not merely increase the gulf between them (which in Ireland, Newman noted, was fearful) but it will encourage the Church to shrink within itself, and to become in appearance an almost exclusively clerical concern. Such a prospect, far from worrying the Irish clergy, was what they preferred; and in a letter written on 23 September 1856,[3] Newman spoke of their dislike of the upper or middle classes, and of their feeling 'awkward when a gentleman is

---

[1] R. Simpson (see below pp. 111–2). That this is not an exaggeration can be seen from one of the questions on university education circulated in England on behalf of Propaganda in 1864: it was: 'Ought the principle to be admitted that the laity should be more highly educated than their clergy?' (W. ii, pp. 541, 554–5.)

[2] *Idea* IX. 8, pp. 232–3; 476.   [3] *Letters* XVII, pp. 385–6.

converted ... they think that then only Ireland will become again the Isle of Saints, when it has a population of peasants ruled over by a patriotic priesthood patriarchally'. Newman continues by emphasizing their objection to what nowadays we should call the educated laity: 'a gentleman is an evil. . . . The University is for gentlemen. It is then but a provision for perpetuating and aggravating a recognised evil and nuisance.'

Why, therefore, did Newman persevere with the Irish university? His answer is given in the first Discourse when he says that since the Holy See had commanded the establishment of a Catholic university, 'St. Peter has spoken, it is he who has enjoined that which seems to us so unpromising'; and in the passage which follows Newman claims that such a command is itself the prophecy of success.[1]

When, as a result of his Irish experiences, Newman changed his mind about the Catholic university, he reverted to the position he had held before the invitation to become Rector. Newman had then favoured a mixed education as being dictated by necessity. But he had changed his mind in deference to the judgement of the Holy See. In his first lecture 'On the Nature and Scope of Universities' he had expressed the view that 'over and above that attribute of infallibility which attached to the doctrinal decisions of the Holy See, a gift of sagacity had in every age characterised its occupants',[2] so that if the Pope intended a Catholic university in Dublin, it was bound to succeed—a hope which, published in the first edition of the *Idea*, was deleted in later ones. Experience taught Newman to distinguish sharply between the Pope's infallibility and his sagacity, namely, his ability to decide what was expedient for the Church at any particular time. His earlier point of view is also to be found in that lecture[3]; and in 1867 he appears to have sent an amended version of this passage to Rome, entitling it 'on necessary exceptions in fact to the rule that education must not be mixed'.[4] It was not well received.

This brings us to the question already touched upon—how ought the hierarchical authority of the Church to be exercised, not merely within a university, but within the Church at large?

---

[1] *Idea* I. 5, p. 13. We find him repeating this claim as late as 1856; see *Letters* XVII, p. 284.
[2] *A.W.*, p. 320.   [3] *Idea*, pp. 8–10; *S & N*, pp. 16–19.
[4] Oratory Archives, B.4.3.

Newman's experiences in Dublin led him to view the question in terms of a setting of limits; and, as was his method, he sought for an authority within Catholic tradition. He found it in St. Philip Neri. What is especially significant is that, in adopting Philip Neri as his patron, Newman was enabled to move behind the Tridentine curtain to that remaining element of Renaissance humanism which Philip and his Oratorians so fleetingly represent. It is also significant that, in likening St. Philip to Keble,[1] Newman is also adverting to the tradition which formed him.

Around the years 1554–8, at the very beginning of the counter-Reformation, just as the Church was about to reform itself by an unparalleled exertion of the hierarchical authority, a new religious association—the Oratory—was formed on republican principles by Philip Neri. It grew out of the free association of priests and lay-men; and its priests were men of mature years, who had read their theology not in seminaries but universities, and had received ordination only after many years as laymen. The elective and republican nature of the Oratorian Congregations and the principle of free association Newman thought would be especially suitable to the 'ethos' (as he so expressed it) of himself and his companions, used as they were to the freedom of a university.[2] And the Oratorian vocation 'to save men, not from, but in, the world' seemed the most appropriate one for the nineteenth century.

Here is the significance of Newman's reference to St. Philip Neri when he discusses the exercise of the Church's pastoral authority within the university. It must be based upon the integration of grace and nature, and not upon their irremediable opposition. This is what Newman means when he speaks of the university's need for a masculine religion.[3] And once more we can see him going behind the Tridentine curtain to a more primitive ideal—the Benedictine one of growth rather than system, of restoration rather than visitation, correction, or conversion.[4] It is to reunite things

[1] *Letters* XII, p. 25.
[2] See Newman's letter to Dalgairns (31 Dec. 1846, *Letters* XI, 305) in which, having commented unfavourably upon the Thomistic 'rigour' of the Dominicans, he speaks favourably of the Oratorians:
'If I wished to follow my bent, I should join them [the Oratorians] if I joined any. They have a good library, and handsome sets of rooms apparently. *It is like a College* with hardly any rule. They keep their own property, and furnish their own rooms.' [My italics.]
[3] *S.V.O.*, p. 14.   [4] *H.S.*, ii. p. 410.

which were in the beginning joined together by God, and have been put asunder by man. Such was the method of St. Philip Neri, whom Newman describes as learning from St. Benedict what to be, from St. Dominic what to do, and from St. Ignatius how he was to do it.[1] St. Philip, says Newman, relied not on protestations and warnings, but on the counter-fascination of purity and truth[2]; and as Newman makes clear in one of his Dublin University Sermons, this was the method of St. Paul himself, 'the least magisterial of all teachers and the gentlest of all rulers'. For him, says Newman, 'Grace did but sanctify and elevate Nature', leaving him in the full possession of all that was human.[3]

Newman founded the English Oratory in 1848, but it soon developed into two establishments in Birmingham and London respectively. During the whole period of his Rectorship of the Irish university he was faced with the growing differences of spirit between the two houses; and matters came to a head when the London Oratory led by Frederick Faber applied direct to Rome for a change in the rule concerning their dealings with nuns, without consulting Newman, their Founder, or the members of the sister foundation at Birmingham. On the surface it seems like a violent storm in a confined space; but it takes us to the very root of the difficulties which beset the Roman Church in the nineteenth century. Newman is for growth, Faber for autocratic rule. Here, in a nutshell, is that collision between conscience and authoritarianism which remains the unresolved dilemma of Catholicism.

We see it already foreshadowed in the collisions between Philip Neri and Charles Borromeo. Although he acknowledges Philip's influence upon his life, as Archbishop of Milan, he felt obliged to admonish him thus:

it ought to be an express rule among you to obey not only the orders but the mere wishes of His Holiness, with a perfect and prompt submission; on the contrary one sees in you a certain spirit that leads you to some extent to resist or at least to hesitate, instead of being eager and diligent when it is a case of undertaking enterprises which are demanded by the service of Our Lord [the Pope] and the Holy See.[4]

When one of the members of the Oratory, Tarugi, was trying to decide between residence in Rome or Naples, he wrote to Philip:

[1] *S.V.O.*, p. 228.   [2] *Idea*, p. 235.   [3] *S.V.O.*, p. 114.
[4] Meriol Trevor, *Apostle of Rome, the Life of St. Philip Neri* (1966), p. 198.

'Your Reverence has the reins of my will in his hands, tight with a vow, and you can pull me to which side you will.'[1] But Philip would not pull: he told Tarugi to make up his own mind.

Here is the drama of Newman, Faber, and Manning three hundred years before it is played out, even down to Newman's insistence upon rational self-responsibility. It was this principle which he applied with more success than is usually supposed in the planning and conduct of the Irish university; and it was the same principle he tried unsuccessfully to apply to Faber's desire to be 'a cadaver in the Superior's hands'. Newman's reply tells us exactly how he thought authority ought to be exercised within the Church: 'I can't command people about like so many soldiers or pieces of wood.' Let Providence 'gently to work our separation . . . as fruit ripens on the tree and falls; you all force me to take a knife and cut it off. I repeat, I cannot fight with facts.'[2]

The issue of principle on which Birmingham and London divided—whether the imposition of a decision by Rome was to be solicited and its promulgation obeyed 'under pain of mortal sin', or whether it was merely to be seen as 'likely to bring propaganda down upon us'[3]—depends upon the attitude adopted to the Church's authority to verify and the context of that mediation within the nature of men, their consciences, and the conditions of their society. The London Oratorians (in company with Manning, Ward, and the Ultramontanes generally) conceived the authority of the magisterium as a divine ordinance to be strictly imposed upon unregenerate nature in all its manifestations—personal, educational, social, and political. Newman, on the other hand, was prepared to draw a different lesson and to trust his instincts as they had been formed within the English tradition which had made him a Catholic.

Ecclesiastical authority can rightfully require an obedience to what is essential for the ordering of the Church as a polity or institution, but it cannot supersede conscience. What Newman is moving towards is a placing of ecclesiastical authority within a larger context—that of the Church as constituting what is now called the whole people of God. The distinction it will lead him to

[1] ibid., p. 246.
[2] Correspondence with F. W. Faber, February to December 1849, *Letter* XIII, pp. 62, 77, 336.
[3] See *Letters* XVII, p. 59.

make may be seen in outline in his *Discourses on the Scope and Nature of University Education*, where he distinguishes between the place of theology in the university from the exercise of the pastoral authority of the Church; and it is this distinction that after twenty years of suffering and frustration he will clarify in terms of one between the kingly and prophetical offices of the Church.

But Newman is approaching a watershed. He will make one final effort at explicit affirmation—to make more precise the distinction between the roles of the magisterium and of the faithful within the total Church community. Its tragic rebuff will then require him to develop his idea by a species of *via negativa*, indirectly, step by step, and in terms of its denial by the authorities in England and Rome. And it is this which determines the method of exposition which must now be adopted, since, henceforward, it was to be by a series of unlooked for calls, occasions, frustrations, and personal encounters that Newman was to be obliged to render his idea of the Church brilliantly explicit. The process was to take a generation.

VII

THE MIND OF THE CHURCH

WHEN, in November 1858, Newman retired from the Rectorship of the Catholic university, he hoped that he would be left alone to write a sustained and substantial work of theology; but he was to be drawn almost immediately, and once more against his will, into a controversy which was to involve all those principles for which he had fought so fruitlessly in Ireland.

A Catholic periodical, the *Rambler*, which had been started by an Oxford convert, Frederick Capes, in 1848 was now being edited jointly by another Oxford convert clergyman, Richard Simpson, and by the young Sir John Acton, who had joined Simpson as co-editor at the age of twenty-three in 1857. Although the circulation of such a paper was small (the number for May 1859 sold just over 800 copies, and the editors considered 1,000 to be a very healthy figure),[1] its influence was out of all proportion to its circulation. Its aim was to rehabilitate Catholic thought in a non-Catholic world, and it did so by combining standards of scholarship previously unknown in Catholic journalism with attitudes critical of ecclesiastical authority which had become equally uncustomary. By the beginning of 1859 it became certain that, unless special measures were taken, the review would be censured in the forthcoming Pastorals of the English bishops. Both sides turned to Newman as the only acceptable intermediary.

One of the alleged sources of irritation had been the style in which many of the articles in the *Rambler* had been written; and for this Richard Simpson was held to be responsible: 'he writes about the Church in a sort of sore tone, and at times as if from without,' wrote a Catholic layman to Newman[2]; and Newman's first task was to persuade Simpson to resign, on condition that the threat of censure would be withdrawn. Since the co-editor, Acton, was equally unacceptable to the authorities, Newman was left with the reward traditionally reserved to over-scrupulous intermediaries:

---

[1] Birmingham Oratory, memo. dated 29 June 1859.   [2] *W.* i, p. 486.

either he must bring the *Rambler* to an end, or himself become its editor.

So runs the accepted version of the dispute; but a closer examination and fresh evidence seem to indicate a more complex background.[1]

The converts to Catholicism who followed Newman into the Roman Church were a new kind of laity accustomed to thinking about their religion to the extent of thinking their way into the Church. For a time the *Rambler* became their focus; and the problem to which it gave rise was if it were laudable for a layman to use his intellect to enter the Church, was it not also laudable for it to be used to serve the Church?

The more practical question was raised by the unemployed status of many of these laymen who had made great sacrifices to join the Church: 'it is *cruel* that so many able men are doing *nothing*',[2] Newman was to write in March 1851; and his objection to restoring the hierarchy and making Wiseman a cardinal was that: 'We want seminaries far more than sees. We want education, *view*, combination, organization.'

Instead of a formal, frontal assault in full papal panoply, Newman favoured flexibility—'a great organization, going round the towns giving lectures, or making speeches . . . starting a paper, a review, etc. The great difficulty to this plan would be the Cardinal's status, would it not?'[3]

But this would have involved making use of laymen, especially the convert laymen; and here there were not only ecclesiastical barriers—Newman notes Bishop Ullathorne's 'horror of laymen'[4] —but social ones, which were probably the most fundamental.

The crisis which Newman was about to pass through was once more about the place of the laity in the Church, but it raised deeper issues about the nature of the Church itself. What came to be put at issue was Newman's conception of the *width* of the Christian community. This had formed the basis of his policy of associating clergy and laity in a common higher education; and it was what caused him to support the educated laity in their effort to discuss the relationship of the Church to its context within a new and challenging society in the pages of the *Rambler*.

---

[1] I have discussed this in greater detail in my edition of *On Consulting the Faithful in Matters of Doctrine* (1961). (*O.C.T.F.*)

[2] *Letters* XIV, p. 239.   [3] ibid., pp. 213–4.   [4] ibid., p. 252.

The questions which opened up were to what extent is the truth mediated by the Church relevant or even meaningful in the absence of lay consultation? Yet if the laity ought to be consulted does this not compromise the authority of the magisterium? Is this not a restatement of the Protestant view (and heresy) that the laity determine and regulate the Church? Was not Newman merely repeating what Coleridge had advocated and Maurice was subsequently to develop?

The course of the controversy needs to be studied in some detail in order to appreciate the issues which divided Newman from his opponents, of whom their spokesman, Dr. Gillow of Ushaw, was highly typical; but also because Newman avoids the charges I have summarized only by means of a carefully balanced and discriminating analysis.

He drew upon his patristic studies to raise the fundamental questions which lay at the root of his failure with the Irish University. What do we mean when we speak of the mind of the Church; and how is it determined, for example, when the teaching function of the bishops is silent? Is the mind of the Church wider than the mind of the magisterium?

Newman's courage in bringing matters to a head theologically should not be overlooked. The publication of 'On Consulting the Faithful in matters of doctrine' in the *Rambler* for July 1859 produced an effect within the Roman Church almost greater than that produced within the Church of England by the publication of *Tract XC* some 18 years previously.

It was not until 21 March 1859, that Newman made his decision to edit the *Rambler*.[1] It had taken weeks of prayer and deliberation, and he may have been moved to it by the fear of what Simpson would do if the *Rambler* ceased to be carried on, since Simpson had threatened that if his resignation destroyed the review, he would make the whole affair public and claim compensation from the bishops for financial loss. Newman accepted the *Rambler* as 'a bitter penance',[2] and only at the express wish of Bishop Ullathorne and Cardinal Wiseman. His short-term policy was to take it out of the front line of controversy.

Newman believed that the review had placed itself in its present false position for three reasons: it had treated of theology proper, it had done so in magazine fashion, and it had allowed laymen to do so. 'It requires an explanation when a layman writes on theology', and given the existing difficulties of the Holy See, especially in a missionary country such as England, a layman could only write in its support; to publish criticisms of authority was to court inevitable disaster, and for a convert, like Simpson, to do so was merely to substantiate the general proposition: 'all converts are dangerous'.[1]

Newman still believed that, without compromising principle, a different tone and choice of subjects were possible—(to read the *Rambler* today is to wonder what all the fuss was about)—but Acton's ironical comment that 'people are quite as sensitive about other things as about theology'[2] was closer to the truth.

In his Advertisement to the new series of the *Rambler*, Newman was at pains to do nothing which would 'damage the fair fame of men who I believed were at bottom sincere Catholics'. Newman thought it 'unfair, ungenerous, impertinent, and cowardly to make in their behalf acts of confession and contrition'; and he deliberately avoided saying anything about changes in matter, drift, objects, and tone.[3]

The first of the new series, for May 1859, seems innocuous enough. It begins with a review article, entitled 'The Mission of the Isles of the North', on the sermons, lectures, and speeches delivered by the Cardinal Archbishop in the course of his late tour in Ireland. The treacle of eulogy is spread thick indeed. 'No other public man in England,' we are told, 'could have answered to the demand thus made upon his stores of mind with the spirit and the intellectual power which the Cardinal [Wiseman] displayed on the occasion.'[4] There are other articles on the 'Religious Associations in the Sixteenth Century', the 'Development of Gothic Architecture', the 'Ancient Saints', and one by the Baron d'Eckstein on Lammenais. There are certain Literary Notices, in one of which appears *Lectures and Essays on University Subjects* by John Henry Newman, to which the feeling comment is appended that 'it does but supply another instance of [the author's] lot all through life, to have been led to its publication not on any matured plan or by any

[1] *O.C.T.F.*, pp. 4–7; *W.* i, pp. 482–5. The reason for Newman's attitude is given in *Letters* XVII, p. 504: he was opposed to laymen writing theology, 'not because they are laymen, but because they are *autodidaktoi*'.

[2] A. Gasquet, *Lord Acton and his Circle* (1906), the annotated copy by Edmund Bishop in the Downside Abbey Archives, pp. 49, 51.

[3] *W.* i, p. 494.   [4] *Rambler*, vol. XI (1859), p. 2.

view of his own, but by the duties or the circumstances of the moment'.[1]

But this appeal was passed over by those close but unsympathetic readers who were concerned only to find grounds for their prejudice that the new series would be no different from the old. There were only two points in that May issue which could have been selected for attack: a letter in the correspondence section which ended with the question: 'how far is it allowable, or desirable, for laymen to study theology?' and certain remarks buried deep in the small type and double columns of the commentary on Contemporary Events.[2] Unsigned, they were written by Newman as editor, and dealt with the judgement of the English bishops on the proposed Royal Commission on elementary education. They contained the following remarks:

we do unfeignedly believe ... that their Lordships really desire to know the opinion of the laity on subjects in which the laity are especially concerned. *If even in the preparation of a dogmatic definition the faithful are consulted*, as lately in the instance of the Immaculate Conception, it is at least as natural to anticipate such an act of kind feeling and sympathy in great practical questions. [My italics.]

This passage, and in particular that part of it in italics, was the point chosen by the *Rambler*'s opponents, of whom the chief was Dr. Gillow, professor of theology at Ushaw, who had previously reported an article by Döllinger to the authorities. It was a sound tactical choice, as the bishops were extremely sensitive to the education question, and had been exposed to some pertinent and expert criticism in previous numbers of the *Rambler*; and if we are to understand why Newman felt it necessary to defend contributions to the old series of the *Rambler* in the first number of the new, it is necessary to know something about a question, which, even now, is not without its contemporary significance.

The state of public elementary education was causing such concern that all parties agreed that more information on the way in which existing arrangements worked was required; and in 1858 the Newcastle Commission was appointed to report on measures likely to extend 'sound and cheap elementary instruction to all classes of the people'. One of the main problems was how to reconcile the

[1] *Rambler*, XI, p. 115.   [2] ibid., pp. 109, 122.

freedom of denominational schools with public control over the subsidies which they received.

In default of any official guidance from the bishops, the *Rambler* had treated the matter of Catholic co-operation with the Commission as one still open to discussion, and had published two articles in January and February 1859. Although unsigned, they were written by Nasmyth Scott Stokes[1]; and they reflect the qualities of their author, being expert, weighty, yet moderate in tone. They begin, it is important to note, with

due submission to ecclesiastical authority, desiring nothing but to promote the welfare and progress of the Church; and we revoke and wish unsaid any word which may seem to tend in an opposite direction. ... In stating actual facts, we desire to furnish materials for a judgment rather than force a conclusion of our own.[2]

The argument is as follows: that although no Catholic was a member of the Commission, one could have been appointed if representations had been received in time. Failure to make such representations was the responsibility of the Catholic Poor-School Committee ('which communicates so rarely with its supporters and the public, and finds so few opportunities to rouse and inform the Catholic body upon educational questions').[3] Catholics should co-operate with the Commission, not only because they were in receipt of public funds and could be compelled to give evidence, if Parliament so determined, but because open cooperation would help dispel bigotry and the suspicion that 'Catholics make bad citizens of a free state'. A positive policy of opening wide the doors would let the world learn that building grants had been spent on schools and teachers' houses and not on churches and presbyteries, that Catholic education was not a hole-and-corner mixture of jugglery, immorality, and sedition, but calculated beyond doubt to train useful citizens and sound Christians.

There was a deeper danger still, and this was that the existing denominational system, so complex and costly, would be

---

[1] A convert and the first secretary of the Catholic Poor-School Committee, a body set up to deal with the government on behalf of the bishops, who were still not legally represented. Stokes became one of the Catholic school inspectors in 1853 and was promoted senior inspector in 1871, thus making him a colleague of Matthew Arnold in the inspectorate. Later he served on the Royal Commission on Primary Education in Ireland. See *O.C.T.F.*, pp. 9–10; *Rambler*, XI, pp. 17–30; 104–13.

[2] *Rambler*, XI, p. 20.   [3] *Rambler*, XI, p. 106.

superseded by some kind of State-supported schools. On these grounds Catholics should welcome the Commissioners' representatives into their schools, so that they might witness the effectiveness of their religious teaching. No principles would be conceded, because the Commissioners were not inspectors, but appointed for a particular occasion, and they were concerned not with the matter of religious instruction but with its method. Were Catholic poor-schools so unlike others that no kind of comparison could be arrived at?

The author concludes the February article by asking what will be the consequence of Catholic isolation, if the grant is withdrawn and schools of a sufficient standard cannot be provided. He cites the similar controversy taking place in the United States and quotes from Brownson's Review the warning that less harm will come to a Catholic child who attends a well-run State school in which he may be compelled to read the Protestant version of the Bible, than to one who is placed in a Catholic school, under half-educated and ill-paid teachers, whose manners and influence can do little to elevate or refine him, so that there will perhaps be more difficulty in preserving to the faith the children educated in such schools than those educated in the State schools of the country.[1]

The judgment delivered by the bishops, which Newman printed in the May Rambler,[2] was supplemented by extracts from the Pastoral of Bishop Ullathorne of Birmingham, whose discussion of the subject was characteristically more thorough, cogent, and illuminating. Commissioners were no different from inspectors, a sacred and religious principle was at issue, the concession demanded was equivalent to a surrender of the very ground on which Catholic inspectors had been demanded and obtained, the distinction between matter and method was denied ('only a Catholic can understand the mind and spirit of a Catholic'),[3] and the presence of a Commissioner's representative at religious instruction would confer upon him in the eyes of the children an impression of the State's exercising authority in matters religious. One or two, here and there, had used the public press as a weapon against the conduct of the episcopacy, and might have separated the faithful from its pastors in a matter involving ecclesiastical freedom, episcopal prudence, and religious discipline.

In his editorial note, Newman immediately apologizes: 'we did

[1] Rambler, XI, pp. 112–13.   [2] ibid., New Series, I, pp. 117 ff.   [3] ibid., p. 119.

not know that the Bishops had spoken formally' (decisions apparently taken in the November were not communicated until the Spring). His second remark which contained the cause of all the trouble is worth quoting in full:

Acknowledging, then, most fully the prerogatives of the episcopate, we do unfeignedly believe, both from the reasonableness of the matter, and especially from the prudence, gentleness, and considerateness which belong to them personally, that their Lordships really desire to know the opinion of the laity on subjects in which the laity are especially concerned. If even in the preparation of a dogmatic definition the faithful are consulted, as lately in the instance of the Immaculate Conception, it is at least as natural to anticipate such an act of kind feeling and sympathy in great practical questions, out of the condescension which belongs to those who are *forma facti gregis ex animo*. If our words or tone were disrespectful, we deeply grieve and apologise for such a fault; but surely we are not disrespectful in thinking, and in having thought, that the Bishops would like to know the sentiments of an influential portion of the laity before they took any step which perhaps they could not recall. Surely it was no disrespect towards them to desire that they should have the laity rallying round them on the great question of education with the imposing zeal which has lately been exemplified in Ireland, in the great meeting which was held at Cork. If we have uttered a word inconsistent with this explanation of our conduct—if we argued in a hard or disrespectful tone—if we put into print what might better have been conveyed to their Lordships in some other way—we repeat, we are deeply sorry for it. We are too fully convinced of the misery of any division between the rulers of the Church and the educated laity— we grieve too deeply, too bitterly, over such instances as are found, either in the present day or in the history of the past, of such mutual alienations—to commit ourselves consciously to any act which may tend to so dire a calamity. It is our fervent prayer that their Lordships may live in the hearts of their people; of the poor as well as of the rich, of the rich as well as of the poor; of the clergy as well as of the laity, of the laity as well as of the clergy; but whatever be our own anxious desire on the subject, we know that the desire of the Bishops themselves is far more intense, more generous, more heart-consuming, than can be the desire of any persons, however loyal to them, who are committed to their charge. Let them pardon, then, the incidental hastiness of manner or want of ceremony of the rude Jack-tars of their vessel, as far as it occurred, in consideration of the zeal and energy with which they haul to the ropes and man the yards.[1]

[1] ibid, pp. 122–3.

Newman's nautical metaphor is significant. Earlier on, in speaking of his policy for the *Rambler*, he had recommended the policy of Wellington in the lines of Torres Vedras; and such naval and military metaphors come naturally to one who burned to see the Church take advantage of its emancipation and become, once again, a community on the march.

Unhappily, nothing so effectively demonstrates the dimensions of the gulf which divided not only the bishops from the laity, but more particularly the converts from their fellow Catholics than does this clash over the education question. It was all the greater for being unconscious; since what the clash so dramatically demonstrates is to what extent the presuppositions about the relationship of Church to society held by converts such as Stokes and Simpson had been formed within the ecclesiology of the Church they had left. Taking for granted, as most of them did, that 'happy anomaly'[1] and 'blessed accident'[2] of a working union of Church and State, they assumed as Roman Catholics that this overlapping relationship of Church and society, in which each was the 'be-friending opposite'[3] to the other, was perfectly normal. Hence not only their trust in the possibility of a working relationship with the government over Catholic education, but their assumption that as expert laymen they were entitled to expect a collaborative relationship with their bishops in such a matter of mutual concern. Without realizing it their behaviour assumed the role of the layman to consist in exercising that double function upon Church and society which Coleridge allocates to the clerisy in *Church and State*.[4]

The bishops, to the extent that they were educated men,[5] had been formed in foreign seminaries and upon alien principles: they were Englishmen only in name. They tended to interpret the currency of English life—Blue books, Gladstone, and Matthew Arnold—in terms of Italian politics (as Newman had noted of

---

[1] Newman in *Moz.* I, pp. 450–8.
[2] Coleridge, *Church and State*, p. 59.   [3] ibid., p. 124.
[4] When vol. ii of the *Parochial Sermons* was republished in 1868, Newman retained its dedication, dated 21 Feb. 1835, which speaks of his 'cheerful conviction that the English Church amid many defections still holds her influence over an attached and zealous laity'.
[5] The consequences of a general 'absence of education' among Catholics are frequently discussed by Newman: it makes them appear 'raw'. 'In the after dinner conversation of priests, and the recreations of nuns,' for example, 'they are to be cheerful, and they have nothing to be cheerful upon. So they are boisterous or silly' (*Letters* XIV, p. 183, 28 Dec. 1850).

Cullen's attitude to the Young Irelanders). To them the gap between the verifying function of the Church and its context within a society increasingly committed to secular and liberalizing policies was unbridgeable and theologically inevitable. Their conception of the Church was patriarchal—that of a family to be protected from 'the world' with which it was inevitably bound to collide. For them it was not a question of how they could take meaningful decisions in the absence of lay consultation, but of how to resist concessions which would bring their patriarchal authority into question.

In a letter to Simpson, Bishop Ullathorne made it clear that the bishops deemed it 'absolutely unnecessary that the Catholic community should be informed of the grounds of our proceedings'.[1] In April, Simpson could not resist producing his own version of the affair in a long letter intended for publication in Montalambert's *Le Correspondant*.[2] It is passionate—the sense of injustice still burns strongly—and rather diffuse, and it seems not to have been published; but it has its insights. Simpson speaks of this 'coup against the laity', in which

the English Hierarchy has been victorious; not over its enemies but over its friends; no new converts have been made, no enthusiasm excited, no burst of charity or zeal called forth by their artillery and their blows. They have triumphed over their own army, and have excited not the enthusiasm of Christian conquest, but the passions of civil war.

He quotes a letter he has received from a most influential layman, a representative of one of the old Catholic families:

this whole story is a warning to all who by writing or public life of any kind wish to serve the cause of religion as independent laymen, or in any other quality or office than that of Bishops. If no other office is recognised, let us have it so declared. If all Catholic literature is to be confined to Bishops' Pastorals, and politics to be merely their echo, let it be known to all whom it may concern. If the dictum attributed to the Cardinal, 'the only function of the laity is to pay', be really the law of this land, let us know it, that we may get out of it into some more Christian country.

Simpson comments that

this jealousy of the laity is a natural result of the strictness of the administrative organization which is now considered to constitute the

---

[1] 8 March 1859 (Downside Abbey Archives).
[2] A MS. letter written for Montalambert's *Le Correspondant*, but never published (*c.* April 1859) and now in the Downside Abbey Archives.

strength of the clergy. . . . The compactness of the clerical union makes
it a caste; it has a separate professional education and separate habits of
thought. . . . The laity are to be kept in ignorance of all religious questions except those in the catechism, in order to misuse their obedience
to a body of directors professionally educated to manage their religion
for them. Religion is turned into administration, the clergy into
theological police, and the body of thinking laymen into a mass of
suspects, supposed to be brooding on nothing but revolution, and only
kept together by motives of fear, and by the external pressure of a
clerical organization.

The effect on British Protestant opinion of the bishops' policy of
non-co-operation over the education question is, Simpson goes on
to say, merely to arouse contempt. The question of religious
education is no longer political but social, and can best be settled
by negotiation, compromise and all the other arts that constitute
the British political way of life: 'we strive to make the stream run
up hill again, and make it a political instead of, or as well as, a
social difference'.[1]

It is important to remember that these observations were made
before Newman's interview with Ullathorne. It was on 22 May
that this famous meeting took place, at which Newman was told
that even the May number of the *Rambler* was too disturbing for
Catholic taste:

There were remains of the old spirit. It was irritating. Our laity were
a *peaceable* set; the Church was *peace*. They had a deep faith; they did
not like to hear that anyone doubted.

Newman's record of the meeting continues:

I stated my own view strongly . . . he saw only one side, I another;
that the Bishops etc., did not see the state of the laity, e.g. in Ireland,
how unsettled, yet how docile.
   He said something like 'Who are the laity?' I answered (not these
words) that the Church would look foolish without them. He said,
'Could there not be an *Irish* Magazine?' I said, who was to conduct it?[2]

In vain did Newman try to convince Ullathorne that the reason
for his going to Ireland in the first place had been 'the hope of
doing something towards those various objects for which I had
consented to undertake the *Rambler*. . . . He would not allow the

---

[1] Simpson, MS. Letter, pp. 17–20.
[2] Birmingham Oratory, memo. dated 22 May 1859.

weight of anything I said'; and when Newman reminded him of
his initial unwillingness to take on the editorship, Ullathorne
turned to him abruptly and said: 'Why not give it up?'

It was agreed, in fairness to the proprietors and to Newman's
own pocket, that he should give up the *Rambler* after the next
(July) issue. There, 'with no sort of unpleasantness', the conversation ended.

Newman's relief was tempered, as the news of his resignation
circulated, by a growing sadness, and then by an increasingly
familiar sense of frustration. Those converts who thought as he
did regarded the event as a sign of the bishops' inability to rise to
the challenge of the times, and various exclamations of despair are
recorded in letters to Newman:

'We must wait for a convert Bishop,' wrote one correspondent[1];
while another, H. W. Wilberforce, wrote: 'I deeply feel that our
Bishops do not understand England and the English. Either the
Catholic laity will kick, or, what I rather fear, they will more and
more fall below Protestants in intellectual training and have no
influence on the public mind.'[2]

Once again Newman felt that his mission had been repudiated.
He tried to console himself with the reflection that 'it may be
God's will it should be done a hundred years later', but he could
not hold back from the bitter reflection that 'when I am gone it
will be seen perhaps that persons stopped me from doing a *work*
which I *might* have done'.[3] Again he felt obliged to defend himself
against misinterpretation (a motive which, as the *Apologia* was to
show in five years' time, was always the most powerful to produce
his best and most characteristic writing). This essay is the result.

On Consulting the Faithful in Matters of Doctrine was published
in the next and, for Newman, final number of the *Rambler*[4]; and
both its subject matter and style gain added significance when they
are related to the background which has already been described.

It is clear from the way in which Newman links the *Rambler* issue
with that of the Irish university and speaks of his particular
mission that not only is the existence of a lively and educated laity
fundamental to his conception of the Catholic Church and to his

[1] *W*. i, p. 501.   [2] MS. Letter, 19 July 1859. (O)
[3] *W*. i, pp. 499–500.
[4] The *Rambler*, vol. i, new series, Part II, July 1859. All references are to the
collated text published by me in *O.C.T.F.* (1961), which embodies the amend-
ments made in 1871.

theology, but that the encouragement of such a laity is one of its most immediate needs. Some eight years previously, in 1851, and before his Irish adventure he had referred to the laity as at all times 'the measure of the Catholic spirit; they saved the Irish Church three centuries ago, and they betrayed the Church in England. Our rulers were true, our people were cowards.' [1] He was now to turn his attention to what appeared to be almost the reverse situation; and there is no doubt that he had been stung into this by the controversy over the *Rambler* and the spirit that it had manifested. What had scandalized him had been the attitude to the laity adopted not merely by the bishops but by the one whom he most admired, Ullathorne. Even to him, a layman seemed, spiritually, to be a kind of 'boy eternal', rather than a responsible adult partner, whose right it was to be consulted on matters within his competence; and it is this point which Newman chooses to subject to the strictest theological examination.

On Consulting the Faithful in Matters of Doctrine begins with what, at first sight, appears to be a rather donnish disquisition on the difference between the idiom of English and the theological use of Latin. In the latter sense 'consult' means to take counsel with, but idiomatically the meaning includes ascertaining a matter of fact as well as asking a judgement. [2] Thus consulting the faithful involves asking, as a matter of fact, what the belief of the faithful is, as a testimony of that apostolical tradition, on which alone any doctrine may be defined, and it was in this idiomatic sense (to consult the faithful, as we consult a body of evidence) that the word was used in the passage of the previous number of the *Rambler* to which objection had been taken. Newman reminds his readers, not without irony, that we cannot re-model our mother tongue, and reproves those who desire that perfect technical accuracy of expression demanded in a Latin treatise for jumping to the conclusion that its absence is a sign of self-will and undutifulness. [3]

He now takes the offensive and asserts that even in the technical theological sense the laity have a right to be consulted, since the body of the faithful is one of the witnesses to the fact of revealed doctrine, because their consensus throughout Christendom is the voice of the infallible Church.

[1] *Pres. Pos.*, p. 360.   [2] *O.C.T.F.*, p. 54.   [3] *O.C.T.F.*, p. 62.

Yet although at various times this consensus of the faithful can make up, for example, for the silence of the Fathers, infallibility is not, strictly, *in* that consensus, but rather the consensus is an indicium or instrumentum to us of the judgement of that Church which *is* infallible.[1] Nevertheless, doctrines have been defined and determined at the request of the faithful—indeed, such deference has been paid to them, that their impatience has sometimes almost been feared; but this was always because such demands were the faithful reflections of the pastoral teaching, and the people were a mirror in which the bishops saw themselves. Newman again permits himself an ironical aside when he adds: 'I suppose a person may *consult* his glass, and in that way may know things about himself which he can learn in no other way.'[2]

Furthermore, the common accord of the faithful, of populations and of nations, is—as St. Augustine points out—one of the chief factors which holds us, justly, within the bosom of the Church; and 'in matters whereupon the Scripture has not spoken clearly, the custom of the people of God, or the institutions of our predecessors, are to be held as law'.

Newman concludes this part of his argument by summarizing the five characteristics of the consent of the faithful.[3] It is to be regarded as a testimony of the fact of the apostolical dogma; as a sort of instinct, or *phronema*, deep in the bosom of the mystical body of Christ; as a direction of the Holy Ghost; as an answer to its prayer; and as a jealousy of error, which it at once feels as a scandal.

The second and fifth of these characteristics take us to the heart of Newman's teaching. The *phronema*, that instinct deep within the mystical body of Christ, is obviously a counterpart to the *phronesis* or illative sense which, in the individual, is that power to make a real, as opposed to a notional, assent in judgements of faith and conscience.

The fifth characteristic is related to Newman's justification of a liberal education: that what is true in a natural sense can never be contrary to Revelation; and it is significant that he should quote the following passage from *Anglican Difficulties* by way of elucidation: 'it is the property of life to be impatient of any foreign substance in the body to which it belongs', since it was almost in these

---

[1] ibid., p. 67.   [2] ibid., p. 72.   [3] ibid., pp. 73–4.

words and from such attitudes that he was to base his case for admitting Catholics as undergraduates at Oxford: young men must be free to make mistakes in order to acquire that real independence which gives vitality to the spirit and, thereby, the power to expel error.

Newman now returns to consider in detail the evidences for this witness of the faithful during the Arian controversy. Theirs was the voice of tradition, and the Nicene dogma was maintained during the greater part of the fourth century not by the unswerving firmness of the Holy See, Councils, or bishops, but by this *consensus fidelium*.[1] There was, therefore, a temporary suspense of the functions of the *Ecclesia Docens*, since the body of the bishops in speaking variously, one against another, failed in their confession of the faith. Later in considering the details of the evidence, Newman remarks that the *Ecclesia Docens* is not at every time the active instrument of the Church's infallibility[2]; by which he means that it may speak with divided voices or not at all, and then the consensus of the faithful constitutes an authentic instrument of the apostolic tradition.[3] What is certain is that, in the fourth century, such an absence of effective leadership caused laymen to express their sense of the truth that was within them in a way profoundly displeasing to those in authority.

Newman now turns to the evidence for the fidelity of the laity during the Arian heresy.[4] He concludes by arguing that the consent of the faithful is one of those theological presuppositions of Catholic doctrine which become clear only when required for use, as for example when the contemplated definition of the Immaculate Conception was under discussion. He goes on to remark, with an irony which the events that precipitated his reflections richly justify, that although Arianism may not return and that this age is one which can preeminently dispense with the testimony of the faithful ('and perhaps this is the reason why the 'consensus fidelium' has, in the minds of many, fallen into the background'),[5] yet each constituent portion of the Church has its proper functions, and no portion can be safely neglected.

Newman now enunciates the cardinal theological principle which he clearly felt to be involved, not merely in the historical question

---

[1] ibid., p. 77.   [2] ibid., p. 86.
[3] See also footnote to sect. 2 in 1871 text, *O.C.T.F.*, p. 116 [1].
[4] ibid., pp. 86 f.   [5] ibid., p. 103.

THE MIND OF THE CHURCH

of Arianism, but in those unhappy controversies which had arisen
as a result of his frustrated efforts to educate the laity and to see
them established in the economy of the Church of his time:

> Though the laity be but the reflection or echo of the clergy in matters
> of faith, yet there is something in the 'pastorum et fidelium *conspiratio*',
> which is not in the pastors alone.[1]

Devotion starts from below. Enthusiasm must be encouraged.
The *Ecclesia Docens* is happier when she has enthusiastic partisans
about her,

> than when she cuts off the faithful from the study of her divine doctrines
> and the sympathy of her divine contemplations, and requires from them
> a *fides implicita* in her word, which in the educated classes will terminate
> in indifference, and in the poorer in superstition.[2]

From his earliest Anglican days, Newman's emphasis had always
been on the fullness of the Catholic idea; and in the Oxford
University Sermon which had anticipated the *Development of
Christian Doctrine*, he speaks of that idea as the secret life of
millions of faithful souls, of centuries passing without the formal
expression of such truths, and of St. Mary's keeping all these say-
ings in her heart and becoming thereby our pattern of faith, both
in the reception and the study of Divine Truth.[3]

The mind of the Catholic Church is formed, therefore, not by
the strict and systematic imposition of authority (as Maurice had
alleged), but by means of a growth, socially, over 'a large mental
field'[4]; and this mind of the Church is composed of sensibilities
'found' by the words of Scripture and 'realized' by the discharge
of their religious responsibilities within society at large.

Under the pressure of inevitable change heresies arise; and it is
these which oblige the Church more positively to define the content
and implications of Revelation: thus arises the development of
doctrine which is a 'more intimate apprehension, and a more lucid
enunciation of the original dogma' by the Church. 'But what is the
Church as separate from popes, councils, bishops and faithful?'[5]

The importance of *On Consulting the Faithful* is, as Professor
Owen Chadwick points out, that it is Newman's first attempt to

---

[1] *O.C.T.F.*, p. 104, cp. Newman in 1842: 'The Church has authority only
while all the members conspire together'. *Moz.* ii, p. 400.
[2] *O.C.T.F.*, p. 106. [3] *O.U.S.*, pp. 313, 323. [4] *Dev.*, p. 36.
[5] Newman to Acton, 8 July 1862, cited in Owen Chadwick, *From Bossuet to
Newman: the Idea of Doctrinal Development* (Cambridge, 1957), pp. 243–4.

resolve publicly one of the major difficulties in his theory of doctrinal development: how, before a definition, is the mind of the Church to be discovered?[1] What is 'the process by which, under the magisterium of the Church, implicit faith becomes explicit'?[2]

This contention is conclusively supported by the documents. On 21 April 1859 Acton wrote to Simpson saying that Newman was in great spirits at having the *Rambler*; an article, 'editorial as it appears, on the Education question' was being written by Newman for the next (May) issue; and in July, says Acton, 'he means to review Gillow'. Bishop's pencilled insertion against this sentence is: 'Was it in the *Consulting the Laity* paper that this idea issued?'[3] Dr. Gillow had just published a sixty-four page pamphlet denouncing Döllinger's article in the *Rambler*, which had attempted to provide the evidence and justification for a statement by Acton in the *Rambler* for August 1858 that St. Augustine was the father of Jansenism.[4] To Gillow's rigidly syllogistic mind this meant that either St. Augustine taught Jansenism or he did not; and that if he did not, such a proposition could be made only by a fool or a knave. Since it was made with the backing of a theologian of Döllinger's eminence, it was not a foolish utterance but one arising from the worst motives; so it must be forcibly and immediately denounced to Rome.

Such a mind, imprisoned within its black and white logical categories, must have been quite incapable of understanding either the development of heresy or the development of doctrine; and Newman may have had it in mind to give Gillow a history lesson upon the complexities which inevitably attend upon the rise, flowering, and suppression of a particular heresy—in this case Arianism—and upon the way in which the mind of the Church actually makes itself manifest.

Döllinger had himself written to Newman on 26 May asking whether he ought to reply to Gillow's pamphlet: 'You have thrown out bait in the *Rambler* to make me enter into the ticklish question of the historical ignorance prevailing in the common divinity of the schools.'[5] But it seems to have been felt that further intervention by Döllinger would only increase the injury to the *Rambler*.

---

[1] ibid., p. 183.   [2] Newman to Acton, ibid., p. 244.

[3] Gasquet, *Lord Acton and his Circle*, p. 70: see p. 105 above, note [2].

[4] *Rambler*, X, p. 135. This is more fully discussed in *O.C.T.F.*, pp. 3–4.

[5] *O.*, 26 May 1859.

The unpublished correspondence between Newman and Gillow, which is preserved at Birmingham Oratory, is worth special consideration in this context, since it establishes even more precisely what Newman had in mind when he was writing his article.[1] Dr. Gillow held the chair of theology at Ushaw for twenty-three years, and at his funeral in 1877 it was said of him that 'the plain words of scripture, the authoritative teaching of the Church, the infallible decisions of the Holy See, the testimony of reason, the irresistible evidence of physical or mathematical science—those alone satisfied his mind.' He was a man of parts—architect, chemist, and inventor—but he had his limitations: he was something of a crank: he invented a watch, for example, by which he insisted on regulating the College chronometer.[2]

The correspondence begins on 12 May, when Gillow sent Newman a copy of his answer to Döllinger and protested against certain statements and principles in the previous (May) *Rambler*, which 'appear to me very objectionable'. He instanced especially the words: 'If even in the preparation of a dogmatic definition the faithful are consulted, as lately in the instance of the Immaculate Conception.'

Newman's reply on 13 May was curt and tart. He admitted responsibility for the passage objected to and asked for the objections to be more specifically stated. Of the policy of previous *Ramblers*, he said: 'I have had no more to do with the Magazine, directly or indirectly, before this number, than, I suppose, you have had.'

Newman sent the correspondence to Ullathorne who, in his reply of 15 May, seems to side with Gillow as against Newman. Speaking of the Pontifical Letter (*c.* 1848) referred to in the *Rambler* article, Ullathorne says:

its sense was to invite each Bishop to ascertain the sentiments of his clergy, and, in prudent ways, the feelings of the laity, on the subject of the Immaculate Conception. . . . From the special injunction of prudence as to our mode of ascertaining the sense of the people, I understood that we were to ascertain that sense not from the people themselves, but from their pastors, who generally gave their proof from the devotions in use.

[1] The correspondence between Newman, Gillow, and Ullathorne which now follows (pp. 119–21) derives entirely from the Letter Books (12 May–2 Sept. 1859) at the Birmingham Oratory. (*O*.)

[2] See Joseph Gillow, *Dictionary of English Catholics* (1885).

Speaking of the relation between the Church teaching and the Church taught, he goes on to say:

the impress can only be as the seal impressed, and if, having the seal, we find on it no signs of the impression it is supposed to have made, the impression must have come from another source.

Newman adopts the analogy of the seal and uses it, substantially modified, later on. Meanwhile, Gillow was eager to continue the correspondence, and in his next letter (15 May) admitted to having read the May *Rambler* in the same critical spirit as he had read the previous ones. Now that he knew that Newman had become the editor, he professed himself satisfied: right had triumphed over wrong, the bishops' control had been established, and the *Rambler*'s orthodoxy at last secured.

Yet he stuck to his guns. The offending phrase about consulting the faithful implied:

that the infallibility of the Church resides in the Communitate fidelium, and not exclusively in the Ecclesia docente. Else the infallible portion would consult the fallible with a view to guiding itself to an infallible decision. But the above principle would be characterised as at least *haeresi proxima*.

Newman replied by return on 16 May. He anticipates many of the analogies (e.g., the barometer) used subsequently in the article, and objects to Gillow's view that the infallibility of the Church is *exclusively* in the *Ecclesia docente*:

I understand Fr. Perrone to say, on the contrary, that it resides per modum unius in both, as a figure is contained both on the seal and on the wax, and primarily in the mind of the engraver.

In a further letter, dated 25 May, Newman asks Gillow if he is not confusing the infallibility of the Church with 'the power and prerogative of definition' which alone belongs to the *Ecclesia docens*:

It is very difficult to be quite accurate in one's wording of scientific truth, even when one makes it a *point* to be accurate. I can quite understand how you came to take my *un*scientific and familiar word 'consult' in a theological sense, as if it ascribed a 'judicium' to the consulted parties, viz., because you are a theologian. The question is, whether the ordinary English layman would have so understood the passage.

After the publication of the *Rambler* article in July, Gillow returned to the attack. In a letter of 28 August, he flatly contradicts Newman's claim that there could be a suspense of the functions of the *Ecclesia Docens*, and asserts that a *fides implicita* is what the Church rightly demands. To assert otherwise would be 'a caution to the faithful to be on their guard against the Church'. Thus the tendency of the article might be

to induce speculative minds to think disparagingly of the infallibility of the Church, and to conceive that though the Church as a whole may be infallible, yet either of its parts, the Ecclesia docens or the Ecclesia discens may fail: or at all events, that if either of these parts be infallible, that infallibility does not reside with the ecclesia docens but the ecclesia discens. Thus they may be led to place the disciple above the Master. The step between this and placing the private judgement above the doctrinal authority of the Church is not a wide one. As I am conscious that I must attribute the appearance of this article to myself as having given occasion to it at least in some measure, I therefore deem it a duty to say this much of my impressions regarding it.

From Newman's notes on the original letter, it is clear that he at first meditated a brief but friendly reply; but after reflection he must have decided that in view of the length of Gillow's letter, he must once more try to teach him a more sensitive verbal discrimination. In his reply of 2 September, Newman protests that 'suspense' did not mean 'failure': 'I think it has a meaning far lighter even than "suspension".' The 'body of bishops' was 'the actual mass at the particular time spoken of'—no more. As for the *fides implicita*, he repeats that 'he merely speaks of the possibility of our inculcating on the faithful a sort of *fides implicita* which would terminate in the evils which he specifies'.

The implications of Newman's answer to his own question— how, before a definition, is the mind of the Church to be discovered —were quite obvious to his opponents. If the Church had a duty to consult the faithful, then it also had a duty to manifest itself fully as a *conspiratio* of priests and laity, as distinct from the existing practice of acquiescing in a laity which was either superstitious or indifferent, and capable of a merely notional assent in matters of faith.

His answer also led him to part company with Acton, whose preoccupation with the Church's political record had caused him to conceive the Church as co-terminous with the actions of its priestly officers, and conscience as that individualizing faculty which was bound to collide with the inevitable consequences of unbridled priestly power. For Newman such a view allowed insufficiently for the limitations of the individual conscience, which could claim infallibility only in so far as it reflected the verdict of the whole world: 'Securus judicat orbis terrarum' was what had brought him into the Church, and it lies at the heart of his conception of the *consensus fidelium* as the infallible voice of the Church. This is to see the Church under its mystical and not its political aspect, to see it as the mystical body saving *in spite of* the actions of its officers. It is clear that Newman sees the individual conscience (*phronesis*) as being fulfilled only in the *phronema*, or communal conscience of the whole Church: one was the mirror to the other, in which we could sometimes see ourselves more clearly, and by which our individual moral insights were fulfilled, completed, and sustained. Under this, its mystical aspect, the Church is more than a political assemblage or aggregation of individual consciences: it is a real, because dynamic, community possessed of the therapeutic power which can quicken, purge, and save the individual consciences of its members; and it alone is able to secure that associated sensibility—intellectual and spiritual—which is the secret of the whole, or holy, man.

Thus Newman was able to take the claims of the papacy in his stride in so far as he saw them as the means necessary to keeping the mystical body in being as an actual and existing community. The Pope was a ruler, not a philosopher—'he strangles while they prate'; and in his person the Church addressed the wild intellect of man with blows not words, adopting not the philosopher's pallium but the cope, broidered with mystic characters.[1]

But amidst all his correspondence, meetings, and misunderstandings with the chief actors in this tragedy of the higher Catholic journalism, Newman never denies their basic contention: that the nature of the opposition they encountered was itself a symptom of the Church's ill-health and malfunctioning. What he did insist on, at the risk of being labelled a sophist, was that this disease required a deeper and more theological analysis. The achievement of *On Consulting the Faithful* is that it removes the argument from the realm of policy and discipline and places it firmly within the context of theology; it has ceased to be a series of charges and

[1] *W.* i, p. 559; ii, p. 226.

counter-charges, of a dispute about the bishops' behaviour over a particular question of educational co-operation, and has become an argument about the laity's place in the very heart, mind, and structure of the Church. The reception of Newman's article, where it was not hostile, was uncomprehending. Ullathorne had written to say he thought that 'the defender of the word "consult" has not succeeded . . . it was understood as intended in defence of laymen who had written theology in the *Rambler*. [and] was merely used, *more gladiatorio*, as an argument in defence of the *Rambler*'s antecedents'.[1] Citing Johnson's Dictionary, he went on to claim that the primary sense of the word both in English and Latin was 'to take advice', and that Newman was using it in the figurative and secondary sense 'to have regard to'.

Manning's response is given in a letter, 22 September, whose moderate and sympathetic tone is particularly interesting in the light of later developments:

our conversation in the Library about the article in the *Rambler* has been many times in my mind, and I wish you would write and print a sermon on the office of the Holy Ghost in the Church, in which you could bring out 'in ordine theologico' what 'in ordine historico' as in the *Rambler* is confusing to common readers.[2]

The fire-eating Dr. Gillow reappears, this time joined with Bishop Brown of Newport, who wrote to the Secretary of Propaganda at Rome, Archbishop Bedini.[3] He begins by speaking of the disturbing influences of the Birmingham and London Oratories, which, filled as they are with converts rather than with 'original Catholics', foster Protestant notions and feelings, 'whilst a Catholic training of the mind, so essential to converts, can hardly be hoped for'.

The *Rambler* article is then referred to, and the offending argument related.[4] Bishop Brown says that he had written to Dr. Gillow suggesting 'that he should publish a refutation of the statements of Dr. Newman'; but Gillow had replied saying

he thought of replying to it, but was induced to retire from a course which ought to be taken by some one higher in authority; that he had

[1] *O.*, 3 July 1859.   [2] *O.*, 22 September 1859.
[3] 'Newman's Delation', some hitherto unpublished letters: by the Rev. Vincent F. Blehl, S.J., *Dublin Review* 486, winter 1960–1, pp. 296–305.
[4] In *O.C.T.F.*, pp. 75–7.

written upon the subject to Newman, *receiving an unsatisfactory answer*.
Perhaps the high authority of the Holy See is the best to deal with the case—It is most painful to see published by one whom we regarded [sic] as the best of our converts allegations and arguments . . . which might now seem to be the writing of a Calvinist.

No reply was received, and the bishop followed this letter up with another dated 30 October, in which not only does he refer to the objected propositions and proofs as 'sophistical and dishonest', but he goes on to charge the argument of the final paragraph of the essay concerning the effects of a *fides implicita* with being 'quite as bad as anything which went before it—in some respects, worse'.

He includes an extract from a letter from Gillow, who refers to the article as

the most alarming Phenomenon of our times, and has made the old Catholics feel that they do not know where they can place their confidence. It has contributed to widen still more the division between the old Catholics and the Converts, which it appears to me the latter have been setting up ever since their reception into the one fold. They have a strong party . . . they have got into their hands the chief portion of the Catholic press, and if the breach continues to open as it is now doing, we shall see sad results.

In Bishop Brown's third letter the passages objected to are translated into Latin—it is ironical to remember that this was done in order to produce greater theological precision—since he translates the term 'body of the bishops' as 'corpus Episcoporum' and 'general councils' as 'Concilia Oecumenica': statements which taken in their *Latin* sense could indeed be said to border on heresy.

Propaganda took up the case; and a series of most unfortunate misunderstandings developed[1] in which requests for clarification sent to Newman through Wiseman and Ullathorne were never received; and Newman's silence was misinterpreted, so that he remained 'under a cloud' at Rome until the visit there of the Oratorian Fathers St. John and Bittleston in May 1867.

'From that time,' wrote Newman, 'all sorts of suspicions and calumnies have attended my name. And, since we began the [Oratory] School, have been both increased, and directed against it. . . . I shrink from a society which is so unjust towards me.'[2]

---

[1] These are described in *O.C.T.F.*, pp. 38 f.   [2] *A.W.*, p. 257.

The depth of suspicion and the measure of his withdrawal were such that not even the success of the *Apologia* redeemed him, as can be seen in a memorandum written as late as 1874. He notes that until 1859 he had written almost a book a year, but from then until 1874 he had written only three or four; and

the cause of my not writing from 1859 to 1864 was my failure with the *Rambler*. I thought I had got into a scrape, and it became me to be silent. So they thought at Rome, if Mgr Talbot is to be their spokesman, for, referring to the *Apologia* to Ambrose in 1867, he said of me: 'He had ceased writing, and a good riddance—why did he ever begin again?' I certainly had myself in 1860 anticipated his view in 1867 of my services to religion.[1]

That Newman was not exaggerating can be seen from the letter written the same year by Talbot to Manning, concerning the address presented to Newman, signed by upwards of two hundred of the laity, led by the Duke of Norfolk, in which the phrase occurred: 'We feel that every blow that touches you inflicts a wound upon the Catholic Church in this country.' In his letter Talbot says that 'if a check be not placed on the laity of England they will be the rulers of the Catholic Church in England instead of the Holy See and the Episcopate'.

'It is perfectly *true* that a cloud has been hanging over Dr. Newman' ever since the *Rambler* article, and that 'none of his writings since have removed that cloud'. Of the laity, Talbot goes on to say that 'they are beginning to show the cloven hoof. . . . They are only putting into practice the doctrine taught by Dr. Newman in his article in the *Rambler*.' Talbot then asks his celebrated question:

What is the province of the laity? To hunt, to shoot, to entertain. These matters they understand, but to meddle with ecclesiastical matters they have no right at all, and this affair of Newman is a matter purely ecclesiastical. . . . Dr. Newman is the most dangerous man in England, and you will see that he will make use of the laity against your Grace.[2]

In 1871 Newman produced a third edition of *The Arians of the Fourth Century*, and added to the appendix, as Note V, an abbreviated version of the *Rambler* article. He took this opportunity to reply to objections previously made in a lecture at the Roman

[1] *A.W.*, p. 272.   [2] *W*. ii, pp. 143; 146–8.

College by the Jesuit theologian, afterwards Cardinal, Franzelin, and first drawn to Newman's attention in 1867.[1]

The changes in the 1871 version are significant. The section dealing with the charge that there was a temporary suspense of the functions of the *Ecclesia docens* and that the body of the bishops failed in their confession of the faith was meticulously revised,[2] errors were corrected, references to the source material were inserted, and certain of the more controversial references were suppressed. References to St. Basil's persecution and to his being treated with suspicion and coldness by Pope Damasus are deleted[3], so is St. Hilary's charge that the ears of the laity were holier than the hearts of the priests,[4] as well as the assertion that 'the ecclesia docens is not at every time the active instrument of the Church's infallibility'.[5]

The proofs of the fidelity of the laity were less drastically condensed,[6] but errors were corrected, references to the source material made more precise, some indications that they were from English editions suppressed, and the italicizing of the more significant (and therefore inflammatory) passages abandoned. Certain references to the turbulence of the Roman people were cut out,[7] but the most significant deletion is that of a reference to the Arian persecution as having nearly effected a union of certain Novatian and Catholic churches, 'for as they both *held the same sentiments concerning the Divinity*, and were subject to a common persecution, the members of both Churches assembled and prayed together. The Catholics possessed no houses of prayer, for the Arians had wrested them from them.'[8]

The *Rambler* affair sank deep into Newman's mind, and he drew two lessons of profound significance from it. The first concerned the independence needed by Catholics, priests and laity, in order to achieve that spiritual and intellectual vitality which alone would protect them from the spirit of the age and make the Church a fit place for the reception of converts. Newman came to see that this independence would never come about as long as the regime of Propaganda ruled the affairs of this country:

This age of the Church is peculiar—in former times, primitive or medieval, there was not the extreme centralization which now is in use.

[1] *O.C.T.F.*, pp. 109–18.   [2] ibid., pp. 77–86.
[3] ibid., p. 83: para. 16.   [4] ibid., p. 84: 20.   [5] ibid., p. 86: 22.
[6] ibid., pp. 86–101.   [7] ibid., p. 97: 18.   [8] ibid., pp. 96–7: 15.

If a private theologian said anything free, another answered him. If the controversy grew, then it went to a Bishop, a theological faculty, or to some foreign University. The Holy See was but the court of ultimate appeal. *Now*, if I, as a private priest, put anything into print, Propaganda answers me at once. How can I fight with such a chain on my arm? It is like the Persians driven to fight under the lash. There was true private judgement in the primitive and medieval schools—there are no schools now, no private judgement (in the religious sense of the phrase) no freedom, that is, of opinion. That is, no exercise of the intellect. No, the system goes on by the tradition of the intellect of former times.[1]

Simpson made the same point in 1859, but he had taken his analysis much further.[2] He attributed the change in the function and status respectively of clergy and laity especially to the French Revolution. Traditionally the laity had been the protectors and advisers of the clergy, who had received an education abroad in pre-revolutionary times which had been the envy of the Protestants:

our priests brought back a tone and a manner which savoured of the salons of the Faubourg St Germain and an intelligence that might recal[l] Bossuet and Fénelon. They were *independent gentlemen*. . . . The strength which then mainly consisted in the force of individuals must now be sought in discipline and organization; a clergy of a different calibre, of different education, and different origin must make up for individual want of weight by corporate union, by unquestioning obedience to absolute direction and by administrative unity.

A further consequence of the system was, as Newman discovered, that matters requiring a theological attention were evaluated diplomatically, in terms of their power to cause good or bad 'impressions', pain or pleasure; and the penalty of defeat was no longer the precision of formal condemnation, but the unending frustration of 'life under a cloud'. In 1863, he had written:

And who is Propaganda? Virtually one sharp man of business, who works day and night, and dispatches his work quick off, to the East and the West . . . a quasi-military power with a preference for quick results and the scalps of beaten foes.[3]

Ambrose St. John's richly evocative portrait of the proceedings in Rome in 1867 at which Newman was 'rehabilitated', and especially his portrait of the suave yet ebullient Cardinal Barnabo,

---

[1] *W*. i, p. 588.   [2] Simpson, MS. Letter, pp. 4–5.
[3] *O*. Letter to Monsell, 13 Jan. 1863.

Prefect of Propaganda, testify to the consequences of such a jurisdiction, from which this country was not released until 29 June 1908. The past was discussed in terms of whether or not in failing to attend Manning's consecration breakfast, Newman had shown a want of conformity to the Pope's mind; Barnabo's manner would alternate between warmth and evasion: in one outburst of downright heartiness, as St. John calls it, he could say: 'I know Manning best, but I love Newman.' His secretary, Mgr. Capalti, looked at matters in the same spirit, and his solution to the question of how the Catholic members of the university of Oxford should be cared for was: 'let them have there a good priest to make their confessions to, but not a man like Newman—that would be to encourage them'. And when St. John tried to get a word in edgewise, this is how the conversation ended: 'Then we are all agreed, and the whole thing can be settled in two words—good bye—there is a Patriarch waiting for me—basta—you will see the Cardinal tonight.'[1]

The consequences of the failure to distinguish between the needs of diplomacy and theology caused Newman, once again, to seek for the analogue of an existing situation in the early Church; and this produced his second and even more significant lesson.

His discovery that the development of the Arian heresy corresponded to the development of the Church of England had contributed to his conversion; and he now thought that he had detected the seeds of an earlier heresy, Novatianism, in the behaviour of those who opposed his conception of the fullness of the Church, which he believed it was the purpose of his work to propagate.

At present things are in appearance as effete, though in a different way, thank God, as they were in the tenth century. We are sinking into a sort of Novatianism—the heresy which the early Popes so strenuously resisted. Instead of aiming at being a world-wide power, we are shrinking into ourselves, narrowing the lines of communion, trembling at freedom of thought, and using the language of despair and dismay at the prospect before us, instead of, with the high spirit of the warrior, going out conquering and to conquer.[2]

Such a spirit was personified in Newman's erstwhile disciple, W. G. Ward, the editor of the *Dublin Review* and the foremost

[1] *W*. ii, pp. 158–62. [2] *W*. ii, p. 127.

critic of Newman's methods and proposals for educating the Catholic laity. In Ward, Newman felt that he was experiencing all over again that narrowness and intolerance of the worst kind of Evangelical Protestantism from which he had freed himself at Oxford:

Pardon me if I say that you are making a Church within a Church, as the Novatians of old did within the Catholic pale, and as, outside the Catholic pale, the Evangelicals of the Establishment. As they talk of 'vital religion' and vital 'doctrines', and will not allow that their brethren 'know the Gospel', or are Gospel preachers, unless they profess the small shibboleths of their own sect, so you are doing your best to make a party in the Catholic Church, and in St. Paul's words are dividing Christ by exalting your opinions into dogmas. . . . I protest then again, not against your tenets, but against which I must call your schismatical spirit. [1]

This narrowness, the very key-note of 'provinciality'—as Matthew Arnold noted in his own analysis of the same spirit [2]— had narrowed the Church down to a point where it was failing in its mandate to open itself to all men. Instead it was producing people who dwelt in a small world and thought it to be a big one, who preferred the so-called 'Catholic' atmosphere to the challenge of the world outside, and who—in failing to consult the laity or to allow for a true private judgement—were, in Newman's constantly reiterated words, 'failing to prepare the Church for converts'. [3]

But more was at stake than this. If in the controversy with Gillow, Gillow was right and Newman wrong then the Church was to be conceived as divided into two castes—the clerical or dynamic element; and the lay or passive element; and the converts were indeed guilty of shattering the peace of the Church with imported heresies. If Gillow was right then the charge of Romanism put by Coleridge and developed by Maurice was also vindicated—that a layman's function was simply to be obedient to the clergy, even at the expense of conscience and personal integrity.

Newman's determination to subject such presuppositions to a detailed theological analysis was an act of considerable courage, but it was also necessary for his continuing survival within the

---

[1] *W.* ii, p. 233.

[2] In that essay in which Newman is commended for his urbanity. (*Essays in Criticism*, Oxford, 1914, p. 50.)

[3] *W.* i, p. 584.

Roman Catholic Church, since the width of his conception of that Church was now at risk. He had left the Church of England because it refused to bring itself into conformity with the width—chronologically and terrestrially—of Catholic tradition; yet the Church he had joined seemed also to be in the grip of a similar inertia. Expecting to find in the Catholic Church a community which was wider and socially more 'radical' than the Establishment, Newman found instead a body narrowed upon its clergy in a fashion which had alarming historical parallels—hence his deliberate reference to Novatianism.

Newman's achievement consists in his successful maintenance of a delicate but exact theological balance: in asserting the essential life-giving properties of the laity, he yet resists any devaluation of the proper authority of the magisterium[1]; but if the mind of the Church is wider than the laity or the magisterium taken in isolation from each other, it follows that the function of each can only be defined in terms of a general theory of the Church, and that such a theory would have to provide a fresh answer to the question—by what is the Church regulated, if not by the authority of the magisterium?

The importance which Newman attached to theology provides the clue to his eventual answer—that the inevitable but desirable dialectic or *conspiratio* of pastors and faithful people is regulated by theology. And Newman's emphasis upon the laity in his writings and work for education is because he sees their restoration to a due position within the fullness of the Church as essential for the development of theology: it is a condition for the development of a meaningful theology by which the Church can live and develop that it take place within the context of the whole people of God.

For this reason Newman saw the university as the focus in which the fullness of the Catholic idea might best be realized, since if the

---

[1] In a correspondence with Matthew Arnold about the Irish University question, Newman writes (3 Jan. 1876) that since the Council of Trent, 'the Holy See has been suspicious of a University life, as dangerous to the priestly character'; and he goes on to say that in the Catholic Church, 'the people are the *matter*, and the hierarchy the *form*, and that both together make up the Church. . . . The Anglican Church is also made up of a like form and matter; though, here, in consequence of the genius of Anglicanism, the power of the matter predominates.' (Quoted by David J. DeLaura, *Matthew Arnold and John Henry Newman* (Texas, 1965), p. 670.)

intellectual layman were religious, and the devout ecclesiastic intellectual, they would learn, by acting upon each other in a common community, how to act upon society at large. But if the laity were to accept that the 'obsequium' owed to religion were 'rationabile', then the power of what is living must be trusted to eject what is false from its system. This—a claim to be allowed to risk mistakes—implies a corresponding obligation to accept reproof; and if it is our privilege to speak out, it is Rome's to speak back, always provided each side speaks with *warmth* and *definiteness* to the other.[1]

Newman's vision is of a manly discipline. It is also a very English one—'We must have knocks. Ha! Must we not?'—and it was more appropriate to Arnold's Rugby than to Wiseman's Westminster. Hoping that it would be his vocation to bring about such opportunities either at Dublin, Birmingham, or Oxford in the founding of an Oratory, he had claimed that 'from first to last, education, in this large sense of the word, has been my line'.[2] And it was on these grounds that he had come to the rescue of the *Rambler*. Yet his appeal on behalf of the testifying power of the whole people of God was not merely rejected, but its explicit statement was delated to Rome as heretical. This was not merely a personal defeat. It was, for his generation, the direct rejection of the prophecy which Pusey had made of Newman's role within the Church he joined. The prophet 'from another part of the vine-yard' had come, had spoken, and been silenced—and with that silencing went the possibility of a work of internal transformation within the Roman Church such as might have produced the consequences Pusey anticipated.

[1] *W*. ii, pp. 226; 397–8. See above pp. 94–5.
[2] *A.W.*, p. 259.

II

THE *VIA NEGATIVA*

VIII

APOLOGIA FOR A SILENT CHURCH

(i) *Intellectual and theological integrity*

IN the long Journal entry for 21 January 1863 [1] from which I have already quoted, Newman looks back over his life as a Roman Catholic and assesses the reasons for its failure so far: it had been a dreary life (the word is repeated several times) of unrelieved frustration, in which the centre of the conflict was over how the authority of the Church is to be regarded. If it were merely to be imposed, as by the sword, then this necessitated the Temporal Power, and required a feudal social order (rapidly crumbling) in which the rulers determined the beliefs of their subjects—thus if the nobility were converted, the world would be restored to Catholic obedience. '"Il governo" is all in all in their ideas,' writes Newman; and the accusation that he was 'doing nothing' resulted from his failure to make 'splendid conversions of great men'.

'But I,' wrote Newman, 'am altogether different.' He was indeed. And the difference now condemned him to a *via negativa* which prevented him from affirming his idea of the Church other than as a response to its denial by an authority whose tyranny reached its climax in 1870.

The first steps, however, were taken in the autumn of 1863 when Dr. Döllinger, then at the height of his powers and influence as Professor of Church History at Munich, and driving-force of the liberal Catholic movement in Germany, held a Congress at the Benedictine Monastery at Munich. Lasting for four successive days from 28 September to 1 October, and attended by nearly a hundred

[1] *A.W.*, pp. 253–60, esp. pp. 257–8.

professors, authors, and doctors of divinity, it was hailed by Acton as marking 'the dawn of a new era'.[1]

Döllinger intended the Congress to be the first of a series of meetings which, by healing the internal dissensions of Catholic scholars, might help to create a faculty of theology in Germany comparable to that of the Sorbonne and capable of producing divines of the type of Petavius, Bossuet, and Arnauld. He believed that the seminaries produced excellent priests but no scholars, and that unless priests could receive a university education they would fall into a social seclusion and lose all influence over the male part of the population.

The Congress elected Döllinger to be its president; and the theme of his inaugural address[2]—the need to resolve the conflicts between religious authority and scientific enquiry—could equally have been Newman's; but expressed in public and at such a time, his remarks merely exacerbated the divisions then existing within German theology.

Nearly one-third of the membership of the Congress came from Munich—a school whose emphasis upon the study of ecclesiastical history was still regarded by conservatives with suspicion. Other schools such as Mainz, which was fierce for the spiritual and temporal rights of the Holy See, the Index, and a strict Scholasticism, sent either their second team or eminent scholars who preserved a disappointing and 'obstinate silence'. At the other extreme, Tübingen—the home of Möhler, that other pioneer in the theory of doctrinal development—was not represented. Against such a background, Döllinger's three conditions for theological renewal must have seemed brilliant, but disquieting: Catholic divines must answer their adversaries in their own language, and 'by using all the means which the progress of the age supplies'. Then, by separating what is 'transitory, foreign and accidental' from what is essential in Catholic doctrine, theologians must present that doctrine 'in all its organic completeness', recognizing as they did so that the very effort required was itself 'a valuable contribution to our self-knowledge'. Lastly, theology must give to the Church 'the property of the magnetic mountain in the fable, that drew to

---

[1] The following account draws upon Acton's 'The Munich Congress', *Home and Foreign Review*, no. 7, Jan. 1864, 209–44, as republished in Acton, *Essays on Church and State*, ed. Douglas Woodruff (1952), pp. 159–99. (*E.C.S.*)

[2] *E.C.S.*, pp. 180–8.

itself all the iron in the ship, so that the ship fell to pieces': by examining all that 'the separated communities have brought to light' and by sifting truth from error, Catholic theologians should then frankly accept and claim these new aspects of the truth 'as the legitimate though unrecognised property of the one true Church'.

Of this renewal Germany was the rightful home, 'since no nation has cultivated so successfully the sciences which are the eyes of theology, viz. history and philosophy'. And Döllinger's address concludes with the plea that truth should be refined in the fire of contradiction: 'the presence of different systems is not an evil, but an advantage . . . freedom is as necessary to science as air to life'. Then follows the distinction which his opponents were to repudiate so forcibly: 'A real dogmatic error against the clear and universal teaching of the Church must be pointed out and re-tracted; but a purely theological error must be assailed only with the resources of scientific discussion.' Errors of this latter kind must be refuted on their own grounds or not at all: 'in theology it is only through error that truth is attained'.[1]

Döllinger's thesis strikingly anticipates the experience of the Second Vatican Council—that the Church must see itself as per-petually in movement between poles that have been variously described as reactionary and progressive, or essentialist and existentialist[2]; but in the light of the foregoing argument we can also see the conflict as one between those who believe that the Church can exercise its verifying function only if it is radically separated from its context within society, and those who assert with Döllinger and Newman that the Church must be contextually relevant.

The first position—the essentialist—was adopted not only by the theologians of Mainz but corresponded to the majority view at the First Vatican Council. It was the position adopted by Dr. Gillow in his controversy with Newman; and it conceived the deposit of faith to be a series of clear and definite formulations [3] which left little room for interpretation. At the First Vatican Council, Bishop Ullathorne noted that it was the Spanish theolo-

[1] ibid., p. 188.
[2] E. Schillebeeckx, *Vatican II: the real achievement* (1967), pp. 7 ff.
[3] See Newman's Letter to Flanagan, 1868, and its discussion below in chapter 10, p. 175.

gians who were its most fanatical exponents: 'One might think from them that fixed and hard ideas, pushed to the furthest extreme, were just the cure for all human ills. They very much need a dose from Dr. Newman's *Grammar of Assent*. They seem to fancy that men and women, the actual creatures of this world, are spirits living on fixed ideas, and devoid of disturbing elements.' It was painful, Ullathorne continued, to hear such men arguing about the human race who knew so little about it.[1]

This was the theological basis of the extreme Ultramontane position; and it had the further consequence of requiring so radical a separation of Church from society that the only kind of acceptable relationship was one where society conformed itself to a political ideology manifestly deduced from theological first principles—usually those of Church order. This identification of sociological and theological categories ruled out all possibility of a reciprocal action of Church and society; and Christendom—the integral union of Church and State—was the medieval norm to which the nineteenth century must conform.

The alternative or existential position, although held by Döllinger, Newman, and the schools of Tübingen and Munich, corresponded to the minority position at the First Vatican Council. It wished to see the Church (without sacrificing its doctrinal integrity) *exist* more fully in the world, not as the world ought to be, but as it was. It accepted the emerging open society, not as the second best alternative to a revived Christendom but as an inevitable starting-point; and it welcomed the opportunity thus provided for the Church to develop a new and fuller understanding of its doctrines. It assumed that Church and society could learn from each other, and that a reciprocal or mutual relationship was the best.

In 1863, however, Döllinger's existentialist programme heralded not the dawn of a new era, but the reverse. Too much in advance of its time, it was—as Acton said—like arguing the temporal power at Turin. In spite of a telegram of good wishes sent by the Congress to Pius IX, the papal reply came in the following March in the form of a Brief to the Archbishop of Munich.[2] It has produced some celebrated epitaphs.

[1] Cuthbert Butler, *The Vatican Council* 1869–70 (1962), p. 368.
[2] The Brief is dated 21 Dec. 1863, but it was not published until 5 March 1864. (Acton, *History of Freedom* (1907), pp. 481–2.)

By re-emphasizing the need for an entire obedience to the decrees of the Roman congregations, the Brief affirmed that the
common opinions and explanations of Catholic divines ought not
to yield to the progress of secular sciences, and the course of
theological knowledge ought to be controlled by the decrees of the
Index. Although the distinction between dogma and opinion was
not denied, its recognition was reduced to the smallest possible
limits; and Acton saw that on such terms the *Home and Foreign
Review*, the successor to the ill-fated *Rambler*, could no longer be
published.[1] The Brief, therefore, brought to an end the most
advanced piece of lay Catholic journalism the English-speaking
world had so far produced.

Newman made an annotated translation of the Brief, and came
to the same conclusion; and he noticed that at the crucial passages
the language was least exact, as the following extract shows (his
annotations are in brackets):

all Catholics are bound in conscience in studying the contemplatrices
scientiae (the theories of science?) for the good of the Church . . . to
submit themselves to the doctrinal decisions of the Pontifical congregations, and to those theological verities, which, by the consent of Catholics,
cannot be opposed without incurring theological censure. (N.B. Is this
the case of Galileo?)[2]

Newman's answer was that the Brief went even further, by
insisting that it was not enough for the theologian to stick to his
subject and the scientist to his; instead, the Catholic scientist
ought to keep theological conclusions before him in treating of his
science. If this were so, there was no alternative but 'simply to be
silent', while scientific investigation proceeded in other and non-
Catholic hands.[3]

We cannot understand why the *Apologia* was written or the
measure of its achievement unless we see it against the background
of the Munich Congress, and the suppression of its hopes by the
Munich Brief. Newman felt himself to be immured within a
Church of silence. Kingsley's gratuitous attack was, however, a
different matter.

The charge that 'truth for its own sake had never been a virtue

[1] Acton's analysis as expressed in 'Conflicts with Rome' (*Home and Foreign
Review*, April 1864, pp. 667–96), and as republished in Acton, *History of
Freedom and other Essays* (1907), p. 483.
[2] *W*. i, pp. 641–2.   [3] *W*. i, p. 567.

with the Roman clergy' was made in the pages of *Macmillan's Magazine* in the following January (1864).[1] It was made, as it were, *en passant*; and Newman at first thought the attack upon himself to be by a young fellow who hoped to make 'a cheap reputation by smart hits at safe objects'.[2] But when he learned that the author was so eminent a person as a Chaplain to the Queen, Professor of Modern History at Cambridge, and tutor to the Prince of Wales, he felt obliged to take matters further, and to ask for a full withdrawal or substantiation. When a satisfactory retraction was unforthcoming, Newman's reply was explosive. Kingsley's arrow aimed at random had gone straight to the target. How could a man, holding the views of conscience and the integrity of the person in which Newman had been educated, square these with an allegiance to Rome?

This question, in a more dramatic and offensive form, repeated the criticisms made by Coleridge and Maurice of the inevitable moral corruption consequent upon the claims of the Roman Church to be self-determining. It amounted to this—that if the Church is indeed a moral union of persons, then since the Roman Church has now suppressed the expression of personal integrity in the interest of system and authority, Newman had forfeited that obligation to tell the truth in which as an Englishman he had been educated, and was instead committed to a life of silent deceit by foreigners who were his ecclesiastical superiors.

Kingsley's attack was thus upon his integrity generally, and a point-by-point refutation by itself would have been useless; this is what Newman meant when he accused Kingsley of poisoning the wells. The only effective reply would be one which 'had a corresponding antagonist unity in my defence'; and this Newman saw lay in answering Kingsley's pamphlet, with its question: What then does Mr. Newman mean? 'He asks . . . not about my arguments . . . but about that living intelligence, by which I write, and argue, and act.'[3]

The merit of the *Apologia* is that Newman succeeded in bringing many necessary but by no means similar elements into a living and compelling unity. First he was able to show, by the application of the principle of development to his own life, that his conversion to Catholicism had been a growth and not a betrayal of previous principles; this established his integrity. But he was also able to

[1] *Apo.*, p. 6. [2] *Apo.*, p. 10. [3] *Apo.*, pp. 98–9.

show the grounds for preferring the Church of Rome to the *via media*. Next, at a time when the Church had been instructed to remain silent and to refrain from argument, Newman was enabled, in his description of what Catholicism really was, to imply a theory of what it should and must become. Not merely did he avoid infringing the prohibition, but he secured a greater degree of support from his fellow Catholics than he had had since his conversion.[1]

The *Apologia* was conceived and written in instalments; and the main part, *A History of my religious opinions*, was not published until Thursday, 5 May 1864; but at the end of the pamphlet war with Kingsley and before writing this history of his religious opinions, Newman had received an important letter from Acton (10 April 64). Acton reports that several of Kingsley's friends and relatives admit that Newman's

dialectics were triumphant, but that you did not take, as you were not bound, or even invited to take, the general defence of the Catholic clergy . . . and they see in your omission another proof of your skill and good judgment. . . . In these minds, therefore, . . . the effect of the controversy is adverse to the Church almost in proportion as it is favourable to you.[2]

Acton urged Newman to widen the discussion and to 'enlighten not only the Protestants but such Catholics as have got a little confused' by recent policies. Acton is clearly referring to the circumstances which occasioned the Munich Brief and to the closure of the *Home and Foreign Review*.

Where Newman stood is made quite clear in his letters. In the summer of 1863 he had written to Miss Bowles that English Catholicism was under the rule of Propaganda—'a quasi-military power'—and that to write theology was 'to fight under the lash'.[3] In the letter to Monsell already cited,[4] he had spoken of the freedom enjoyed by theologians in the Middle Ages ('which have a manliness and boldness of which now there is so great a lack') before authority intervened.

His reply to Acton—'your letter is a very valuable one . . . you

---

[1] *W.* ii, pp. 35–6.
[2] Hugh A. MacDougall, *The Acton-Newman Relations* (New York, Fordham, 1962), pp. 91–2.
[3] *W.* i, pp. 586 ff.
[4] *O.* Letter of 13 Jan. 1863; see above, chapter 7, p. 127.

may be sure I shall go as far as ever I can'—makes us see that the
climax to the *Apologia* was intended to be both defence and
prescription; if Catholics approved the defence, then they were implicitly subscribing to the principles it implied; and authority was
challenged to repudiate not a critic (as it had Döllinger and Acton)
but a defender. Newman had put his conversion to the hazard.

This is the most courageous of all Newman's actions, and it is
aesthetically fitting that it should occur at the climax of the work.
He outlines the theology of the Catholic Church which caused him
to become a Catholic—and the risk he ran of being repudiated by
his own side, if it were calculated, was so from the most serious
motives. And, what is more, his tone has the assurance, not of one
who loses (as, until this time, Newman himself had lost) but of one
who wins.

Starting with an apprehension of the existence of God which is
simultaneously that of our separation from him, Newman establishes the need for Christianity to be embodied in a visible and
infallible Church; nothing else can withstand the 'wild living
intellect of man'. But what is to be the function of reason within
such an infallibility; is it to be broken, as the Munich Brief seemed
to favour? No, says Newman. The Church's power is given for
edification, not destruction; and the conflict of reason and authority
is inevitable and to be welcomed, since it is the dialectic out of
which the Church grows and develops.

In the great ages of theological growth 'how slow is authority in
interfering . . . the controversy proceeds year after year and Rome
is still silent', until 'after a long while . . . authority is called upon
to pronounce a decision, which has already been arrived at by
reason'.[1] If this were not so, we should indeed be 'fighting under
the lash'; and authority, in thus beating the freedom of intellect
out of us, would have abused its privilege. Newman drives the point
home by quoting Shakespeare—'O, it is excellent to have a giant's
strength, but tyrannous to use it like a giant'[2]; and he concludes by
saying that the greatest evil the Church must guard against is the
loss of its Catholicity, by becoming contracted 'within the range of
particular nationalities'.[3]

How sensitive Newman continued to be to the charge of
Romanism made by Coleridge and Maurice and repeated by

[1] *Apo.*, p. 357.   [2] *Apo.*, p. 349.   [3] *Apo.*, p. 359.

Kingsley can be seen in his reference to the dangers to which theology was exposed by being thus contracted within the range of one nationality—the Italian.[1] Maurice had spoken of the tendencies of Latin minds to narrow Christianity to their own conceptions; but Newman is doing more than repeat what he had said when he spoke of the dangers of a fresh relapse into Novatianism. He is implying the *width* of the context within which a meaningful and relevant theology can alone develop: it positively requires the nourishment afforded by different and conflicting traditions.[2]

But Newman is also criticizing by implication those who, by failing to distinguish the political problems of the Church in Italy from the spiritual authority of the Church in the world, were perpetuating a dangerous confusion of theological and political categories—to the extent that the Pope, Pius IX, could speak in 1859 of the Papal States as 'part of the robe of Jesus Christ, which remained whole even on the hill of Calvary'.[3] Such confusion had been at the root of the failure to develop the Irish university; but there was little chance of a more general theory of the Church being developed until the issue of papal authority had been settled. Was the Pope, as Pius IX appears to have believed,[4] the sole witness to Tradition, or were there definable limits to the exercise of papal authority? This was the unsettled question which rendered abortive Döllinger's efforts at the Munich Congress; and until it was settled Newman believed that to be silent and patient was the right course. One of the greatest difficulties was 'to say precisely what it is that is to be encountered and overthrown'; and in too eagerly attempting to develop a dialogue between reason and authority, the Church and the world, there was the risk of 'chasing phantoms' and of complicating matters further, 'which are already complicated without my interference'.[5]

---

[1] 'But the Latin race will not always have a monopoly of the magisterium of Catholicism. We must be patient in our time; but God will take care of his Church—and, when the hour strikes, the reform will begin.' (*W.* ii, pp. 554–5.)

[2] It is interesting to note that a number of Cardinals, including Antonelli, objected to the calling of the First Vatican Council on the grounds that it would bring German and French theologians to Rome and upset the authority of the Roman Congregations. (E. E. Y. Hales, *Pio Nono* (1956), p. 276.)

[3] Hales, op. cit., p. 201, citing P. Pirri, *Pio IX e Vittorio Emanuele II dal loro carteggio privato*, II pt. 2, 135.

[4] Butler, op. cit., p. 355.

[5] *Apo.*, pp. 353–4.

(ii) *The distinction between religious and social motives*

Thus far in the *Apologia*, Newman has succeeded in showing that a Church which, from the outside has seemed to be a Romanist system tyrannically imposing silence, is, when responded to as a whole and from within, the very symbol of Christ's incarnation. In thus establishing his personal integrity and that of his fellow Catholics, Newman had removed the poison from the wells; and he was now sure of a fair hearing. He now faces each of Kingsley's charges in a point by point refutation, 'lest I should seem to be evading difficulties'.[1] This he deemed to be the only way of ending the controversy once for all; but he had also a more fundamental purpose.

Having established the need for a freedom and diversity of theological investigation within the Church, Newman wishes to emphasize the converse—the need to safeguard the sacramental nature of the Church: it is good that Grace should co-operate with nature; but Nature is under the judgement of Grace; and authority has been given to the Church to be the means of recalling men to an acknowledgement of their absolute dependence upon Christ.

In reminding Kingsley of such claims and of their implications he uses almost the same words as Maurice in his dispute with Ludlow over the future of Christian Socialism. Like Maurice, Newman is ever on his guard against those who are too much at ease in Zion and too ready to allocate the respective spheres of action as between God and man, Grace and nature. The instincts that caused Maurice to oppose Ludlow in 1852 and to break the Pelagian and theocratic tendencies of the Christian Socialist Movement are from the same tradition as those which caused Newman to assert the prior claims of Grace, and to reiterate the Tractarian distinction between Christian teaching and political expedience.

In order to understand why Newman thought Kingsley's case important enough to require thorough refutation, we need to remember that since Newman regarded the Church of England as essentially a national institution, he saw it as particularly vulnerable to political and social pressures, and as liable to be 'corrupted' by them.[2] In this last section of the first edition of the *Apologia* he asserts that 'the Nation drags down its Church to its own level'; and although his attitude to the Church of England was milder

[1] *Apo.*, p. 416.   [2] *Moz.* i, p. 449. (August 1833.)

since he had been a Catholic than before,[1] it was because, 'when I was an Anglican, I viewed it as repressing a higher doctrine than its own; and now I view it as keeping out a lower and more dangerous'.

Thus his attack on muscular Christianity, which he so denominates for the first time, is upon a pernicious social development of that dogmatic liberalism which the Oxford Movement was formed to combat. He sees in Kingsley a leading example of that unbridled individualism which, 'in taking man's side and not God's',[2] was knocking the life out of the institutions it had inherited.[3] It is not appropriate for the Christian to *force* the success of Christian policies: the powers of the Church are given for edification not destruction; and the Christian is in the world not as its overlord but its servant. He must take heed of what is implied in the injunction to be born again. It means yielding to the action of Grace,[4] to substitute 'meekness for haughtiness, passiveness for violence, and innocence for craft'. The temptation was to substitute reason for conscience and thereby 'to do good that good might come, that is to act *in order* to their success, and not from a motive of faith'.[5]

Newman's emphasis here is crucial. It falls upon a distinction between acting from a religious motive—from conscience 'perhaps in despondency, and without foresight'—and from a political or social motive—which is at bottom 'a calculation of results'.[6] This

---

[1] *Apo.*, pp. 396, 398.

[2] Somewhat ironically, the ill-fated *Rambler* for July 1859 contained a review of Kingsley's sermons, *The Good News of God*, which charges Kingsley with virtually protesting 'against the supernatural', and making himself 'the mouthpiece of the religious tendencies of the present age . . . which takes man's side and not God's'. (*Rambler*, New Series, I, p. 250.)

[3] *S & N*, p. 142.   [4] *Apo.*, p. 340.   [5] *Apo.*, pp. 385–6.

[6] This is from the very sermon, *Wisdom and Innocence*, which Kingsley singled out for attack (*S.S.D.*, 305). How deeply rooted this distinction is in Newman's thought may be seen from a sermon preached in St. Mary's, Oxford, on 2 April 1837 (*P.S.* iv, pp. 18–36). It was on the sin of Balaam—a man 'high-minded, conscientious, honourable', yet whose endeavour was 'not to please God, but to please self without displeasing God'; who had for his object not God's will, but 'certain maxims, rules or measures, right perhaps as far as they go, but defective because they admit of being subjected to certain other ultimate ends which are not religious'. The result of Balaam's sin was that he was no longer 'content with *ascertaining* God's will, but he attempted to *change* it'. Newman returns to the subject in a sermon, 'The Religion of the Pharisee, the Religion of Mankind', preached in the University Church, Dublin in 1856. (*S.V.O.*, pp. 15–30.)

is why Newman claimed that 'a lazy, ragged, filthy, story-telling beggar-woman, if chaste, sober, cheerful, and religious, had a prospect of heaven, which was absolutely closed to an accomplished statesman, or lawyer, or noble, be he ever so just, upright, generous, honourable, and conscientious, unless he had also some portion of the divine Christian grace'.[1] Now it was precisely this analogy which Kingsley claimed 'strikes at the root of all morality',[2]—a difference of principle if there ever were one, and one which, coming from a Christian pastor who happened to be the tutor of the future King Edward VII, needed to be pressed.

Newman associates Kingsley with the growing tendency towards commercial and colonial imperialism which, as one who belonged to an older generation and another tradition, he found distasteful. In the full text of the Letter to Jelf not published in the *Apologia*, he specifically refers to 'that older system which has of late years indeed been superseded'.[3] Restored by the Romantics—who, after the drought of the Enlightenment had revived feelings of 'awe, mystery, tenderness, reverence and devotedness', this was the tradition to which the Oxford Movement belonged.[4] But it was again superseded by rationalism and calculation, or by what Coleridge called 'the over-balance of the commercial spirit'.[5] Newman defines the emphasis to be resisted as Pelagian—that we are saved by works rather than by faith, by leadership rather than by love. Both he and Coleridge conceived the contrast as one between two worlds—an older one which valued poets, philosophers, and theologians, and sanctioned the generous unworldliness of the whole (or holy) man; and a new one of shrewd, knowing men of business and imperial rule, whose piety was dangerously unlearned and unenlarged.[6]

This contrast also throws light on the limitations of Kingsley's Christian Socialism as they are revealed by his later political

---

[1] *Apo*, p. 340.   [2] *Apo*, p. 47.   [3] *V.M.* ii, p. 386.
[4] *Apo*, pp. 262, 195.   [5] *C & S*, p. 359.
[6] See above, chapter 3, pp. 42–4; and also, Coleridge (Notebook entry *c*. 1808–10), *CN* 2598: 'Let England be (Sir P. Sidney), Shakespere, Spenser, Milton, Bacon, Harrington, (Swift), Wordsworth, and never let the names of Darwin, Johnson, Hume *furr* it over! If these too must be England, let them be another England—or rather let the first be the spiritual Platonic old England & the second with Locke at the head of the Philosophers & Pope of the Poets, with the long list of Priestleys, Paleys, Hayleys, Darwins, Mr. Pitts, Dundasses, &c &c be representative of commercial G. Britain/these have their merits, but are as alien to me, as the Mandarin Philosophers and Poets of China. . . .'

attitudes: he was anti-semitic, opposed to the freeing of slaves in
the American Civil War, and was provoked by the Crimean War to
write that bloodthirsty manifesto—*Westward Ho.* Newman not
only objected to the Crimean War as evidence of our growing taste
for war 'as if it were our forte'—'why will we not be content to be
human?'[1] he asks; but as early as 1832 he had voiced his mistrust
of the new policy of trusting in 'trade's master-keys' and in forts
'earned upon hostile ground'.[2]

It is particularly important to see Newman's theological judgements in the *Apologia* in relation to his social and political opinions,
since they give some indication of how his views on the relationship
of the sacramental Church to modern society were evolving.[3] They
also provide further evidence of a common tradition since, in
Kingsley's arrogant rejection of essential theological distinctions,
Newman detected the same danger as that which had provoked
Coleridge to write the *Lay Sermons.* It is of a religion so unlearned
and of a piety so restricted as to be unable to rise above 'a calculation of results' to any 'enlarged systems of action'.[4] Newman's
social vision, so closely akin not only to Coleridge but to Matthew
Arnold, is of a society which is becoming uniquely post-Christian,
in which controversy is not 'between the hosts of Heaven, Michael
and his angels on the one side, and the powers of evil on the other;
but it is a sort of night battle, where each fights for himself and
friend and foe stand together'.[5] Thus Newman's analysis of the
shortcomings of English religion was not merely religious polemic
as many, including Pusey who congratulated him upon it, and
Arnold could see. Christianity itself was set upon 'a darkling plain,

> Swept with confused alarms of struggle and flight,
> Where ignorant armies clash by night.[6]

[1] 'Who's to Blame' (a sustained criticism of the Crimean War policy
published in the *Catholic Standard*, 1854), republished in *D.A.*, pp. 306–62;
see esp. p. 333.

[2] From the poem *England*, of which the second stanza begins—'Dread thine
own power.' (*V.V.*, p. 89). On 4 September of the same year he writes to a
former pupil, J. F. Wood, 'The country seems to me to be in a dream, being
drugged with this fallacious notion of its superiority to other countries and times'
(cited by A. D. Culler, *The Imperial Intellect* (1955), p. 81).

[3] They should be read in relation to his correspondence (1860–3) with the
historian T. W. Allies which is discussed below in the General Conclusion,
chapter 16.

[4] See above, chapter 3.

[5] *O.U.S.*, p. 200 (1839).   [6] M. Arnold, *Dover Beach.*

In making an affirmation about the Church, the *Apologia* is also sounding a warning to both social and religious dogmatists. Although we cannot as yet say precisely what is to be encountered,[1] the outlines of the question are beginning to emerge. It will no longer be one of the expedience of Christianity for society, but of its truth and of the grounds for personal certitude.

(iii) *The argument from Personality*

It is generally accepted that the peculiar merit of the *Apologia* is that the various points which it has to make are developed without sacrificing the dominant unity which it achieves. It is also accepted as convincing testimony to the integrity of Newman's growth to Rome as repudiating nothing Catholic in the theological tradition from which he had come, and which he had hoped to foster in the Church he joined. As a whole, Newman admitted, the work counted against the Church of England[2]; yet the reason for its unique and continuing success is that his affirmation or apologia, by being placed upon its proper footing in terms of a life lived, is moved out of the realm of polemic, and provides us with a successfully *realized* example of Newman's theological method. His theory of religious assent is not merely stated in the *Apologia* but evoked, or to use Newman's term, *realized*,[3] since by bringing his whole soul successfully into activity before us, Newman is providing us with a further development of his 'method of personation'. In the *Grammar of Assent*, Newman says that to ascertain 'what I am, in order to put it to use',[4] he must begin by speaking of himself[5]; and in his unpublished Philosophical papers Newman writes: 'metaphysics should always be written in the first person',[6] since for each man 'his hermit spirit dwells in his own sphere'[7]; and in matters of belief the individual must speak for himself, and 'egotism is true modesty'.[8]

Time and time again Newman speaks of 'undervaluing cut and dried arguments' in favour of his rule 'to tell people my *feelings* about events which happen to me. I think people are perplexed till a key is given them, and then at once they thankfully accept it and use it.'[9]

---

[1] *Apo*, pp. 353, 428.   [2] *W*. ii. 24.
[3] Mark Pattison noted that 'realize' was one of Newman's favourite words (*Essays*, Oxford, 1889, II, p. 303).
[4] *GA*, p. 264.   [5] *GA*, pp. 292-5.   [6] *D.E.M.S.*, p. 12.
[7] *D.E.M.S.*, p. 142.   [8] *GA*, p. 292.   [9] *Letters* XV, p. 280.

The key he gives us in the *Apologia* is that, when it is a matter of religious assent, we must trust persons and not logic [1]; since the revelation of God to each one of us is both gradual (or *economical*) and uniquely personal: 'Accordingly, I considered that He, in His superintending providence, took man by man, each in his own way, a way which cannot be analysed or generalised by science, and supplied the means of certitude suitable to each; . . . giving in each case a perfection to a process in itself imperfect'. [2]

Our assent is verified not by logical criteria, therefore, but by our acts [3] and within the actions of the worshipping community. It is above all an assent to a personal question: 'What think ye of Christ?'—and in making this response to a person we learn that our response to His Church must be of the same kind, as being a response to a personal unity [4] which is yet compatible with a detailed response to its component aspects and demands.

In the Church of silence enjoined by the Munich Brief and in which Newman stood as he wrote the *Apologia*, the sacramental or integral response only was encouraged, and a more detailed and explicit attention specifically discouraged; but the method of the *Apologia* fixes our priorities. Our response to the Church is always greater than to a balance of pros and cons, since it is to a personal unity. What the *Apologia* implies is an idea of the Church as an organism whose *full* function is to maximize, without destroying, the personal unities of which it is composed to the extent that an

---

[1] *Apo*, pp. 264–5; *GA*, pp. 259, 264.

Continental commentators on Newman frequently refer to his 'personalism', by which they mean that he affirms 'une valeur intellectuelle et une qualité absolue dans la personne même'. (Maurice Nédoncelle, Introduction to the French edition of the *Apologia*, pp. 70–2, Paris, 1966.)

In his *Ludwig Wittgenstein*, A Memoir, 1958, p. 71, Norman Malcolm speaks of Wittgenstein's impatience with 'proofs' which attempted to give religion a rational foundation, and although Wittgenstein disliked Newman's theological writings, 'which he read with care during his last year at Cambridge', his decision to begin his *Philosophical Investigations* with a quotation from St. Augustine's *Confessions*, was 'not because he could not find the conception expressed in that quotation stated as well by other philosophers, but because the conception *must* be important if so great a mind held it'. (See above, chapter 2, p. 16.)

[2] From a cancelled passage of the MS. of the *Apologia* in which Newman develops his claim that Butler's argument from probability becomes, in matters of religion, 'an argument from Personality, which in fact is one form of the argument from Authority'. (*Apo*, Oxford ed. 1967, p. 30, and notes, p. 498.)

[3] 'Life is not long enough for a religion of inferences . . . Life is for action . . .: to act you must assume, and that assumption is faith.' *D.A.*, p. 295.

[4] *Diff*. i, p. 6.

attack upon the integrity of any of its members for being its members, and particularly upon its priests,[1] is an attack upon the integrity of the Church, as that personal unity so constituted as to mediate Christ. It is not the Church, as a mere external rule or polity, which verifies and to which the absolute assent of faith is given, but Christ. The Church provides the locus or means of verification: it is Christ who verifies, but a Christ who is approached only through His Church and its sacraments.

However silent the Church may be, it is still valid; yet our faith in it as the mediator of Christ seeks understanding; and that understanding must survive the challenge of unbelief. This was especially the case in Newman's time when, under the stimulus of rapid scientific expansion, forms of explanation alternative to Christian belief were beginning to proliferate. The need to bring the Church and its explanations into a relevant relationship to this new world was becoming increasingly urgent, as the Munich Congress rightly affirmed, yet since theological explanation derives from the believing community whose language it is, if that community disparages theology and insists upon silence, then that silence becomes terrible indeed. Only the saint, the superstitious, and the indifferent may survive within it.

[1] 'But the case is very different when the religious rite is insulted, and the individual for the sake of the rite.' *Pres. Pos.*, p. 188 (1851).

IX

THE CONTEXT OF A COMMON CULTURE

(i) *Conscience and the Church*

THE *Apologia*, by its success, enabled Newman to renew old friendships and to gain a respect among Protestants he was never to lose. The Catholic response was mixed; and in its higher reaches the society that had been so unjust to him remained so: Rome still preferred him to remain unemployed—at 'dishonoured ease' in the 'cold shade', as he himself described it.[1] Archbishop Manning, for example, came to regard Newman as the chief source of a particular danger—that of 'an English Catholicism. It is the old Anglican, patristic, literary, Oxford tone transplanted into the Church. It takes the line of deprecating exaggerations, foreign devotions, Ultramontanism, anti-national sympathies. In one word it is worldly Catholicism.'[2] It was still the *via negativa*.

The *Apologia*, by obliging Newman to relive his past so intensively, gave him a more developed insight into the complexity and extent of his roots in English tradition; but the evidence points to something deeper than the understanding that he had but carried on 'children of the Movement of 1833 to their legitimate conclusions'.[3] Instead, and in spite of the mounting temper of ultramontane intransigence within the Catholic Church, Newman's correspondence and activity reveal a growing awareness of the necessary relationship between the Church and its cultural context. It is as if, in writing the *Apologia*, he had come to understand the extent of the danger to which the Church is exposed when it cuts itself off from society and insists on pursuing a collision course with the spirit of the times.

What seems implied is an idea of the Church in relation to society with which Coleridge has made us familiar—that our encounter with the Church is most real if it takes place in a be-

---

[1] *A.W.*, p. 264.
[2] In a letter to Talbot, Feb. 1866 (E. S. Purcell, *Life of Cardinal Manning* (1896), vol. ii, pp. 322–3).
[3] *W*. ii, p. 57.

friending, overlapping of Church and society, or when, to paraphrase Tillich,[1] our religion has for its form the national culture,
and that culture has our religion for its substance. Newman's
appreciation of such values in English culture increased rather than
diminished; and in his later writings and correspondence the term
'*mixed*' as denoting an essential and wholesome common ground
for Catholic and non-Catholic begins to appear.

But there is also evidence of what might justly be called a
developing oecumenical intention on Newman's part. This can be
gathered from the correspondence over the re-issue of his Anglican
sermons, and the republication in a definitive edition of all his
works, which the successful reception of the sermons now encouraged. In writing to thank the man at whose instigation and
under whose editorship the work had begun—the Revd. W. J.
Copeland, Vicar of Farnham, Essex [2]—Newman said:

Unless you had broke the ice, I could have republished nothing which I
wrote before 1845–6. The English public would not have borne any
alterations—and my own people would have been much scandalized had
I made none. They murmured a good deal at the new edition of the
Sermons, as it was—but, since you, not I, published them, nothing
could be said about it. After this beginning, I took courage to publish
my Essay on Miracles, and the *British Critic* Essays, uncorrected, but
with notes corrective of the text. This too made some disturbance, but
very little. And then I published at Rivington's my University Sermons;
and then I went on to *mix* [my italics] Anglican and Catholic essays
together; and now I hear no criticisms on these measures at all—and I
have even dedicated a volume of my Historical Sketches, half of it
written as an Anglican, to an Irish Bishop. My view has ever been to
answer, not to suppress, what is erroneous—merely as a matter of
expedience for the cause of truth, at least at this day. It seems to me a
bad policy to suppress, Truth has a power of its own, which makes its
way, it is stronger than error.[3]

An earlier letter makes Newman's developing oecumenical intention quite plain when, in acknowledging the use which 'Dissenters'
had made of his republished sermons, he said:

---

[1] Tillich, *The Protestant Era*, p. xvii. See above, chapter 3, p. 41.

[2] I have discussed Newman's purpose in greater detail in 'Newman's own
guide to the reading of his works', in *Newman, a Portrait Restored* (1965),
pp. 112, 116.

[3] *O*. 20 April, 1873 (*W*. ii, p. 396 in part).

I have answered them, that I thought, as things are, the first step towards unity was a union of Feeling, and that if I were prospered to do anything whatever towards laying the necessary foundation, on which higher strata of truth might be deposited at some future day, I should have received a great favour and mercy from the Giver of all good.[1]

This important statement of Newman's oecumenical intentions must be set alongside his remark that 'the division of Churches is the corruption of hearts',[2] and Copeland's statement in the Preface[3] to the *Selections of Parochial and Plain Sermons* published in October 1878 that their purpose was 'the promotion of mutual sympathy between estranged communions and alienated hearts'.

To the early '60s belong also the letters between Newman and the historian Allies, which represent the nearest Newman goes to outlining an explicit relationship between the Catholic Church and a modern, pluralist society; but I propose to examine these in the General Conclusion. There is, however, a letter to Monsell[4] which shows Newman's movement towards a positive acceptance of the 'mixed' character of contemporary English society:

> The age is such, that we must go by reason, not by force. I am not at all sure that it would not be better for the Catholic religion everywhere, if it had no very different status from that which it has in England. There is so much corruption, so much deadness, so much hypocrisy, so much infidelity, when a dogmatic faith is imposed on a nation by law, that I like freedom better,

and he goes on to say that it is better for the Church 'to fight for its supremacy'.

These are the considerations we should bring to Newman's frequent references to the Establishment as a 'breakwater' or 'bulwark against infidelity'. Whatever his criticisms of the theological claims of the Church of England, he very firmly accepted 'the English *nation* as a body',[5] and as the form of a Christian culture, or, as he called it, ethos. And it was his growing understanding of the role of the Establishment as teacher and realizer of a Christian ethos,[6] his

---

[1] Letter to Copeland, 26 November 1868.   [2] *S.S.D.*, p. 133.
[3] P. vi.   [4] *O*. Letter of 17 June 1863.
[5] Letter to P. de Lisle, 1 July 1857.
[6] Newman's distinction in the *Apologia* (*Apo*, pp. 394–5) between the National Church as 'a witness and teacher of religious truth' and the Catholic Church as 'an oracle of revealed doctrine' is the very distinction which leads Coleridge to distinguish the *Enclesia* from the *Ecclesia*.

appreciation of the moral benefits of a mixed society, and his growing oecumenical sympathies which explain why Newman reacted so very strongly against the announcement of the First Vatican Council in 1870. He spoke of it as 'thunder in the clear sky'; and in a letter to Lady Simeon, he said: 'We have come to a climax of tyranny. . . . For years past my only consolation personally has been in our Lord's Presence in the Tabernacle.'[1]

When Gladstone published his protest against the Decrees of the First Vatican Council, he was repeating more politely what Kingsley and before him Maurice had urged: that Catholics, committed as they were to the principle of 'Romanism' with its unquestioning obedience to an infallible pope, could not hold the same doctrine of conscience as Protestants. They were, therefore, untrustworthy members of a modern state.[2] This charge struck at the heart of Newman's acceptance of a mixed or common culture; and his answer asserts the dialogue in conscience between the individual and his Creator to be the very foundation of a common Christian assent: 'When Anglicans, Wesleyans, the various Presbyterian sects in Scotland, and other denominations among us, speak of conscience, they mean what we mean, the voice of God in the nature and heart of man, as distinct from the voice of Revelation.'[3]

And the unity of Christians consists in this acceptance of conscience 'as the aboriginal vicar of Christ': it witnesses to the implicit, as distinct from explicit, exercise of Christ's offices of Prophet, Priest, and King, so that 'even though the eternal priesthood throughout the Church could cease to be', the 'sacerdotal principle would remain' in the exercise of conscience.[4]

Just after the Vatican Decrees had been passed, Newman wrote in a letter of the many high ecclesiastics in Italy and England 'who think that to believe is as easy as to obey—that is, they talk as if they did not know what an act of faith is'.[5] Newman shows his concern at the atheism implicit in such a blind acceptance of imposed authority by adding that it may well be the act of a man 'who will believe anything because he believes nothing'. In a Church, so much under the influence of the Ultramontanes, so much given to equating faith and obedience, and therefore so rigidly systematic, centralized, and clericalized, there was an urgent need to

---

[1] O., 18 Nov. 1870. [2] Diff. ii, p. 179.
[3] A Letter to the Duke of Norfolk. (Diff. ii, p. 247.)
[4] ibid., pp. 248–9. [5] W. ii, p. 332.

re-state the rights of conscience; and Newman treated Gladstone's charge in the same way as Kingsley's: in the course of a defence, he implied a criticism, and then stated a positive idea of the Church—this time in its relation to the conscience of its members.

In the subsequent *Letter to the Duke of Norfolk* (1875) Newman remarks, in passing, that however pure the Church's power might be at the summit, it suffered from 'a great deal of Roman malaria at the foot'[1]; and he reminds his fellow Catholics not only of the supremacy of conscience, but of the functional autonomy of the spiritual and the temporal in Church and State which the rise of Christianity required and made inevitable. He quotes Ranke to the effect that, nowadays, although, 'the spiritual and secular powers may come into near contact, may even stand in the closest community . . . they can be thoroughly incorporated only at rare conjunctures and for a short period'.[2]

But the foundation of Newman's argument is that however the Pope's infallibility might be interpreted it could never supersede conscience—hence Newman's challenge that he would drink 'to the Pope, if you please—still, to Conscience first, and to the Pope afterwards'.[3]

Such sentiments allied Newman with the liberal Catholics and with Acton in particular; and the question may be asked whether Newman concedes too much in the interests of English political liberty: are not freedom of speech, thought, and moral action *in effect* incompatible with the exercise of papal infallibility? Could it be our duty in conscience to deny an *ex cathedra* pronouncement by the Pope?

The answer provided by Newman is that any such collision would be merely apparent, since it is logically impossible: the deliverances of a true conscience and the dictates of a *de fide* papal pronouncement are derived from the same source—God; and an apparent contradiction would, on analysis, be found to spring either from a misinformed conscience or a mistaken interpretation of what it was which was being infallibly defined. Newman draws attention to the skill, time, and integrity which are required before the true implications of an infallible pronouncement can be accurately and certainly established. He quotes Bellarmine to establish the grounds on which a Pope's authority may lawfully be

[1] *Diff*. ii, p. 297.   [2] Quoted in *Diff*. ii, p. 204.
[3] *Diff*. ii, p. 261.

resisted—if he assaults a man's person, or his soul, if he 'troubles the state', or strives to destroy the Church.[1] Newman adds, *contra* Gladstone, that he gives an absolute obedience neither to the Queen nor the Pope; and he added later in a Postscript that some Ultramontane theologians have even held 'that a Pope who teaches heresy *ipso facto* ceases to be pope'.[2]

The ability to say what exactly is infallibly defined requires theological skill; mistakes may be made, and some new writer may maintain that 'the Pope's act does not imply what it has seemed to imply, and questions which seemed to be closed, are after a course of years re-opened'. Here, says Newman, 'there is a real exercise of private judgement and an allowable one'.[3]

In drinking first to conscience and then to the Pope, Newman is showing what, for a theologian, is the correct logical priority, but he is also re-stating the principles enunciated in his essay *On Consulting the Faithful in Matters of Doctrine*[4]—that the power within us which is able to know the difference between right and wrong (the illative sense or *phronesis*) is the counterpart of that instinct 'deep in the bosom of the Mystical Body of Christ'[5] (the *phronema*) which characterizes the mind of the Church at its deepest and widest—the *consensus fidelium*. It is this correspondence which guarantees our ability to recognize what, in an infallible pronouncement, is infallible; but a successful interpretation demands that two conditions be satisfied: 'the principle of minimising, so necessary, as I think, for a wise and cautious theology' must be applied; and the active 'co-operation' of the whole Church must be forthcoming. Newman is thus insisting that the right course is likely to be that 'which commits the Church least', and the best that which associates the whole people of God in a definition which is 'more or less perspicuous . . . in proportion to the quality of the men who meet together in Councils', to the thoroughness of the preparatory investigation, and to the experience and knowledge available. Newman cites Molina in his support; but he cannot forebear the ironical comment: 'So much on the circumstances under which the Vatican Council passed its definition.'[6] There is no doubt that Newman would, under certain circumstances, have

---

[1] *Diff.* ii, p. 243.   [2] ibid., p. 359.   [3] ibid., pp. 333–40.
[4] See above, chapter 7, p. 115. The revised and abbreviated edition of this essay had been published by Newman as an appendix to his reissue of the *Arians* as recently as 1871.
[5] *O.C.T.F.* text, p. 73.   [6] *Diff.* ii, pp. 332, 307–8.

agreed that it might be the layman's duty to think and then to say—with 'definiteness' and 'warmth'—what, under conscience, he was bound to utter; and it is perhaps a comment on the qualities respectively of Vatican I and Vatican II that the latter Council could include such an injunction in one of its Constitutions.[1]

By thus placing papal infallibility within the context and authority of theological interpretation, and by placing that theological interpretation within the Church as a whole, Newman showed how to prevent the arbitrary extension and abuse of papal power which Acton so much dreaded. An infallible pronouncement would seem to function in the manner of Berkeley's 'operative principle'[2]—it must first be used to be understood; and until the Church as a whole has used such a pronouncement, it cannot be sure what part of it has been infallibly defined.

The function of the Pope in relation to the conscience of the faithful is also clarified. It is not to tyrannize over the Church, but to keep it free, by acting as a counter-balance to the equally infallible powers of the bishops in Council and of the *sensus fidelium* —'the championship of the Moral Law and of conscience is his raison d'être'.[3]

Thus 'Rome ought to be a name to lighten the heart at all times', he wrote to Bishop Ullathorne on 28 January 1870,[4] in what he refers to as 'one of the most passionate and confidential letters that I ever wrote in my life'. Instead, the announcement of the First Vatican Council had come like 'thunder in the clear sky' telling us 'to prepare for something, we know not what, to try our faith, we know not how'.

Newman's protest is therefore at the irrelevance of the action. Judged by the criterion that the function of an oecumenical Council is to speak to all nations in their condition, then the First Vatican Council, by being imposed rather than demanded, and by being chiefly concerned to extricate the Pope's spiritual authority from his involvement in Italian politics, was—from the standpoint of

---

[1] *Lumen Gentium*, para. 37, speaks of the laity as being 'sometimes obliged to express their opinion on those things that concern the good of the Church'.

[2] See above, chapter 1, pp. 12 f.

[3] *Diff.* ii, p. 253. See Bishop B. C. Butler's judgment that Vatican II encourages the interpretation that 'there are not three infallibilities . . . [but] a single infallible Church . . . exercising her infallibility . . . in three different modes'. (*Theology of Vatican II*, 1967, p. 112 and note.)

[4] *W.* ii, 287–8. A more correct text in C. S. Dessain, *John Henry Newman* (1966), pp. 137–8.

the Church universal—contextually irrelevant.[1] But even so, and in spite of his conviction that the Council had fallen into the hands of an 'aggressive insolent faction', who were determined to treat the Faithful 'as the Faithful never were treated before',[2] Newman kept his balance as a theologian.

Since 'the highest of all teachers' was also 'the least luminous', Newman could not rest on the unaided power of conscience as the sole alternative to the abuse of authority. He qualifies his account of conscience by speaking of it as requiring for its fulfilment 'The Church, the Pope, the Hierarchy [who] are in the Divine purpose, the supply of an urgent demand.'[3] Although to deny conscience was to deny the presence and power of the indwelling presence of Christ, that voice of God within us is incomplete, and requires the Church and its sacraments for its true identification, location, and fulfilment. Here is the source of Newman's divergence from liberal Catholicism as represented by Acton—a divergence completely consistent with his position theologically. Both Newman and Acton were for the separation of Church and State, in the sense of their autonomous functioning; and Newman would not have cavilled at Acton's statement of the central problem of Catholicism as 'how private virtue and public crime could issue from the same root'.[4] They both opposed, therefore, the Ultramontane *intégrisme* that saw the Church as confined to one mode—the political ultra-devotional. It was this which provoked Newman's rhetorical question to Ullathorne—'when has definition of doctrine *de fide* been a luxury of devotion and not a stern painful necessity?'[5]

But after 1870 the papacy, for Acton, was 'the fiend skulking behind the crucifix'.[6] His religion became his flag, while his

---

[1] See Cuthbert Butler, *The Vatican Council* 1869–70, pp. 161, 169.

The Bishop of Savannah, Georgia, objected to the Council's preoccupation with 'the obscure errors of German idealists' when it would be more to the purpose 'to condemn the theory that negroes have not souls; and he proposed a canon anathematizing any who dare assert that blacks are not of the human family'. Even 'the strongly Ultramontane theologian' Abbé Gay, thought the Council to be too much concerned 'with errors hardly known outside the schools, too little with those that trouble men's minds and are a peril to society'.

Notice has already been taken of Bishop Ullathorne's comments (ibid., pp. 368–9) in the discussion of the Munich Congress in chapter 8 above, p. 135.

[2] *W*. ii, pp. 287–8.

[3] *Diff*. ii, p. 254.

[4] Acton, *Historical Essays* (1907), p. 301.

[5] Dessain, *John Henry Newman*, p. 138.

[6] Acton, *Correspondence* (1917), p. 56.

politics became his faith.[1] He was never able to see an alternative
to papal autocracy other than an autonomous conscience. Yet this
was to obliterate that very distinction between conscience as a
divine agent and as a moral principle which Newman had felt to
be what divided him from Coleridge. Depending upon the Church
for its explication and fulfilment, conscience is as much the effect
or sign of a healthy spiritual sensibility as its originating cause;
and the relationship between conscience and the Church, between
freedom and authority was a matter, therefore, requiring delicate
discrimination. Even before 1870 Newman hints at the principle
which ought to govern that relationship when, in speaking of the
vexed question of university education, he says that the best course
is what 'will commit the Church least'.[2] And if we interpret this
remark in accordance with his 'principle of minimising' we can see
how Newman is moving towards a view of the authority of the
magisterium as likely to be best protected when its encroachments
are most resisted. But the question remains—by what principle is
such a resistance to be determined? The answer is to be found in
Newman's second thoughts on the Catholic university.

(ii) *Unity of ethos*

The Vatican Council brought to the surface Newman's second
thoughts on the Catholic university.[3] After his return from Ireland
he had, on two separate occasions in 1864-5 and 1866-7, been
prepared to establish an Oratory in Oxford, but even this possibility
was finished: conditions in the last two years, he wrote in 1872,
'have altered everything'; and he believed that Catholics in
Oxford would now be obliged to engage in 'a vast polemical
undertaking, for which we are not prepared'.[4] The tendencies
which had caused him to speak in 1866 of the Church as narrowing
itself down into 'a sort of Novatianism' had been so much
strengthened that Newman observed on 25 March 1872, 'we think
"to overcome the world" by "going out of it"'.[5]

    The way in which Newman changed his mind about the
Catholic university bears upon his growing understanding of the

---

[1] *Letters to Mary Gladstone* (1904), p. 199.
[2] *O*. Letter to Augustus Betell, 10 December 1864.
[3] The evidence now presented, unless otherwise attributed, derives from the
Letter Books of the Birmingham Oratory. (*O*.)
[4] Letter to J. Spenser Northcote, 7 April 1872.
[5] Private memo, vol. 66.

need for the Church to be related to its context within a mixed or common culture; but it also throws light on the setting which Newman had now come to believe to be appropriate for the development of an effective theology. His purpose in wanting to go to Oxford had not been to introduce controversy 'into those quiet circles and sober schools of thought which are the strength of the Church of England'.[1] It was, rather, 'to show a side of the Catholic religion more theological, more exact'; and this at a time when 'the Pope is not a theologian', and theology had, in consequence, 'gone out of fashion'.[2]

By March 1867, in a correspondence with Sir Justin Shiel, Newman had come to consider the Catholic university to be 'a speculative perfection, which cannot be carried out in practice',[3] and he seems no longer opposed to young Catholics going to Oxford. Until Manning's appointment as Archbishop in 1865 the attitude of the bishops to sending Catholics to the English universities had varied. Ullathorne, if left to himself, would have established a Catholic Hall at Oxford in the '60s,[4] and many Catholic institutions, Downside among them, affiliated to London University for external examinations in the '40s; but Oxford, because it was the home of the Anglican Establishment, was anathema to Manning and the convert Ultramontanes; and a series of increasingly stringent prohibitions bedevilled the discussion of university education for Catholic laymen until 1895, when laymen were at last allowed to go to Oxford and Cambridge—some twelve years after the comparable permission to laymen in Italy.

If the Catholic laity had had but a quarter of the robust independence of Sir Justin Shiel, things might have been very different. Replying to Newman, Sir Justin speaks of 'the fanaticism . . . of Dr. Wiseman and Dr. Manning', and goes on to say: 'I assume to myself an absolute independence in the management of my secular affairs, in which I include education.' He dismisses as ridiculous the notion of 'foreign prelates and Jesuits of Propaganda'[5]—that faith and morals would be jeopardized by an Oxford education. But this was very much a minority view: Newman was prevented from going to Oxford, even at his own bishop's request, to found

---

[1] *W.* ii, p. 58.   [2] ibid., p. 374.
[3] *O.* 22 March 1867 (*W.* ii, p. 136).   [4] *W.* ii, p. 52.
[5] *O.* 27 March 1867.

an Oratory, in case his presence there should encourage Catholics to defy the bishops and send their sons to Oxford.

Yet, as Newman said, 'necessity has no laws'[1]; and he was even suspicious of the theological status of the prohibition; but where else could these young men be sent? It was soon to be no longer a matter of the fate of two hundred old Catholic families but of the urgent necessities of a newly emerging Catholic middle class; and it would not be possible to persist for much longer in a policy that 'Catholic youths might not have a career', because this would require them to be 'better educated than their priests'.[2]

In 1874, Manning's solution, and the one he had persuaded Rome to recommend, was officially adopted: the establishment of a Catholic University College in Bayswater. It lasted four years. The academic staff was distinguished but not autonomous; and the laity continued, as in Dublin, to be held at arm's length. The aim of the institution was to ensure that its pupils were 'vigilantly protected from all contact with the intellectual errors of National Education'.[3]

It was assumed that Newman would support this fresh attempt at a Catholic university, but in a letter to one of its sponsors, the President of Oscott, he says bluntly: 'I should not propose a Catholic university, for I think our present rulers would never give us a real one'—and he adds—'nor a Catholic college at Oxford'.[4]

Newman's primary condition for a Catholic university had been the full participation of the laity in teaching and governing; and, as McGrath[5] points out, his constitution for the Irish university involved as little dependence upon external authority as possible. Yet for the clergy to concede power to the laity involves an understanding of and sympathy for that very theology of consultation put forward in *On Consulting the Faithful*, for which Newman was delated to Rome. It also involved conceding as a matter of principle, rather than of expediency, rights to the laity in the temporal sphere, which were then (1870) being disputed. Manning and his supporters, for example, had petitioned for the Temporal Power of the papacy to be made a doctrine *de fide*.[6]

Yet the principle of academic autonomy is implicit not only in

[1] *W*. ii, p. 149 (from *S & N*, p. 14).   [2] *W*. ii, pp. 554–5.
[3] From the *Report* (1872) of the Hierarchy's Commission, cited in A. C. F. Beales, 'Catholic Higher Institutes' (*Dublin Review*, 1962, no. 491, pp. 82–4).
[4] *O*. 9 April 1872.   [5] *McGrath*, op. cit., pp. 381–2, 384.
[6] *W*. i, pp. 521 f.

the government of Newman's university, but in the liberty of a teacher to pursue his subject to its limits; theological primacy in theory must be won in fact, and theology becomes, if it can, the queen of the sciences on the university's terms and not its own. This is what Newman meant in speaking of the philosophy of an imperial intellect[1]; its purpose is to discriminate rather than to simplify, to understand rather than to condemn. The educated Catholic has nothing to fear from the world of liberal values by which he is encompassed, since truth cannot contradict truth; but it is a truth which can be achieved only 'by many minds working together freely',[2] and failure to observe this principle in, for example, a Catholic institution for higher education would have two fundamental consequences.

The theology taught would become unreal (although in essence correct and true) since its methods and vocabulary would have no relation to the intellectual standards, methods, and needs of the secular climate of opinion. An education in such a purely notional theology would produce neither educated priests nor devout laymen, but dissociated personalities, neither properly educated nor effectively devout. Its subservience to a theology which was contextually irrelevant would make a low intellectual standard inevitable, since questions would cease to be open, and emphasis would fall upon the formal correctness of answers rather than upon their relevance or meaning. Newman records an amusing encounter with a Jesuit who wished 'to indoctrinate the lay youths in philosophy'[3]; and amongst his papers for February 1872 is a brief and almost illegible note on what a Catholic university is not. It is not, 'a place to get up petitions for the Pope's temporal power, and be *deposed* if a man won't sign it, or to print in its Gazette the Pope's dogmatic Bulls, or *docete gentes* in Mathematics, or oblige a dissector ever to be bringing in Providence'.[4]

Newman's second thoughts pose two major questions—would it be to theology's advantage if it were studied in an open rather than in a Catholic university; and is a Catholic university in fact possible in a mixed or open society? In order to take all knowledge for its object, a university must reflect the society in which it grows, because only thus can it provide that inclusiveness which alone makes possible the enlargement of mind that is the hallmark of its

[1] *Idea*, p. 461.   [2] *W*. ii, p. 49.   [3] *W*. ii, p. 197.
[4] *Letters*, vol. 66, memo. attached to 23 Feb. 1872.

graduates. In a university the primary emphasis must be, there-fore, intellectual; where, for whatever reason, an institution cannot or will not reflect the intellectual diversity of its society, it remains —if it is Catholic—a seminary; nor, if this is recognized for what it is, need we deplore it. A seminary or school, where the emphasis is on moral rather than intellectual development, is a necessary stage in education; but we can only escape the latent tautology if we realize that a Catholic society produces a Catholic university primarily because it is a society, and not because it is Catholic: in a mixed or non-Catholic society, Catholics are able to produce only seminaries or contributions to an existing university.[1]

That this is a reasonable interpretation of Newman's later think-ing can be seen from his willingness, in spite of personal disinclina-tion, to found an Oratory at Oxford, if he were asked. But profound reservations are to be seen in his letters of this time. 'By mis-management,' he says, 'the whole question has got into that tangle, that it can't be satisfactorily solved',[2] and if a Catholic Hall were established, he feared it would encourage what is nowadays called the ghetto-mentality: 'Catholics in Oxford will be few and then despised, or many and then feared and hated.'[3] In 1863 Newman thought the point of principle turned on whether Catholics could be taught by Catholic tutors, but a note added in 1875 shows that he considered the dilemma too great even for this solution, since he now concluded that 'a College at Oxford, so isolated as not to have the influx of Oxford opinions, was an impossibility'.[4]

The effects of the Vatican Council were a further aggravation; and in a letter to Lord Howard of 27 April 1872, Newman shows that his mind had slowly but decisively changed:

On the whole I do not know how to avoid the conclusion that mixed education in the higher schools is as much a necessity now in England, as it was in the East in the days of St. Basil and St. Chrysostom. . . . In a large university, there are good sets and bad sets; and a youth has a chance of choosing between them. In a small, exclusive body there is no

---

[1] 'A Catholic nation, *as a matter of course*, establishes Catholicism, because it is a Catholic nation . . . the establishment is the spontaneous act of the people . . . the Catholic people does it, and not the Catholic Church. It is *but an accident* of a particular state of things . . .' Newman to Allies, 5 March 1861, in M. H. Allies, *Thomas William Allies* (1907), p. 131.

[2] Letter to Lord Howard, 4 May 1872.

[3] Letter to Ambrose St. John, 26 August 1863.

[4] ibid. (note added in 1875).

choice; and one bad member ruins for a time the whole community. *Thus the open university, when complemented by a strong mission, may be even safer than a close Catholic college.* [My italics.]

Here is Newman's change of mind. He not only reverts to the position he had previously held on mixed education,[1] but adopts a minimizing attitude to authority; yet I wish to argue that he changed his mind as much from a concern for theology as for the education of the laity. The two concerns are, in fact, interrelated, and they are further related to Newman's developing understanding of the changes necessitated by the Church's position in a mixed society. It was not merely affection for old friends and for Oxford that caused him to become increasingly pained by the alien aspect of the Catholic Church. His vision went beyond that of his opponents, Manning, Ward, and Talbot, who had done so much to ensure that the Church 'should present just that aspect to my fellow countrymen which is most consonant with their ingrained prejudices against her'.[2]

'Catholics did not make us Catholics,' he had said, 'Oxford made us Catholics'[3]; but his exploration of his Anglican roots leads to more than a fresh appreciation of the origins of his idea of the Church, it leads him to a deeper and more urgent understanding of why the Church must realize itself within the context of a common culture which—mixed, open and liberal—is the common ground on which all Christians may meet within what a later thinker has called a community of analogy. To insist, within such a context, upon the production of Catholic institutions as ends in themselves is to be unreal, since the question which has first to be settled is what ought to be the relation between the Catholic Church and this common culture.

Newman speaks of universities as having originally been established 'in order to preserve the *equilibrium* between clerical and lay education'[4]; and in serving this purpose they also establish an equilibrium between the Church and the culture of the times. The nineteenth century, however, was a period of extreme disequilibrium for the Church, both internally (in the relations

[1] When Allies suggested that an Oratory in Oxford constituted a change in principle, Newman replied on 7 March 1867 by citing the passages in *S & N*, pp. 13, 18, on mixed education to the effect that in the circumstances 'to attempt more is to effect less'. These are marked in Newman's copy, but were not reprinted in the *Idea*.

[2] *V.M.* i, p. xxxvii.   [3] *W.* ii, p. 57.   [4] *H.S.* iii, p. 242.

between clergy and laity) and externally (in the relations with society). It was Newman's view that an equilibrium could only be recreated by the renewal of theology; but this would have to be a theology which by being made relevant to the times was able to make sense of them. Such a theology could, however, only be achieved within the framework described in the *Idea of a University*, since 'truth is the guiding principle of theology and theological enquiries',[1] and truth can be achieved only by 'many minds working together freely'.[2]

It was the absence of such a theology which had been the cause 'of our late and present internal troubles'[3]; but—and here was the risk of a vicious circle—without such a theology a Catholic university such as he had conceived was impossible. Furthermore, it was not sufficient to require the laity to support such a university: it must be so constituted as to mirror in its constitution, regulations, and actions that theological principle of the *conspiratio* of pastors and faithful people which the Church requires for the widest and deepest expression of its mind.

In abandoning the idea as 'a speculative perfection', Newman did not abandon his idea of the Church from which his conception of the university was derived; and even his second thoughts—that a mixed society requires a mixed education—throw further light on his idea of the Church. If it were mistaken to remove the laity from their involvement in a mixed and open society, then—in the long term—something more positive would have to be envisaged than the minimizing principle that what commits the Church least will best overcome its alien aspect.

Newman's oecumenical references and intentions now become particularly relevant. The positive foundation he seeks to see established is what he calls the growth of 'a better sort of religious sentiment'; and his purpose in republishing his works was to establish such a foundation on which 'higher strata of religious truth might be deposited at some future day'. As he specifically describes the process as one of 'levelling-up' it is reasonable to suppose that what he calls the 'open university' would most likely be the place to provide the means and opportunity for such a work.[4]

[1] *V.M.* i, p. xli.   [2] *W.* ii, p. 49.   [3] ibid., p. 374.
[4] Letter to Mother Margaret Mary Hallahan *c.* 1870, in Dessain, *John Henry Newman*, p. 160: '... there must be a great move of the national mind to a better sort of religious sentiment. Wesleyans, Anglicans, Congregationalists, Unitarians, must be raised to one and the same (what we used to call at Oxford)

The implication of Newman's argument would seem to be that in a society whose institutions are open and require no conformity to test acts, the place for Catholic theology is in an open university, not only because it is a legitimate subject of study in an institution taking all knowledge as its object, but because, for the Catholic layman, his further theological education ought to take place in the same place and at the same time as his further intellectual education.[1] But there is another consideration.

To place Catholic theology and the higher education of priests and laity within such a context would enable all Christians and other men of good will to help bring the fruits of a common culture to bear upon the formation of the Church; and this was that 'unity of ethos among those who otherwise differ'[2] at which Newman aimed. It would also assist an inherited Establishment to transform itself into a common culture rooted in a wider range of theological agreement and no longer restricted to a governing class. It is within such a context that we must seek the common element of which Pusey prophesied.

Although Newman was not encouraged to publish his reflections upon the changing nature of theological studies or on the contributions the laity might make to them, we can see from *My Campaign in Ireland* that he thought laymen should apply themselves to certain areas of theological investigation, and in particular to the philosophy of religion and to the problems which arise in the interaction of religion and culture.[3]

"ethos". That is the same moral and intellectual state of mind. To bring them to this is "levelling-up"'.

[1] I have discussed this matter further in the Introduction to *Theology and the University* (ed. Coulson, 1964).

[2] Letter to Copeland, 13 Oct. 1877.

[3] 'I would exclude the teaching in extenso of pure dogma from the secular schools, and content myself with enforcing such a broad knowledge of doctrinal subjects as is contained in the catechisms of the Church or the actual writings of her laity. I would have them apply their minds to such religious topics as laymen actually do treat, and are thought praiseworthy in treating . . . [because] . . . I am professing to contemplate Christian knowledge in what may be called its secular aspect. . . . I should desire, then, to encourage in our students an intelligent apprehension of the relations . . . between Church and Society at large.' (*Campaign*, p. 162.) 'Theologians inculcate the matter and determine the details of that revelation; they view it from within, philosophers view it from without, and this external view may be called the philosophy of Religion, and the office of delineating it externally is most gracefully performed by laymen. In the first age laymen were most commonly the Apologists. . . . If laymen may write, lay students may read.' (ibid., p. 165.)

In conversations between 1885 and 1890 with his biographer, Wilfrid Ward, we can see something of what he might have required. He is reported as stating that theological schools should become more intimately alive to contemporary problems in subjects other than theology, since developments in science and history, for example, by changing the data could invalidate certain traditional theological expositions. The paramount need was for the fair and candid discussion between 'representatives of the special sciences and the theologians', since only by such means could justice be done to the 'absolute necessity of certain concessions on the part of theology'. Theologians must be trained to recognize those changes in other disciplines which change the data of theological studies.[1]

But no one knew better than Newman why the times were unsuitable for publishing or even projecting such a programme. 'The Nihilism in the Catholic Body, and in its rulers' raised internal problems of greater urgency—'They forbid, but they do not direct or create.'[2] The Church had first to get the descriptions of itself right—of its powers and of their mutual relationship—before a convincing and profitable account of its context within a mixed society could be attempted. It was to this that Newman now turned—how to make sense of the Church's present position in relation to its past and, in particular, how to determine the relations between authority and the autonomy proper to intellectual and theological investigations. By what principle could such apparently contradictory tendencies be regulated? And—even more fundamentally—how was it possible so to describe the Church as to show that it was both a personal unity and yet an inevitable ferment of seemingly discordant practices, opinions, and parties?

[1] *W.* ii, pp. 497–500.   [2] ibid., p. 486.

III

THE FINAL AND EXPLICIT FORM

X

THE REGULATING PRINCIPLE

AFTER the troubles produced by the publication of his *Letter to the Duke of Norfolk*—a work so unpopular in Rome that Newman's bishop had been asked to secure some kind of retraction [1]— Newman settled down to republishing his works. He was now 76 years of age; yet although no further 'occasions' were to present themselves to him publicly, there was one encounter he was determined to have before he died. It was with that most formidable and final of adversaries—the Newman of his Anglican past.

He chose to publish the fruits of this encounter in the form of a preface to a re-issue of his *Lectures on the Prophetical Office of the Church* (1837) under the general title of *The Via Media of the Anglican Church*. This he published in 1877; and its Preface contains his description of the Church in its final form. Its comparative neglect may arise from its publication in the form of a preface to works which his enemies were unlikely to read; but it may also arise from the deceptive simplicity of its form and expression.

Newman's final and explicit formulation of his idea of the Church both supplements the incomplete definitions of Vatican I and anticipates the Constitution *On the Church* (*Lumen Gentium*) of Vatican II; and by doing so it expresses an idea of the Church at once more oecumenical and more traditional. Its immediate influence was slight—although, as I wish to show, it did directly influence von Hügel's celebrated analysis of religion into three elements—but it anticipates much that is to be found in later European writing on the Church, particularly in Blondel. By sharing our contemporary presuppositions, Newman asks our kind

[1] Dessain, *John Henry Newman*, p. 145.

of questions; and this is why he anticipates the more oecumenical teaching of *Lumen Gentium*—that we must first understand our response to the Church *as a whole* before we can effectively define how we should understand its component parts.

In the manuscript of his Preface [1] Newman writes that he wishes to speak 'of the Church concretely as the body of Christ'; and he achieves his purpose—to show how the apparently contradictory faces of the Church may be reconciled without compromising their antecedent unity—by deriving his definition from the three offices of Christ:

He is Prophet, Priest, and King; and after His pattern, and in human measure, Holy Church has a triple office too; not the Prophetical alone and in isolation, as these Lectures virtually teach, but three offices, which are indivisible, though diverse, viz. teaching, rule and sacred ministry. This then is the point on which I shall now insist, the very title of the Lectures I am to criticize suggesting to me how best to criticize them.

Christianity, then, is at once a philosophy, a political power, and a religious rite: as a religion, it is Holy; as a philosophy, it is Apostolic; as a political power, it is imperial, that is One and Catholic. As a religion, its special centre of action is pastor and flock; as a philosophy, the Schools; as a rule, the Papacy and its Curia. [2]

Although the words 'imperial', 'political', and 'curial' strike sharply on modern ears, Newman had his reasons for using them, as I hope to show; but what is more immediately significant is that this final and explicit formulation should arise in the editing and reconsideration of a work—the *Lectures on the Prophetical Office of the Church*—which was specifically composed to advocate the claim of the Church of England to be a *via media* between the sectarian extremes of Protestantism and of Romanist corruption.

The conditions which Newman seeks to satisfy take us straight back to Coleridge and to the origins of Newman's idea of the Church in English tradition. They are how to provide a description of the Church which allows us to respond to it as a whole—as an organic unity of persons through whom the verifying presence of Christ is transmitted—yet without resting on this response as self-evident. Our response as a whole must therefore be compatible with those diverse empirical aspects which are represented by the

[1] MS., p. 33. It is dated 7th March 1877.
[2] *V.M.* i, p. xl.

authority of the magisterium, the tradition of Christian doctrine, and the life of prayer and liturgy.

This conception of the Church must, moreover, be as wide as the whole people of God: a narrow or sectarian definition which confines the Church to the clergy and denies a creative role to the laity and to the pastors and faithful in *conspiratio* is quite unacceptable. But given a successful width of definition the further question still arises—by what principle are these diverse aspects of the Church to be regulated? And it is the isolation of this as the crucial question which represents Newman's achievement, and to which his experiences on the *via negativa* inevitably led.

What is of special interest is the extent to which Newman takes as his model that notion of an equilibrium of functions within the individual which makes for the associated sensibility; and his terminology is strikingly reminiscent of Coleridge's account in *Church and State*[1] of the requisite equilibrium between reason, religion, and will in the individual which is a principle to be applied also to society. It is possible, as I have suggested, that this conception influenced Newman when he composed his lectures on University Education; and what is of further significance is the similarity between Newman's *model* or idea of the Church and his idea of a university as a self-equilibrating organism, in which the action of the various disciplines or sciences (including theology) upon each other is the source of their regulation. Here, too, the equilibrium of those functions—intellectual, religious, and theological—which in the individual is the mark of a successful education is, when applied socially to the university, what constitutes it an educating community.[2] The difference is, as Newman now makes clear, that in the Church, theology is singled out as having the authority of the prophetical office to act as the equilibrating principle, since the purpose of theology is truth, and the over-all purpose of the Church is to bear witness to the truth of Revelation.

These modal parallels are of great significance. Not only do they testify to the width of Newman's conception of the Church—that it must be as wide as its context within contemporary culture—

---

[1] *C & S*, p. 263; and 260 passim. See above, chapter 2, pp. 32 ff., and esp. p. 33, footnote: it is noteworthy that the qualities described by Coleridge have as their degenerative form—rationalism, superstition, and tyranny.

[2] See above, chapter 2, pp. 34 ff.

but they also demonstrate the homogeneous character of its development. They also show that the Church as a dialectic of functions is logically prior to the application of its authority; and that this dialectic is organically the same for the individual as for the Church collectively.

The conception of the three offices of Christ as applying both to the Church and to the individual is of great antiquity. The Church is described as performing the offices of Christ as Prophet, Priest, and King in Eusebius[1]; but there is the even older liturgical tradition which is still preserved in the Mass of Chrism for Maundy Thursday. Here the chrism is described as that 'wherewith thou didst anoint prophets, priests and kings'[2]—the chrism here being the sacramental sign of the gift of the Holy Spirit— whose descent showed forth Jesus as the *Christos* who is the supreme Prophet, Priest, and King; and by that chrism every Christian partakes of these triple functions.

The liturgical association of the individual with the three offices of Christ is the *explicit* form of that relationship with God which Newman held to be *implicitly* present in conscience, which is 'a prophet in its informations, a monarch in its peremptoriness, a priest in its blessings and anathemas'.[3]

The question which Newman is posing—by what principle is the dialectic of functions (the Church) regulated; and, in being regulated, purged?—is one which was live enough to Coleridge, Maurice, and others within the tradition in which Newman had been formed. To the victorious Ultramontane party it did not arise; or, if it did, it had been settled in 1870. For them the Church was an authoritarian regime, whose regulating principle was the absolute rule of the Pope; by such means, and by such means alone could the verifying function of Christ through his Church be guaranteed.

This view is credible when it is realized that barely three years after Newman's conversion, the temper of the Church changed radically. In 1848, the Pope abandoned his efforts to come to terms with the liberals and fled from Rome; and during the next twenty

---

[1] Eusebius, *The Ecclesiastical History*, 1.1.3: 7–20.
[2] Preface to the canon of the Mass of Chrism. Cf. the *Traditio Apostolica* of Hippolytus (*c.* 200 A.D.), and Paul Dabin, S.J., *Le Sacerdoce royal des fidèles dans la tradition ancienne et moderne* (Bruxelles, 1950).
I am indebted to Fr. Robert Murray, S.J., for pointing this out to me.
[3] *Diff.* ii, p. 248. See above, chapter 9, p. 151.

years his authority remained in question while his power was steadily eroded. The Vatican Decrees of 1870 did not succeed, in practice, in separating his spiritual from his temporal authority—the party which had attempted to have his temporal power declared a doctrine *de fide*[1] was still in the majority; and the authority of the Church was thought to rest solely on the authority of the Pope—so much so that loyalty to him in his troubles became a test of orthodoxy which applied with special force to converts.

Emphasis now fell on the unity of the Church—with Rome as its focus—rather than upon its diversity; and this was reinforced by a political preference for the loyal but superseded *anciens régimes*. Catholics acquired the habit of living to themselves, withdrawing from the hostile world, and leaving the initiative to liberals, secularists, and Protestants.

No more unpromising climate of opinion could be conceived in which to conduct a significant theology or press such distinctions as that between unity and uniformity; yet by 1877 the effects of Ultramontane autocracy were already raising acute questions about the nature of the Church. The question Newman had answered in his *Essay on Development* had now to be put again: is what, as an Anglican, he had criticized as Romanism and what, as a Roman Catholic, he had experienced as Ultramontanism, an inevitable condition of the Roman Church? And, if it is, does it invalidate that Church's claim to function as 'the visible part' of the Body of Christ?

The extent to which Newman was prepared to press the question may be gauged by his decision to reprint his former criticisms with an ironical footnote: 'There is a certain truth in this remark but a man must have a large knowledge of Catholics and of the effect of their system upon them, to assert with confidence what is here imagined of them.'[2]

That Newman was not merely being ironical at his own expense, can be seen from a letter written to von Hügel at the same time, 30 June 1877, in which Newman said: 'but to argue "the existence of evil in the *Church* is a proof that the Church is not from God",

[1] *W.* i, pp. 521 f. In 1880, in *The Temporal Power of the Pope*, Manning stated his 'first proposition' as 'that the temporal power of the Pope is ordained of God' (cited in *MacDougall*, op. cit., p. 58).

[2] *V.M.* i, p. 102[6]. Almost the same words are used with reference to 'Romanism' and to the view that obedience justifies in a footnote added to page 186 of the *Lectures on Justification* in the revised edition of 1874.

is not going to the root of the matter, but trifling with a mere instance of a great and fearful fact instead of going straight to that fact itself. . . . The disasters and defeats of the Church are presupposed in Scripture.'[1]

As an Anglican Newman had been content, in his *Lectures on the Prophetical Office* (1837), to make a simple distinction between what gave the Church life—the prophetical tradition—and what gave the Church form—the episcopal tradition.[2] The sermons he preached as he moved towards his conversion show a concern to analyse the nature of the Church and its effects upon the world[3]; but his conception of the Church's double aspect remains that of simple corruption—doctrinally by adding to the faith, politically by the abuse of power, and spiritually by encouraging superstition. In 1840[4] he makes his first references to the triple offices of Christ as Prophet, Priest, and King; but these are applied in a general way to thought, endurance, and active life as the three privileges of the Church. It is only when, as a Roman Catholic, he is unceasingly obliged to witness to those conditions which, within the legitimate authority of the Catholic polity, make for life and liberty that Newman finds himself obliged to propound what Professor Nédoncelle has called 'une théologie des abus ecclésiastiques'.[5] It is this which was responsible for his discovery that the traditional application of the three offices of Christ to the Church was intended for more specific purposes than pastoral or liturgical rhetoric.

Squarely he faces 'the writer whom I am undertaking to answer'[6] —as he now describes the Newman of forty years before. He is at last prepared to give his final answer to the Anglican question—is the Church of Roman reformable? Or is it only able to regulate itself by imposing a rigid uniformity? Unless an alternative principle of regulation could be established then the results Newman had anticipated as an Anglican were inevitable: 'when religion is reduced in all its parts to a system, there is hazard of something

---

[1] *O.*   [2] *V.M.* i. 249, 251, 260.
[3] First published in 1843 as *Sermons bearing on the Subjects of the Day*. It was Kingsley's error that he confused such analysis with advocacy.
[4] ibid., Sermon V, pp. 52 f.
[5] Maurice Nédoncelle, 'L'Apologia de Newman dans l'histoire de l'autobiographie et de la théologie' in *Studies presented to Romano Guardini on his 80th birthday*, p. 583. (Echter Verlag, Würzburg, n.d.)
[6] MS. of Preface, p. 38.

earthly being made the chief object of our contemplation instead
of our Maker'.[1] It was this judgement which he did not withdraw
and to which the ironical footnote was appended.

His criticisms of the Ultramontane principle fasten on the
fallacious expedience of its disjunction of the Church from the
world, of Grace from Nature, and on its despairing view of natural
man and secular society as being so feeble that a movement to God
is possible only when coerced by external authority: on such a view,
as Blondel remarked,[2] 'nothing in man echoes or calls to the gift'.
As an Oxford tutor and as a Catholic theologian Newman held
tenaciously to the opposite principle—that 'Revelation . . . does
but complete what Nature has begun'.[3] It had informed his idea of
a university education as it now informed his elucidation of that
principle, alternative to Ultramontanism, by which the Church
has traditionally been regulated. We must attend to the 'recurring'
nature of the 'contrast between the theological side of Roman
teaching and its political and popular side'.[4] In a private letter to
Blachford he puts the point with an Oxonian directness—it is how
to safeguard the Church from the 'Don Pasquales, the pope's lackies
who butter the Pope'. In the same letter he anticipates the line he
will take later in the Preface. In spite of the excesses of individuals,
the Catholic Church has 'its constitution and its theological laws';
and it is these, and not the unaided power of conscience, which
have to be opposed to the institutional excesses of the Church.
'Theology,' he goes on to say, 'is the regulating principle.'[5] Its
absence has been 'the cause of our late and present internal
troubles', since never is religion in greater danger than 'when the
schools of theology have been broken up and ceased to be'.

Here is the nerve of Newman's argument as it is expressed in his
Preface:

I say, then, Theology is the fundamental and regulating principle of
the whole Church system. It is commensurate with Revelation, and
Revelation is the initial and essential idea of Christianity. It is the
subject-matter, the formal cause, the expression, of the Prophetical
Office, and, as being such, has created both the Regal Office and the

[1] *V.M.* i, p. 102.
[2] In Alexander Dru, 'Blondel's *La Semaine Sociale*', *Downside Review*, July
1963, p. 244.
[3] *V.M.* i, p. lxxi.   [4] ibid., p. xxix.
[5] Letter to Blachford 5 Feb. 1875 (partially available in *W.* ii, p. 374).

Sacerdotal. And it has in a certain sense a power of jurisdiction over those offices, as being its own creations, theologians being ever in request and in employment in keeping within bounds both the political and popular elements in the Church's constitution,—elements which are far more congenial than itself to the human mind, are far more liable to excess and corruption, and are ever struggling to liberate themselves from those restraints which are in truth necessary for their well-being.[1]

In failing to recognize the prophetical function as the regulating principle, both Acton and the Ultramontanes were making the same mistake. Both saw the Church in political terms: Acton opposed conscience to papal tyranny, but conscience without theology is at best sensibility, at worst emotion. For the Ultra-montanes, power without theology was exercised in unreflecting imitation of secular power[2]—the Pope must have the status of a Prince, the bishop of a lord mayor and so forth—and it produced that monstrous contradiction between scripture and practice known today as 'triumphalism'. It is theology's function to recall the systems and abstractions of Churchmen to the fullness of their origins in Scripture and in the traditions of the people of God.

Theology is the perpetual critic of abuses and abstractions: it shows that the descriptions of the Church in Scripture, since they are 'educts of the imagination', are in terms of metaphors and symbols, since we are dealing not with static concepts but with developing functions. By these means Newman had come to regard the Church as 'a divine indwelling'; whose 'instruments are not even so much as instruments, but only the outward lineaments of Him'.[3] It was a complex unity of many offices—of the Pope, the bishops, and of the consensus fidelium—whose union was not political but 'musical'. In an unpublished letter to Dr. Jenkins of 6 April 1877, he puts it thus: 'the Pope as the key note, the Bishops the 3rd, the priests the 5th, the people the octave, and the Protestants the flat 7th which needs resolving'.[4]

With the introduction of theology as the regulating principle, Newman explicitly abandons his former distinction between life

[1] *V.M.* i, pp. xlvii–xlviii.
[2] Newman underlines this in the MS. of the Preface (p. 42): 'Thus the natural attempt from time to time of ecclesiastical superiors to force unconditional obedience on their subjects has been met by the whole schola affirming the rights of conscience.'
[3] *Jfc*, p. 196.
[4] *O.*

and form[1] by returning to Scripture for a threefold description of the Church as a community for teaching, worship, and ministry. It is a description in terms of offices or functions, presupposing an antecedent unity, and aiming at an harmonious resolution of institutional, liturgical, and theological claims in which no one element must preponderate at the expense of the others.

This is the ideal: the fact tends to be otherwise:

Truth is the guiding principle of theology and theological enquiries; devotion and edification, of worship; and of government, expedience. The instrument of theology is reasoning; of worship, our emotional nature; of rule, command and coercion. Further, in man as he is, reasoning tends to rationalism; devotion to superstition and enthusiasm; and power to ambition and tyranny.[2]

Hence the practices tolerated in Catholic countries which are at odds with Catholic theology, and the recurring charge of Romanism. Such examples of this notorious 'double aspect of the Church', although remediable, are part of its enduring tendency:

Men talk of our double aspect now; has not the first age a double aspect? Do not such incidents in the Gospel as this, and the miracle of the swine, the pool of Bethesda, the restoration of the servant's ear, the changing water into wine, the coin in the fish's mouth, and the like, form an aspect of Apostolic Christianity very different from that presented by St. Paul's Pastoral Epistles and the Epistle General of St. John? Need men wait for the Medieval Church in order to make their complaint that the theology of Christianity does not accord with its religious manifestations?[3]

The motives for accepting this apparent contradiction are pastoral:

they illustrate at once both these elements of her divinely ordered constitution; for the fear, as already mentioned, of 'quenching the smoking flax', which is the attribute of a guide of souls, operated in the same direction as zeal for the extension of Christ's kingdom, in resisting that rigorousness of a logical theology which is more suited for the Schools than for the World. In these cases then the two offices, political and pastoral, have a common interest as against the theological; but this is not always so.[4]

---

[1] He now applies this distinction to the people and the hierarchy (see his letter to Matthew Arnold, 3 Jan. 1876, referred to above, chapter 7, p. 130).
[2] *V.M.* i, p. xli.   [3] ibid., p. lxvii.   [4] *V.M.* i, p. lxxix.

It is at this point and only after making these reservations that
Newman is prepared to accept the Ultramontane emphasis upon
the institutional character of the Church; and Newman agrees that
her survival depends upon the Church's maintaining, through the
exercise of her kingly or institutional power, 'a strict unity of
polity'.[1]

As I have said, Newman's language falls sharply on modern ears,
but it is chosen deliberately to conciliate the Ultramontane party,
and its subsequent restatement by von Hügel may be more to our
taste. What Newman is saying is that religious sensibility and the
language of theology, like all languages, arise not from self-evident
ideas, but from the life of a community, and that they are meaningful only in so far as they continue to reflect a continuing community
life. Hence the community as such must be safeguarded if the
rights of conscience and the language of theology are to continue
to function. This is the sense which Newman gives to the term
'Tradition' which like 'Scripture' is the expression of this
continuing community.[2]

How far he was prepared to go can be seen in the MS. to his
Preface to the *Via Media*, where he expands para. 26[3] to read: 'I
say, then, that a conclusion of the executive in the Catholic Church

[1] 'The Catholic Church is by its very structure and mission a political power,
by which I mean a visible, substantive body of men, united together by common
engagements and laws and thereby necessarily having relations both towards its
members and towards outsiders. Such a polity exists simply for the sake of the
Catholic Religion, and as a means to an end; but since politics in their nature
are a subject of absorbing interest, it is not wonderful that grave scandals from
time to time occur among those who constitute its executive, or legislative, from
their being led off from spiritual aims by secular. These scandals hide from the
world for a while, and from large classes and various ranks of society, for long
intervals, the real sanctity, beauty and persuasiveness of the Church and her
children.' (ibid., footnote to p. 107.)
 'It is not a mere question of succession. The Catholic Church is not a mere
[spiritual] family or race, the essential idea of which is propagation, but a polity,
of which the essential idea is union and subordination, and of which propagation
is but the condition and necessity.' (ibid., footnote to p. 345.)
[2] 'The early Christians, when teaching and proving Christianity, had nothing
tangible to appeal to but the Scriptures. As time went on, and a theological
literature grew up, the appeal exclusively to Scripture ceased. Intermitted it
never could be. Scripture had the prerogative of inspiration, and thereby a
sacredness and power, sui generis; but, from the nature of the case, it was
inferior as an instrument of proof, in directness and breadth, to Councils, to
the Schola, and to the Fathers, doctors, theologians, and devotional writers of
the Church. (ibid., p. 321.)
[3] p. lxxxiii.

may become a dogmatic conclusion in her theology on the principle that what is absolutely essential to her well-being must be intended by her Divine Founder to take its place among her doctrines.'

But this executive power depends upon what might be called a dialectic of functions within the Church: it must not be exercised in a vacuum. Instead it must expect challenges and clashes. These, however, are to be regarded not as the sources of error and weakness, but as evidence of a power to adapt and to survive, since 'whatever is great refuses to be reduced to human rule and to be made consistent in its many aspects with itself'.[1] Such a conception of the Church and Tradition was diametrically opposed to the official and dominant view of the nineteenth-century papacy; and what saved Newman from the legal fiction current among his fellow Catholics that the Church and Tradition were 'a list of articles that can be numbered'[2] was 'the old Anglican, patristic, literary, Oxford'[3] tradition in which he had been formed. This, by encouraging his Patristic studies, had predisposed him to regard the Church as a living and antecedent unity, complex of definition, perpetually in growth, and seemingly contradictory in its behaviour.

Newman's idea—and it is that which informs *Lumen Gentium*—has never lacked propounders; but its direct influence within his own Church was limited to von Hügel. It seems to have provided the model for his analysis of the threefold elements of religion. This, first published in Part 1 of the *Mystical Element of Religion* in 1908, has had great influence upon Anglican theologians, who have been tempted to regard von Hügel as unrepresentative of his Church and unorthodox in his descriptions of its nature. He conceives it as 'the greatest possible multiplicity in the deepest possible unity', because 'every truly living unity is constituted in multiplicity'—hence his celebrated remark that monism was the enemy of religion. The three offices of Christ—the kingly, prophetical, and priestly—are by von Hügel taken to correspond to the external, intellectual, and mystical elements of the human soul.[4]

Each of these three elements of religion seeks to suppress the other and to exercise a totalitarian domination. Thus when the external or historical and institutional element predominates

---

[1] ibid., p. xciv.

[2] Newman, 'Letter to J. S. Flanagan', 15 Feb. 1868, in *Journal of Theological Studies*, Oct. 1958 (pp. 324–35), p. 332.

[3] See above, chapter 9, p. 148.

[4] *The Mystical Element of Religion* (1923), vol. 1, pp. 66–7.

religion is conceived as a thing fixed in itself and given once for all, and to be defended against all change and interpretation. This is that view which nowadays we have learned to condemn as 'essentialism'—a view which in von Hügel's words conceives the Church as a paste from which 'all yeast must be kept out'.[1]

The proof that von Hügel derived this interpretation of the threefold nature of the Church directly from Newman is reasonably conclusive.

Newman may have met von Hügel in 1869 but there are full records of a week's conversation in June 1876; and it is clear that Newman's influence upon von Hügel was at its height during the '70s—the period of the composition of the *Letter to the Duke of Norfolk* and of the Preface to the *Via Media*. Of the books which most influenced him von Hügel mentions *Loss and Gain*, *The Apologia*, *Anglican Difficulties*, and the *Grammar of Assent*.[2] What is not generally known is that in 1878 he was writing to Newman and suggesting that some of his works, including the Preface to the *Via Media*, should be translated into German.[3]

A good deal of work must have been done, since Newman is writing on 26 January 1879 'of a passage or sentence in my Preface to the *Via Media* which ought to be made clearer', and he sends it in a letter of 4 February 1879.[4]

But Newman gives von Hügel even more than a way of looking at the Church under three modalities, as von Hügel himself admitted when on Newman's death in 1890 he wrote of his influences as 'too general and far-reaching, too secret and deep to be thus tangible and self-evident to a generation bathed in and penetrated by them'.[5]

To both men the enemies of religious insight were shallowness and its ally over-simplification. 'This clarifying business,' von

[1] ibid., p. 71.
[2] O. 13 December 1874.
[3] 'I have long been hoping that I might some day be the means of getting your minor writings better known among the many Germans who do not read English. And now a friend of mine, a Baron Stockhausen, is desirous of translating some of your shorter pieces. . . . We propose to translate . . . the preface to the *Via Media* and the 5 lectures on the notes of the Church, which make up part II of *Anglican Difficulties*—I had also thought of the nine discourses on university teaching.' (9 Nov. 1878.)
[4] Von Hügel directly acknowledges Newman's Preface to the *Via Media* in a footnote to *The Mystical Element of Religion*, i, p. 53, as well as Fechner's *Die drei Motive und Gründe des Glaubens* (1863).
[5] O. Letter from von Hügel to Fr. Ryder, 18 Aug. 1890.

Hügel wrote, 'misleads and impoverishes us.'[1] And although T. S. Eliot was right in saying that we value von Hügel chiefly for his religious sensibility,[2] nevertheless in telling us what a mature religion is like 'from the inside', he also succeeds in expressing the institutional or kingly office of the Church in terms which are, perhaps, oecumenically more acceptable than Newman's. Both men hold this office or element of the Church to be neither an accident nor an unrealized ideal, but a mysterious precondition of effective religion.

There is, however, a difference of approach. Von Hügel was interested in religion generally, Newman in the Christian Church specifically—a difference which is attributable partly to the diminished status of Christian belief at the end of the nineteenth century, and partly to Newman's 'Evangelical' pre-occupation with the presence of Christ. This preoccupation may well have accounted for the 'rigorous' tone of his sermons which von Hügel found 'depressing'.[3] What Newman gave von Hügel was a logical model for the analysis of religion into its elements; but whereas von Hügel starts with a general theory, with which the three offices of Christ are subsequently shown to be compatible, Newman is entirely concerned with these offices and as they elucidate the structures of the Church. This enabled him to anticipate our contemporary emphasis upon the priestly function of the Church as being, through its liturgy, to embody the people of God. Von Hügel, however, equates the priestly with the mystical, and seems to speak of the Church as if it were but the institutional *element*, instead of that 'Divine Object' to which we must respond as a whole before we can understand or identify its parts.

Nevertheless, von Hügel explicitly acknowledges that it was Newman who 'first taught me to glory in my appurtenance to the Catholic and Roman Church'.[4]

'Cease to worship God in particular places,' he writes,

and your worship will become less vivid, less concentrated ... the history of religion teaches us that it ... requires to be developed *socially*.... And this social worship ... will not be fully normal and

---

[1] Cited in Maurice Blondel, *Letter on Apologetics* (1964), p. 57.
[2] In his review of the *Selected Letters* (*The Dial*, Feb. 1928).
[3] *Essays and Addresses* (second series, 1928), i, p. 242.
[4] *The Mystical Element of Religion*, i, p. xxxi.

complete unless it contains a central element of action as well as of saying and teaching. A simple mental cultus is too brainy for mere man.[1]

We need to be trained, therefore, 'in the creaturely mind, so richly furnished by Church appurtenance'; and to reject this institutional element is to upset the balance within the Church. Thus von Hügel deplored the excesses of the Reformation, because they eradicated 'a difficult and delicate discrimination' which had until then 'been operative within the Christian consciousness'. What differentiates the Church from a sect is its depth and width, and its capacity, therefore, to embrace both the 'movements of World-flight and of World-seeking, of the Civilising of Spirituality, and of the Spiritualising of Civilisation'. And from this capacity arises 'the Church's large and leisurely occupation with Art, Philosophy, the State'.[2]

This was the width of affirmation which Newman found preserved within English tradition; and it was what enabled the convert to share with the cradle Catholic—especially if he were in the tradition of Philip Neri or von Hügel—a broad and deep humanism which accepts the Church as it is—warts and all. Entry into it, however, is both privilege and danger. Von Hügel, for example, often speaks of the Church as his hair shirt or purgatory, because conflict is inevitable in that which, by its perpetual growth, refuses to be confined to one modality. Yet, he concludes, 'What is a religion worth which costs you nothing?'[3]

[1] *Essays and Addresses*, ii, pp. 67–8.   [2] ibid., i, pp. 265, 270, 282.
[3] *Letters to a Niece*, pp. 87, xxxviii.

XI

CONCLUSION

NEWMAN'S *via negativa* is a long and painful one; it is necessary
to trace it chronologically and in its detail in order to understand
how much lies behind the apparent simplicity of his final description of the Church. This provides not only a prescription for the
healthy functioning of the Church, but how the particular malady
of Romanism or Ultramontanism arises and can be cured.

In this final account of the Church in terms of the three offices
of Christ, no specific mention is made of the importance Newman
especially attached to an educated laity. It is theology which is the
regulating principle: it is 'the expression of the Prophetical
Office', and as such has created the priestly and kingly offices. But,
as I shall hope to show, Newman's conception of theology implies
an active and educated laity. There is, furthermore, a fruitful
compatibility between his view of the laity and that advanced by
Coleridge and Maurice, who help to 'spell out' the consequences
of Newman's view—consequences which he himself may not fully
have anticipated, and which he was certainly not encouraged to
explore.

What is more immediately significant is the extent to which
Newman's final view of the Church is faithful to the simple
sacramental tradition with which he began his Tractarian period.
It presupposes that the Church is given once for all and is yet
capable of infinite growth. It is the means appointed by Christ by
which we must come to him; and we must first give ourselves to
the Church and respond to it as a whole, before we can effectively
respond to its component parts or functions, which are its acts of
policy, its liturgical function of making us one with Christ in the
people of God, and its descriptions of itself in the metaphors and
symbols of Scripture. And it is theology which alone can teach us
how to interpret this, the Church's language, and how rightly to
perform the actions which this language demands: action creates
understanding and the conditions for our growth into religious
certitude.

To speak of our response to the Church and its sacraments as being to 'living educts of the imagination', or to symbols 'which partake of the reality they render intelligible', or even to an *idea* presupposing a living unity is to point to a tradition which was in danger of being overlooked by Roman Catholics until Möhler, Newman, von Hügel, and Blondel re-affirmed it. They affirmed once more that the essence of a Catholic's response to his Church is never to a sterilized 'deposit' or to an imposed uniformity, but to a unity which is complex of definition and discernment, because it lives and has the power to bring 'the whole soul of man into activity'. The language is Coleridge's, the insight profoundly Catholic and sacramental. And part of Coleridge's importance for this study is the way in which he shows how to make a creative response to the Church, its sacraments, and its language, and the extent to which this response is similar to that which is today more readily made and taken for granted in poetry, literature, and the arts.

But where Coleridge required no firmer grounds for his assents than self-evident truths or *ideas* which seemed to be partially created by the imagination, Newman bases his assent upon a social unity, to a personal relationship with Christ as mediated by a 'polity' possessing certain distinct characteristics. In contradistinction to Coleridge's *idea* of the Church, Newman adopts what he calls his 'method of personation'; and, as he grew older, spoke less of *ideas* and of their development, and more of persons and of the development of communities and institutions—and of the Church.

By shifting the locus of our response to Christ from such indeterminate entities as self-evident truths and *ideas* to an identifiable people incorporated within institutional forms, observances, and systems of government, Newman anticipates the conception of 'tradition' which is to be found in later theologians, such as Blondel. For Blondel, as for Newman, certitude is what we grow into by rising 'to the light through a practical verification of speculative truths'. And since 'Jesus wrote only in the sand and impressed his words only on the air', his teaching must be sought in that continuing tradition whose 'powers of conservation are equalled by its powers of conquest'.[1] This is the developing experience of Christ, collectively, by the Church; and the con-

---

[1] Maurice Blondel, *Letter on Apologetics* and *History and Dogma* (translated by Alexander Dru and Illtyd Trethowan, 1964), pp. 274–5, 267.

ditions for it to be effectively perceived are the same for Blondel as
for Newman and von Hügel: it must be permitted to live generous-
ly through all its dimensions or, as we should now say, functions of
liturgical embodiment, social action, and theological realization.
And to this trio of functions theology must be restored to its
rightful place 'as the fundamental and regulating principle of the
whole Church system'.

Newman is now able to answer the two questions which troubled
him—is Romanism an inevitable condition for a Church claiming
sufficient power over itself and its members for it to be, in essentials,
everywhere the same? And on what grounds is an educated laity
essential to a healthy functioning of the Church?

Newman answers the first question in terms of the failure of the
theological office to regulate the excesses of the kingly office. When
one aspect or office of the Church is able to gain a totalitarian pre-
dominance then there must always arise that tyranny of the spirit
which was so disquieting a feature of nineteenth-century Roman
Catholicism. It was what provoked most of the upheavals within
the Church, especially after what appeared to be its reinforcement
by the Decree on Papal Infallibility. Newman, in his criticisms of
the policies of Pius IX and in his writings on the Temporal Power;
the Modernists, in their attempts to distinguish the Jesus of history
from the Jesus of the Church; or Blondel, in his opposition to
'L'Action Française'—all revolve round the same question: is the
life of the Church co-terminous with its external and institutional
rule? And each in his own way came to the same answer: the
Church is the multi-dimensional Body of Christ. If its action is
confined to one of its dimensions, then it will fail to fulfil its
mission, which is to show Christ so that he may draw all men to
him.

It is interesting to note how the terms of Newman's diagnosis
are independently confirmed by later theologians, all of whom
testify to the nature of the Church's error as being to confine itself
to one modality, or at the most, two. Von Hügel, who derived most
directly from Newman, spoke of the emotional elements of religion
uniting with the institutional and imposing themselves upon the
analytic and speculative elements.[1] Blondel, more succinctly, refers
to the disease as 'monophorisme'[2]; while in our own time

---

[1] *The Mystical Element of Religion*, i, p. 75.
[2] In *Dru*, art. cit. (*Downside Review*, July 1963), p. 244.

Schillebeeckx has called it 'essentialism'.[1] We might, however, prefer Newman's racier but no less exact remark that the Church had fallen into the hands of the political ultra-devotional party.[2]

Newman remained a Catholic because he believed that the abuse of one function of the Church does not jeopardize its God-given ability as a whole to mediate Christ, and because he held that such abuses are corrigible. He prophesied correctly that there would be a second Vatican Council to put right the excesses of the first. But when the Church does fall into the hands of the political ultra-devotional party, and the regulating principle of theology is denied, then the very principle of a living development is resisted, as is the contribution of an educated laity.

Thus Newman interpreted the denial of the rights of the laity to participate fully in the life of the Church as the symptom of the disease, rather than its cause. As von Hügel pointed out, to neglect theology is to defer an inevitable reckoning with 'the arrears of some 12 generations'[3]; and the consequences of such procrastination go very deep, involving as they must do the whole sensibility. To hold theology in contempt is to precipitate a crisis Claudel describes as 'the tragedy of a starved imagination'.[4]

There is a dramatic irony in Newman's forecast while still an Anglican that 'When the Church displays her proper gifts, she prospers: when she disuses them, she declines.'[5] And it is even more ironical that the chief stimulus in recalling the Church to a re-examination of its mission should have come from forces external to itself, which it had become powerless to influence—the two Great Wars and the social unrest from which they sprang. And it is for this reason that Maurice's challenge remains and must be taken up—that Christ came into the world to found a Kingdom and to regenerate all human society, and not merely to propound a set of opinions,[6] or confine his work of redemption to a self-centred Church. Can we conceive the Church as separate from a nation and its culture without substituting a superseded illusion for a present reality? Has not the Church to stand for that eschatological principle which, rather than holding a society back, helps it to

[1] See above, chapter 8, p. 134.
[2] *W*. ii, p. 374.
[3] Letter to Fr. Tyrrell, 25 March 1908, *Selected Letters* (1927), p. 147.
[4] Blondel, op. cit., p. 21.
[5] *S.S.D.*, p. 243.
[6] *TE*, p. 245; *KC* (1838), iii, p. 387.

understand the principles of its momentum and of its function to bring about the Kingdom of Christ?

Although the idea of Revelation certainly involves the presence of Christ, personally and sacramentally, to the world, is Newman's method of personation wide enough? Is it not fatally circumscribed by its origins in a clericalized idea of the Church, with which, however, it is inevitably bound to conflict? Have we not to be citizens first before we can realize our membership of the Church?

PART THREE

CRITICISM

MAURICE'S IDEA OF THE KINGDOM

XII

AN ALTERNATIVE METHOD OF PERSONATION?

MAURICE'S challenge is the most important that Newman's idea of the Church has to face. It arises from Maurice's application of the sacramental principle to the common everyday life of secular society no less than to the institutional Church. In doing so, Maurice feels himself obliged to come into direct conflict with the Tractarians, since his concern is primarily with relevance and reality. The Church cannot be conceived in a vacuum; its verifying function cannot be discharged without reference to its context within a society which, in the mid-nineteenth century, was undergoing profound social and intellectual change. To conceive the Church without reference to this context was not only to be guilty of unreality: it was to convert the Church into a negative source of needless social instability.

This is a fair statement of an extreme position only—of that adopted by the Roman Ultramontanes and by some of the early Tractarians at a time when the Oxford Movement was having to emphasize the overriding necessity to free the sacramental Church from its Erastian integuments.[1] Even now Newman's superior surgery remains unappreciated; and he is still thought to be fundamentally opposed to the mainstream of what might be called Christian social concern, as it derives from Maurice and his successors. I wish to argue that it is possible to do more than hope that Newman and Maurice may be reconciled[2]: their reconcilia-

---

[1] In the Library of Birmingham Oratory, there is a copy of the first edition of Maurice's *Kingdom of Christ* inscribed 'With the Author's Compliments', and in each volume the signature John H. Newman/Oriel College. It is annotated, especially in vol. III, which is chiefly concerned with Church and State; but whether in Newman's hand or not is difficult to determine. By the time the book was published (1838) Newman had already committed himself to freeing the Church from the State. He discusses the argument in his correspondence with Allies (see General Conclusion).

[2] See Maurice B. Reckitt, *Maurice to Temple: a century of the social movement in the Church of England* (1947), p. 81: 'some may think that a synthesis of Newman and Maurice, impossible in human terms, may nevertheless be attainable in

tion is implicit within the common tradition from which they both derive. This appreciation has been obscured not only because the Catholic Church has appeared to be completely identified with the extreme Ultramontane position until very recently, but because theologians had then the habit of ascribing philosophical differences to denominational principles—a habit of which Maurice himself was certainly not guiltless.

Nevertheless, in 1872 J. M. Capes published a most perceptive comparison of Newman and Maurice in the *Gentleman's Magazine*.[1] With the death of Maurice and, as Capes believed, the completion of Newman's career as a thinker and religious leader, the time seemed opportune to outline 'the parallel and the contrast presented by the two most influential theological teachers of the last half century in England'. In reaction to the absolute individualism which had prevailed in the religious thought of forty years before, both men saw the living presence of Christ as connected with a belief 'in a vast organised institution'. This notion of the Church 'as the spiritual body of Christ' had vanished from the English Church. It was neglected by the Evangelicals, for example, whose view of the Church, based as it was on the purest individualism, was that it was composed of a multitude of single believers, being, in fact, invisible. 'Surrounded, then, by phantom theologies, Newman and Maurice began the labour of their days.' The minds of both men were filled by the conception of that great institution which Newman called the Church Catholic, and Maurice the Kingdom of Christ. 'And in both cases this conception differed from all existing popular English notions, in that it looked upon the living presence of Christ in this body as the one source of its reality, as a spiritual institution, all other ideas of the Church being hypocrisies or barren mockeries.'

Capes now leads us to the essential distinction between Newman and Maurice. For Newman the Church Catholic, 'stood alone in the midst of a world lying in wickedness; and whatever might be said of good men outside its pale, it could have no existence as the Church beyond the limits of a transmitted Apostolical succession of bishops'. Maurice, on the other hand, 'identified the Church

principle, and that if so attained, it would represent the highest which nineteenth century theology and churchmanship could bequeath to succeeding ages'.

[1] J. M. Capes, 'A Parallel and a Contrast', *The Gentleman's Magazine*, 1872, New Series IX, 2, pp. 33–44.

with the whole human race. All humanity, in his view, constituted the Kingdom of Christ.'[1] Capes then refers to that passage in Maurice's *Theological Essays* which is the clearest of all his distinctions between Church and World:

> The world contains the elements of which the Church is composed. In the Church, these elements are penetrated by a uniting, reconciling power. The Church is, therefore, human society in its normal state; the World, that same society, irregular and abnormal. The world is the Church without God; the Church is the world restored to its relation with God, taken back by Him into the state for which He created it. Deprive the Church of its Centre, and you make it into a world.[2]

I have quoted more fully than Capes from this important passage, in order that I can return to it for other purposes later on. Capes concludes by asserting that both men lived in an ideal world: that Maurice's was the ideal world of the future, and Newman's that of the past—a judgement which does less than justice to Newman's idea of the Church, but which can be understood in the light of contemporary Roman Catholic attitudes. Yet, as later commentators have pointed out, the distinction is not between right and wrong views of the Church, but between contrasting accounts of Christ's redemptive work, the roots of which are within the Bible itself. The Church is described as one society among other societies, and to that extent set over against the world; but it is also described as standing for and as making explicit ideas implicit in the very creation of man, which are therefore applicable to the whole of mankind.[3]

On the other hand, Maurice would certainly have agreed with Capes's estimate of Newman and of the tendencies inherent in Tractarianism. In 1837 he spoke of their error as consisting in 'opposing to "the spirit of the age" the spirit of a former age'[4]; and the distinction comes out very clearly in his controversy with

[1] ibid., pp. 36, 39, 40.   [2] *TE*, pp. 403–4.
[3] A. M. Ramsey, *F. D. Maurice and the conflicts of Modern Theology* (Cambridge, 1951), pp. 36–7: 'the roots of the contrast are within the Bible. There the Church is a society, with an historical origin and a boundary, standing over against the world; there also the Church is inherent in the creation of mankind, and definable as the whole race of mankind redeemed. . . . These diverse aspects of the Church have sometimes become doctrines defined in mutual antagonism, but a sound theology demands the validity of both in union and tension.'
[4] Frederick Maurice, *The Life of Frederick Denison Maurice* (1884), vol. i, p. 226. (*Life.*)

Pusey over baptism in 1836/7. Pusey saw the baptismal act as redeeming the child from the sinful world, Maurice saw the act as affirming the child to be what he was already—a son of God in a world redeemed by Christ.[1]

The root of Maurice's objection to the Tractarians, and to the Romanizing principles they stood for, is that instead of acting as if Earth and Heaven had been reconciled by Christ, their theological principles caused them to act, 'as if Heaven and Earth were still separated, as if we had still to effect for ourselves that which the Scripture declares that God has effected, as if there were no Spirit to unite us with the Father and the Son, and with each other'.[2] Whereas, in fact, 'the State is as much God's creation as the Church',[3] since it is the Kingdom of God which is 'the great practical existing reality which is to renew the earth and make it a habitation for blessed spirits instead of for demons'. He saw it as his mission to proclaim 'society and humanity to be divine realities, as they stand',[4] since 'Christ came to establish a Kingdom, not to proclaim a set of opinions'.[5]

And if we want to see why Maurice was never attracted, 'even in fancy', by the Roman claim, we have only to grasp his distinction between a Church and a sect: 'The Church is a body united in the acknowledgement of a living *Person*; every sect is a body united in the acknowledgement of a certain *Notion*'.[6] Irrespective of its size and distribution, the Roman Church, by requiring conformity to a system of doctrine, behaved as if it were a sect rather than a Church—a criticism which was not without foundation.

This distinction takes us to the heart of Maurice's theology; and it springs from what might be called a profound 'personalism'.[7] In his dedication to Derwent Coleridge of the second edition of the *Kingdom of Christ* (1842), when he is writing of the influence

---

[1] ibid., p. 214.   [2] *TE*, p. 415.
[3] *Kingdom of Christ* (1838), iii, p. 76. [*KC* (1838).]   [4] *Life* ii, p. 137.
[5] *KC* (1838), iii, p. 387.   [6] ibid. ii, p. 338.
[7] 'People send me books about final causes, primary beliefs, and so on. I gaze at their covers, wish I could read them, and sometimes actually contrive to do it; but scarcely unless I can find some historical or biographical interest in them and can persuade myself that *a man has been fighting his way to some final cause, or that a nation of men is laying hold of some primary belief*. I wrote to Mill that I could not think of him as the most accomplished of metaphysicians, that I had recollections of him as a human being which effaced the other impression; I do not think he was displeased at that sort of recognition.' (*Life* ii, p. 496; my italics.)

of S. T. Coleridge upon him, he sides with those who 'can feel no affection for a book unless they can associate it with a living man'.[1] He believed that if 'our Secularists' were addressed not as schoolmen but as husbands and fathers, they would cease to be atheists: 'Arguments about a Creator will fall dead upon them. A message from a Father may rouse them to life.'[2]

This approach determined not only his career as a preacher, but his method as a theologian: 'I was sent into the world that I might persuade men to recognise Christ as the centre of their fellowship with each other, that so they might be united in their families, their countries, and as men, not in schools and factions', he wrote in an explanatory letter entitled 'Reasons for not joining a party in the Church' (1837).[3] As a happily married man he had no need of party, since marriage had 'educated him in the kingdom of God', and taught him 'how much the true union of hearts may make party ties unnecessary'.

The charge that Maurice is obscure, and therefore an unprofitable writer persists: 'To use general terms and glowing words is only fit for women and for Sewell of Exeter,' Newman wrote in 1850. 'It is to sewellise, or to mauricise.'[4] And this was an opinion Newman persisted in to the end of his life. In 1885, for example, we find him referring to Maurice as 'provokingly unintelligible'.[5]

There is, of course, a certain diffuseness of style in Maurice: it is something he shares with 'his master' Coleridge. Both men took their stand within existing doctrines and institutions, to ascertain their meaning, and to ascertain the neglected truths which lay in them.[6] What Newman said of Pusey and Keble[7] could, to some extent, be applied to Maurice: he was haunted by no intellectual perplexity. Coleridge, he said, had preserved him from infidelity

---

[1] *The Kingdom of Christ*, new edition based on the second edition of 1842, ed. A. R. Vidler (1958), II, p. 350. (*KC*.)

[2] *Life* ii, p. 428.   [3] ibid. i, p. 240.   [4] *Letters* XIV, p. 181.

[5] 'As to his (Mozley) undervaluing, as you think, Maurice and Hampden, you must recollect that the more active-minded men of the Movement were men who delighted in clearness of thought and statement, such as Hurrell Froude, Ward, etc., and they considered the two writers you have named as most provokingly unintelligible. Yet my dear friend, Ambrose St. John, professed to owe his first steps towards the Catholic Church to Maurice's book on Baptism; and I think we all considered his pamphlet in 1836, *Subscription no Bondage*, a striking one.' (Letter from Newman to Plummer (27 February 1885) cited in F. L. Cross, *John Henry Newman* (1933), p. 181.)

[6] J. S. Mill, *Bentham and Coleridge*, pp. 40, 99, 100.

[7] *Apo*, pp. 162, 495.

before he entered the university.[1] And the root of Coleridge's influence upon him is contained in these words: 'I learnt from him, by practical illustrations, how one may enter into the spirit of a living or a departed author, without assuming to be his judge; how one may come to know what he means, without imputing to him our meanings.'[2]

This training in acceptance developed Maurice's powers of affirmation. Like Coleridge he could say 'whatever *finds* me, bears witness for itself that it has proceeded from a Holy Spirit. . . .' and that 'in the Bible there is more that *finds* me than I have experienced in all other books put together'.[3] It was this that enabled Maurice as a theologian to stand securely within Scripture. It shapes his method as a theologian, and in turn shapes his style. He is concerned with the wholeness of the context, whether it be in Scripture or in the parties which appear to divide the Church. Thus in his commentary on the *Epistle to the Hebrews*, he writes: 'The most exact interpreter is the one who takes most heed of everything which illustrates the book or sentence he is considering; which raises it from a dead utterance to a living one.'[4] Similarly in dealing with party views, he aimed to show 'the great truth asserted by each: that he agrees with each party in the assertion', but 'each is wrong when it becomes the denier of the truth of the others, and when it assumes its portion of the truth to be the whole'. This was 'his method on all subjects'.[5]

Thus his style is as Coleridge's tentative, not as Newman's dialectical; it speaks for the defence, not for the prosecution, and it is that of a discriminating intelligence which 'haunted with the sense of some harmony' seeks to realize the key-note. When philosophers and theologians claim to be unused to such a style, this is a significant disadvantage, since it is the very idiom in which most of the influential literary criticism of our time has been conducted. It has, when it succeeds, that power—to which Dean Church testified—of making real or 'realizing' what for the reader or critic has *found* him. As Hutton shrewdly observed, 'no economy of spiritual power' is possible to such a response: 'in the intensity of his earnestness he wrote on as if in soliloquy'.[6]

[1] *Life* i, p. 177.   [2] *KC* II, p. 354.
[3] Coleridge, *Confessions of an Inquiring Spirit* in *AR*, pp. 295–6.
[4] *H.*, p. 37.   [5] *Life* i, p. 203.
[6] R. H. Hutton, *Modern Guides to English Thought in matters of Faith* (1891), pp. 326–7.

To appreciate Maurice, therefore, we must seek him where he is strong—in an affirmation which is yet critical and intelligent. Sometimes, it is true, his style has the repetitive quality of a rocking-horse; but what I have said may help to explain his preference for dictation, and his wish that when his son grew up, 'he might always express himself as freely, and will not learn to compose'.[1] It may also explain why he refused to assume the words *system* and *method* to be synonymous, and that 'if the first is wanting in the Scriptures the last must be wanting also'.[2]

It is not surprising, therefore, that Maurice's ideas were formed as early as 1831,[3] and that the rest of his life was spent in amplifying rather than developing them. Whereas Newman's idea of the Church can only be grasped in terms of a developing dialectic and requires, therefore, a chronological method of exposition, Maurice's idea must be grasped as a whole before we can appreciate the profoundity of individual and apparently contradictory insights. In an unpublished letter to Newman, in which he compared Newman with Maurice, R. H. Hutton speaks of Newman's 'clear and comprehensive conception of revelation as a coherent and developing intellectual system of the universe' in contrast to Maurice's which is, 'as it were, a broken cluster of deep but insulated insights into God's purposes, which he cares little to weave together and believes the human intellect to be unable to weave together into a systematic whole'.[4]

It is the characteristic of insulated insights that they frequently go deeper into a situation than ones which aim at a greater consistency; and the merit of Maurice's challenge to Newman's idea of the Church is his persistence in points of criticism—such as the charge of Romanism—which however easily they may be answered in terms of theory are still a perpetually recurring practical difficulty. Maurice's insulated insights are therefore the stumbling-blocks which Newman's idea must overcome with complete conviction: they stand for objections which are basic and persisting.

---

[1] *Life* i, p. 310.   [2] *KC* I, p. 236.   [3] *Life* i, pp. 131 f.
[4] 28 Feb. 1863. Oratory Archives. Newman while acknowledging the letter does not refer to the comparison, perhaps because he was then too completely involved in the controversy with Kingsley. Whately compared Maurice's method with that of a Chinese portrait, where each single object is drawn with accuracy, but no one can make head or tail of the landscape. (Cited in Owen Chadwick, *The Victorian Church*, I (1966), p. 350, note.)

XIII

HOW IS THE KINGDOM REALIZED?

THE contrast between Newman and Maurice is best seen in their choice of starting-points. Newman starts with the Church—for him the Bible disappoints, and it requires the Church for its elucidation. For Maurice, it is not merely the Bible which is the starting-point, but the 'strange significance' of its language and its peculiarities; and he speaks of being unable to separate even in his mind, the language of a writer from his meaning.[1] This position can be a limitation—since the meaning can then never be developed or put in more relevant ways—but such a stand does guarantee a continuing respect for the symbolic 'peculiarity' of religious language and sacramental forms. It not only guarantees the depth and integrity of a vision of the Bible as the universal record of God's dealings with man, but it keeps us close to the question—how is the Bible the vehicle of that vision?

Maurice's interpretation of the Bible leads him to conclude that God is actively and organically present to us throughout the whole range of social working, and that our social and political structures must be seen as sacramental of his presence. Maurice now propounds a view which is strikingly contemporary—that social structures, since they precede the formation of the Christian Church, determine most if not all of its characteristics. The Church is not a uniquely new and separate form, but is structured by the social forms which it finds already existing. To start with the Church, therefore, is to perpetuate the medieval mistake of separating the Church from the world and to ignore the historical fact of a Christian culture. The starting-point should be within the realizing principles of this culture as they are embodied in the life and institutions of the nation. What the Bible shows, provided we study it as a whole, and in the light of the purposes which actuated and informed it,[2] is that these social forms are themselves the results of God's dealings with man.[3]

---

[1] *KC* II, p. 163.   [2] *KC* II, p. 159.

[3] cp. Coleridge in chapter 3 above, p. 47: 'What is Christianity at any one period? The Ideal of the Human Soul at that period.'

The Bible is the history of a covenant between God and his chosen people, the Jews, beginning with 'the first call of the patriarch which made them a family, their deliverance under Moses which made them a nation',[1] and culminating in the universal society which Christ came into the world to form, which is the Catholic Church. Here is that transition from family to nation, and from nation to Church which is the basis of Maurice's teaching in the *Kingdom of Christ*; but whereas in Newman the emphasis falls chiefly upon the Church, in Maurice it falls upon the nation: the Old Testament, he says, 'is the great key to the meaning of national society'.[2]

This is a description of social development only to the extent that social structures have grown out of theological prescriptions; and the tone of Maurice's exposition is therefore prescriptive rather than descriptive—this is the way in which society ought to evolve, since for him, as for Coleridge, the Bible remains the Statesman's Manual. The human relationships we find ourselves committed to as members of families and societies are the ways of understanding God's purpose in the Incarnation; but they are also the way by which we are *found* by Christ: 'No doubt the world is full of sacraments. Morning and evening, the kind looks and parting words of friends, the laugh of childhood, daily bread, sickness and death; all have a holy sacramental meaning, and should as such be viewed by us.'[3]

In discharging our responsibilities as family men and citizens we are 'realizing' our understanding of Christ: the fact of our relationship to Christ is grasped within the texture of these relationships, and our capacity to fulfil them arises from our acknowledgement of Christ as the power that makes their achievement possible.[4] This power, by concentrating our attention upon local and personal relations, deepens us and yet enables us to work more effectively in larger contexts; and it is in this sense that the family can be said to create the wider community—the nation. Christ comes into the world, therefore, 'to regenerate all human society, all the forms of

---

[1] *KC* I, p. 244.   [2] *KC* II, p. 237.

[3] *KC* II, p. 81. cp. Newman's Sermon 'Doing glory to God in pursuits of the World' (*P.S.* VIII, p. 165). Newman writes that the Christian should 'feel that the true contemplation of that Saviour lies *in* his worldly business ... while performing it, he will see Christ revealed to his soul amid the ordinary actions of the day, as by a sort of sacrament'.

[4] *KC* I, p. 237.

life,—all civil order, all domestic relationships'; and our regeneration is consequently *social* as well as individual.[1]

A distinction between Church and Nation should be unnecessary: ideally there ought to be one form of society, but a contradiction arises 'between the will of man and the order in which he
is placed'; and we become conscious of belonging to two societies,
'one formed in accordance with the order of God, the other based
upon self-will'.[2] The former is necessary to the latter as the
principle of its life-giving energy[3]; but since this society which is
the Church especially witnesses to those facts which it is natural to
fallen man to deny, it 'must be a distinct body'.[4] Yet because the
relationship of these societies is organic and mutually life-giving,
the Church, though necessarily distinct from the nation, must
never be extra-national. It must never set itself up as something
separate from the nation.[5]

It is because Maurice holds the nation to be as much God's
creation as the Church that he speaks of it as an organic or life-
giving influence rather than an impersonal legal framework; and
this may also account for his using 'state', 'nation', and 'society'
as synonymous terms. The relationship between the nation, which
he defines as 'a law, a language, and a government',[6] and the
Church is so deep and intimate that we cannot say how exactly it
began; all we can do is to note from the transactions between
Nation and Church in the first centuries that they 'pre-suppose a
real, though as yet imperfectly understood *relation*, not such as
could have been produced by a compact, or had the least tendency
to create one'. The nation structures the Church in the sense of
being the principle of its chastisement as well as of its development;
and thus, as I have said, it is an *organic* community, possessing a
conscience, and being neither religiously indifferent nor purely
secularist. The distinction between a Jewish and a Christian Nation
is that the former is a nation professing religion, while the latter
is a nation which recognizes a Church 'as the ground and vital
principle of its own existence'.[7]

I use the word 'organic' not only because Maurice uses it,[8] but
because in spite of its ambiguity it can still be employed of a society

---

[1] *TE*, pp. 245, 248.   [2] *KC* II, p. 151.   [3] ibid., p. 254.
[4] *KC* I, p. 258.   [5] *KC* II, pp. 234, 254, 281.
[6] Cited in A. R. Vidler, *F. D. Maurice and Company* (1966), p. 163.
[7] *KC* II, pp. 239, 257, 306.   [8] ibid., p. 234.

which is sufficiently homogeneous to effect the moral education of its citizens in terms of their station and its duties; and Maurice himself speaks of conscience as testifying to this maxim of 'keeping their places, and doing their work'.[1] The nation is most healthy, therefore, when it is a community of well-defined, localized, and fully personal relationships; it is least healthy when it attempts to construct a universal or international society. Such attempts will continue to be defeated by 'the determination of men to assert their own wills'.[2] This—the basis of his criticism not only of the Roman Church but of the French Revolutionary regime—is characteristically expressed in his sermon on the death of the Duke of Wellington:

> There may be abundance of *religion* where there is no national life; but there is no *godliness*. Destroy all national characteristics, reduce us merely into one great society, and whether the bond of that society is a pope, or an emperor, or a custom-union, the result is the same. A living God is not feared or believed in; He is not the centre of that combination; His name or the name of a number of Gods may be invoked in it, but His presence is not that which holds its different elements together.[3]

Each nation must maintain 'its own integrity and unity' if a real 'family of nations' is ever to emerge. Here, again, Maurice is misunderstood if we think of him as merely reflecting the nationalist aspirations of the time. His point is that our religious beliefs gain their meaning and reality from the depth of our involvement in family, work and social commitment. Without this involvement our religion remains 'notional'; with it, we see the actions of our daily living for what they are—as sacraments of the presence of Christ.

It is from this standpoint that we must approach Maurice's work for the Christian Socialist Movement, his unusual ability to get on with working men who had never before met a parson like him,[4] his foundation of the Working Men's College, and his maxim promulgated in 1838 in the first edition of the *Kingdom of Christ*—'that a Churchman must be a politician'.[5]

Maurice accepts a distinction between Church and Nation to the extent that the Church is constituted 'not in laws, but in a Person'[6];

[1] ibid., p. 329.   [2] *KC* I, p. 220.
[3] In *Sermons on the Sabbath Day* (1853), pp. 93–4.
[4] Chadwick, op. cit., I, p. 354.   [5] *KC* (1838), iii, p. 387.
[6] *KC* II, p. 240.

and throughout his writing the point is continually emphasized that the Church is the in-dwelling presence of Christ; and it is this which brings his theology so fruitfully into identity with Newman's view of the Church; since both men see the Church as fulfilling the offices of Christ as Prophet, Priest, and King.[1]

Once again Maurice's writing strikes a very contemporary note. He sees the creed, our prayers, and the liturgy as signs of a universal society.[2] They constitute an order of signs in which we must place ourselves, if we are to grow out of our own selfish limitations. 'They are the very voice in which God speaks to his creatures,' he says in his tribute to Coleridge, from whom he gained this understanding of signs and symbols. Worship is necessary to us in order that by its means we may 'realize' our fellowship one with another. Thus 'when thou art most alone thou must still, if thou wouldest pray, be in the midst of a family; thou must call upon a Father; thou must not dare to say *my*, but *our*'. By means of an understanding of the forms which our worship has taken, we come to an understanding of the deeds and desires of the world, which otherwise would remain utterly unintelligible to us.[3]

The Church is this order of signs taken in its unity. It is called Catholic because it is intended to be universal; and the office of bishop was instituted to 'transcend national limitations' and to be 'emphatically the bonds of communication between different parts of the earth', so that a more extended 'commerce and fellowship among men' might be established.[4] Maurice does not seem to anticipate the mighty consequences of this view of the episcopal office. What authority, for example, does the bishop have in a conflict between his universalizing power and a local desire to remain narrow and provincial? Were the Gallicans right to resist the Ultramontanes? And what happens when the bishop himself refuses to exercise his office in this way? How would Maurice deal with the Novatian and with the Arian bishops? The latter questions, in particular, were paramount in Newman's mind, because he too held this view of the episcopal office.

Maurice is characteristically more concerned to safeguard the universalizing power of the bishop from Romanist abuses, and in particular from the *premature* universalizing of the Church—an imperfection which he regarded as a necessary consequence of the

[1] *KC* II, p. 125.   [2] ibid., p. 293.   [3] ibid., pp. 36, 42, 53, 363.
[4] ibid., pp. 98–9, 104.

first age of the Church. In this period the Church could not be
identified with any of the existing national societies, and she
tended to overemphasize her independence of national life—an
over-emphasis which was not finally corrected until the Reformation.[1]

But, once again, Maurice's main emphasis falls upon the
essential function of the Church as that of educating its members.
It teaches men 'to rise above their private judgements',[2] in order
that the nation may be formed and reclaimed from its 'secularist'
tendencies. It is not simply a counter-society, 'existing for purposes
wholly foreign to those for which the civil power exists'.[3] Its purpose is not to safeguard its flock in order to shepherd each member
to his own 'private selfish heaven',[4] but to teach all nations, in
order that all things may be restored to Christ. This it does by
explaining man to himself by bringing his world into an intelligible
relationship with him. And the world that Maurice has in mind is
the world which provoked Marx to his analysis of Capitalism, of
the alienation of the workers, and of religion as the opium of those
workers. And it is in this context that this famous passage from the
Kingdom of Christ should be appreciated. What, asks Maurice, is
to be said to the mass of living beings who are imprisoned within
'our awful manufacturing districts'? Are they merely to be told
that, since they have immortal souls which are perishing, they
must ask how to be saved?

Such words spoken with true earnestness are very mighty. But they
are not enough; men feel that they are not merely lost creatures; they
look up to heaven above them, and ask whether it can be true that this
is the whole account of their condition; that their sense of right and
wrong, their cravings for fellowship, their consciousness of being
creatures having powers which no other creatures possess, are all
nothing. If religion, they say, will give us no explanation of these feelings, if it can only tell us about a fall for the whole race, and an escape
for a few individuals of it, then our wants must be satisfied without
religion. Then begin Chartism and Socialism, and whatever schemes
make rich men tremble.[5]

It is this prophetic grasp of the contemporary objection to the
Church as *irrelevant* which makes Maurice so preserve the Church

[1] ibid., pp. 248 ff.   [2] ibid., p. 243.   [3] ibid., p. 276 (my italics).
[4] ibid., p. 282.   [5] ibid., pp. 335–6.
14—N.C.T.

from anything which will make it a tyranny wanting to impose a life-destroying uniformity, or a system of notions which only 'professional Christians' can be bothered to understand. The Church must grow out of effective, and therefore local, personal relationships; and unity will only come as fellowship is promoted with 'national Churches which are willing to acknowledge themselves as parts of a great Catholic body'.[1] It is interesting to notice how close we are coming to von Hügel's definition of the Catholic Church as 'the greatest possible multiplicity in the deepest possible unity'; and if in the following passage 'Ultramontanism' were to be substituted for 'Popery', both Newman and von Hügel would cordially have agreed: 'Popery is continually undermining the Church, and . . . the more you can persuade men to be churchmen, the more effectually you deliver them from popery.'[2]

This strong sense of working out your faith in terms of where you are leads Maurice to propound ways of approaching other Christian bodies which again are strikingly contemporary, and again are to be found expressed by Newman and von Hügel. Maurice believes that the true meanings of the doctrines upon which the parties and sects are formed will be found to be contained within 'the forms of our English Church'[3]; and our approach, therefore, is to enter into these convictions as they are expressed by the members of the denomination concerned. And in one of the most remarkable anticipations of the oecumenical dialogue written in the whole of the nineteenth century, Maurice prescribes this rule of conduct for the theologian:

He will not be impatient to force any notions of his own upon them. His desire will be to meet their feelings and to enter into them. He will be most anxious not to destroy anything which they have received or learnt; to confirm them in their feelings of affection and reverence for their fathers; to strengthen in them by all means the hereditary affections, which their doctrines respecting private judgement so much impair. He wishes to preserve all the faith which they have from the destruction which is threatening it; to unite their faith with that of those from whom they are separated; to make them integral members of the body from which they fancy that it is the object of our pride and selfishness to exclude them. What the result of such a method may be, is in God's hands, not ours. At all events other methods have been tried and have failed, this has not been tried.[1]

Yet there is a crucial question which Maurice was unable to face, it is—what happens when the organic relationship between Church and Nation is denied or fails to work? Even as early as 1836 he was reported as saying that the most difficult thing in these days is for a man to realize his connection with the nation. He noticed that the public societies of his day were utterly opposed to that 'personal distinctness' which was necessarily connected with national life as he conceived it.[2] As he grew older, this gap between Church and Nation grew wider; until, like Gladstone, he had to face the fact that the organic relationship between Church and State appeared to be unworkable.[3]

It is here that the contrast between ourselves and Maurice may seem greatest. The sense of community is, by his standards, now so indeterminate that it can often only be realized in small, neighbourhood or interest groups, and when it can be focussed nationally the frame of reference is so 'de-Christianized' that we are faced by a dilemma. Should we make yet another attempt to invest Christianity with a political ideology, or should we appear to make a virtue of necessity and speak of what we gain by encountering a hidden God? If God chooses or uses secular *incognitos*, may it not even be blasphemous to try to un-mask them?[4]

Yet Maurice also had to face a not dissimilar dilemma. Believing that 'men are social beings by God's constitution, and that they cannot be good for anything when they are not living as if they were',[5] he had felt obliged to accept an invitation to promote 'practical co-operation' among the victims of the Industrial Revolution. It arose when Charles Kingsley and J. M. Ludlow decided to create the Christian Socialist movement to fill the vacuum left by the collapse of Chartism in April 1848. Its aim was to socialize Christians and to Christianize Socialists; but its success was two-edged. It produced the co-operative society movement which by 1883 had 666,000 members[6]; but Maurice's association with so left-wing a political body sowed the seeds of

[1] ibid., p. 334.   [2] *Life* i, pp. 203–4.
[3] See Vidler, op. cit., pp. 173–4.
[4] cp. W. N. Pittenger, 'Secular study and Christian Faith' (*Theology*, Feb. 1962).
[5] Essay on Burke in *The Friendship of Books* (1874), p. 310.
[6] *Life* ii, pp. 10, 35, 162.

that opposition to himself which culminated in his dismissal from the Professorship of Theology at King's College, London, in 1853.

In the year 1852-3 J. M. Ludlow wished the revised constitution to require a specific Christian subscription on the part of the Governors that they might act as 'a true and holy Jesuitry'.[1] All Maurice's instincts were opposed to this step,[2] and the subsequent correspondence between the two men produced Maurice's celebrated description of theology as no longer a synthesizing Queen of the sciences, but as 'the foundation on which they all stand'. He himself therefore was 'only a digger'.

What Maurice seems opposed to is an identification of Christianity and politics in some kind of permanent ideology—'His great wish was to Christianise Socialism, not to Christian-Socialise the universe.'[3] Given Newman's idea of the Church Maurice's stand would be clear—that the Church must preserve a self-determining power in order to develop its insights and explanations. This is the freedom to dig as opposed to the commitment to build. But there is a sense in which theology is both digger and builder; and Ludlow, in his reply, also quotes St. Paul[4] to the effect that it is 'a little out of date for those who know that the foundation is laid (as he [Maurice] has often told me) and who see around them crowds of poor wretches wanting a roof to stand under' to confine the work of Christian reclamation to 'digging'.[5] But Maurice's unwillingness to concede to the Church as polity an adjudicating power over the fruits of its theological building and digging condemned him to a position which appeared theologically to be intransigently conservative. It laid him open to Ludlow's charge that he was too often 'carried away by platonistic dreams about an order and a kingdom and a beauty *self-realised* [my italics] in their own eternity'.[6]

This is not surprising, however, if we see Maurice's dilemma as characteristic of the Anglican position at the time. He appears to be committed to two contradictory positions—that, to realize our Christian insights, it is the duty of every Christian to be a

[1] (This was) the Society for Promoting Working Men's Associations. N. C. Masterman, *John Malcolm Ludlow, The Builder of Christian Socialism* (Cambridge, 1963), p. 143.

[2] *Life* ii, pp. 159–60.   [3] ibid., pp. 41, 132, 136.   [4] I Cor. 3.

[5] Masterman, op. cit., p. 140.

[6] Masterman, op. cit., p. 140. A criticism repeated by Owen Chadwick, *Victorian Church*, I, 360: 'Maurice perpetually shrank from practical measures lest they corrupt the Kingdom of God.'

politician; and that, in order to safeguard its sacramental integrity, the Church cannot be compromised by association with specific political programmes or parties. In practice, if not in theory, Maurice opposed Ludlow on the same grounds as Newman opposed Kingsley [1]—that political and religious motives must be distinguished and not identified. Theologically, however, the dilemma remained unresolved; and this may account for the failure of the Christian Socialist movement to bring itself to bear in that area where it strove most strongly to succeed: it was quite unable to change the structures and policies of the Church of England as a whole, which remained substantially the same at the end of the century what they had been at the beginning.[2]

Newman's idea of the Church as a tri-unity of functions, if adopted,[3] would have resolved the contradiction, since the authority of the Church (and therefore of its sacramental integrity) is compromised neither by the freedom of theological debate nor by the political actions of its members; and it is part of the theological or prophetical function of the Church to work out conclusions which are relevant to local issues and difficulties. Such is not only the function of what Newman calls a theological school, but it has frequently been the cause of its development; and Maurice's use of the term 'nation' is frequently closer to that of 'a school' than to such undifferentiated and generalized terms as 'state' and 'laity'. This can be seen in the circumstances which led to his founding the Working Men's College in 1854. Once again, in practice if not in theory, his ideal of association is remarkably akin to Newman's idea of the Church: it is not so much political or ideological as collegiate—that of an association of 'men as men', of which teachers and learners are equally members.[4] For Ludlow this was

---

[1] See above, chapter 8 (ii).

[2] C. E. Hudson and M. B. Reckitt, *The Church and the World* (1940), vol. 3, pp. 95, 145.

[3] See above, chapter 8 (ii): It is significant that Ludlow believed that Christian Socialism could not become 'a true Church-movement among the people, unless we can *Americanize* the Church by giving her true self-government in convocation', MS. letter, 23.9.50, in Torben Christensen, *Origin and History of Christian Socialism*, 1848–54 (Aarhus, 1962).

[4] *Life* ii, p. 221. Christensen, op. cit., p. 340. The Working Men's College is defined in its prospectus as 'a society of which teachers and learners are equally members ... in which men are not held together by the bond of buying and selling ... in which they meet not as belonging to a class or a caste, but as having a common life which God has given them and which He will cultivate in them'.

to substitute education for Christian Socialism and to evade the question how far God's order required political change.[1] Yet it is also possible to see Maurice as instinctively anticipating that principle of 'collegiality' which is becoming a crucial form of response in a society whose frame of reference has ceased to be Christian. This principle of association already takes forms as diverse as episcopal conferences, oecumenical symposia, study groups, and missions to special areas; and where the Eucharist is the act of their institution, these associations enter into a formal relationship with the universal Church or *Ecclesia*, becoming in a localized or domestic sense a church.[2] If they 'dig' and 'build' successfully they may even coin a new language for the Church; but its acceptance and verification is another matter; and it is here that the authority of the bishop and his obligation to be in communion with his fellow bishops is a creative opportunity. Mistakes are inevitable—so is fierce debate; but local blunders do not commit the Church as a whole.

Maurice's imprecise use of the terms 'Church' and 'Nation' conceals this distinction. Newman was determined to bring it out. It was that between the Church, sacramentally, in the unity of all its functions, and its partial realization within a particular context —as a national Church[3]—or a particular function—as a local school of theology.

Yet, at a time when there was little understanding of the Church as the living body of Christ, it was feasible to confuse the ethos or effect with its cause, and to conceive the nation rather than the Church to be the determining factor; the Church of England was riven by parties, and national unity was more apparent than

[1] See Christensen, op. cit., pp. 139, 142, 364.

[2] *Lumen Gentium* (para. 11), refers to the family as 'so to speak, the domestic Church'; and Coleridge's distinction between the *Enclesia* and *Ecclesia* is not essentially incompatible with this distinction between domestic Churches and the universal Church.

[3] This is Newman's distinction between the national Church as 'a witness and teacher of religious truth' and the Catholic Church as 'an oracle of revealed doctrine' (*Apo*, 394–5; see above, chapter 9, p. 150). That Newman intended the distinction to be taken positively may be seen in *Apo*, p. 396, where he goes on to speak of a Catholic's duty as being that of 'assisting and sustaining' the National Church 'in the interest of dogmatic truth'.

Something of the same distinction is to be seen in the Constitutions of Vatican II—in *Lumen Gentium*, para. 15, and in the distinction in the Decree on *Ecumenism* between the Catholic Church, the Separated Churches, and ecclesial communities (para. 19).

ecclesiastical. A more exact definition of the relation between the Church and its context is needed, however, if we are to escape from the circular argument that the nation forms the Church, and the Church forms the nation; and the most obvious way of extricating the argument from circularity is to concede structural elements in the Church which are not of local origin. In this respect Maurice's discussion of the universalizing powers of bishops is promising, but he does not develop it; since he is anxious to deny those powers of self-determination to the Church which he thought would inevitably entail Romanism. It is this which keeps his conception of the Church vague and disembodied, and requires the nation to be constituted to purify and correct the Church. His way of speaking of the Church as if it were an idea *embodied* in specific nations [1] was plausible only for so long as that intimate relationship between Church and State which prevailed in nineteenth-century England endured. In our own time a fragmented and atomized society obliges the Church either to be more explicit or to cease to have any recognizable functional identity.

What Maurice so rightly holds on to in the integrity of his vision is that the Church, in order to fulfil its mission, must have an intimate relationship to the society in which it finds itself, and better a relationship of dependence than of imposition. And Maurice's point which he urged against the Dissenters should not be lightly dismissed—that it is only when the Church stands wholly aloof from the State that she has least chance of being purified from her irregularities. [2] But, for the reasons I have already given, it would be better to try for a different model to describe how the Kingdom of Christ is established, or how—in other words —the *idea* of the Church is realized within the context of a national culture.

[1] *KC* II, p. 254. Cp. his reference to Plato's *Republic* as being the dream of a universal Church (*Life* i, p. 465).
[2] *KC* II, p. 244.

XIV

HOW IS AN *IDEA* REGULATED?

OF all factors in the common tradition from which Coleridge, Newman, and Maurice derive, the most significant is the frequency with which the Church (and the Kingdom) are spoken of as an *idea*; and it is in this essentially *linguistic* conception of the Church as an institution that we can, I suggest, find the best model for the relationship between the universal Church and its local empirical embodiments. For too long we have been blinded by a purely administrative or juridical concept of this relationship; and Newman was one of the first to point out the dangers when, in a period of theological silence, matters requiring a theological attention are evaluated purely in diplomatic and political terms. It is also Newman who speaks of the 'new language which Christ has brought us'[1]; and to respond to the *idea* of the Church as Newman conceives it is very akin to responding to a language—the structures of the Church reveal Christ, as the best words in the best order reveal their author and authenticate his disclosure.[2]

To fulfil this role the Church must possess a qualified, but residual, power of self-determination. While not denying its dependence upon the world, it must up to a point be allowed to structure itself—with all the risks of abuse which inevitably arise from the assumption of powers and government by men. Yet, says Newman, the Church has had this double aspect from the beginning: hence his claim in the *Essay on Development* that 'this corruption of a thousand years, if corruption it be, has ever been growing nearer death, yet never reaching it, and has been strengthened, not debilitated, by its excesses'.[3] And hence Newman's concern, as he grew older, to fashion what Professor Nédoncelle has called 'une théologie des abus ecclésiastiques'.[4]

What is important is that this concern leads Newman to the

---

[1] *P.S.* V, p. 44.
[2] *Lumen Gentium*, para. 8, speaks of the presence of Christ within the structures of the Church as comparable 'to the mystery of the incarnate Word'.
[3] *Dev.*, p. 410.   [4] See above, chapter 10, p. 170.

same question as that put by Coleridge and Maurice: by asking what is the *idea* of the Church he is ultimately led to ask by what principle is it purged and, therefore, regulated. As we have seen for Coleridge and Maurice the answer was by the nation which in practice meant by the laity. And although this way of putting it was unacceptable to Newman as compromising the authority of the magisterium, nevertheless directly the Church ceases to be wholly preoccupied with the exercise of its kingly or ruling function and admits, even requires, a vigorous, participating and educated laity then descriptions of the Church are no longer acceptable which imply a radical separation from the world, and therefore from the laity. We become obliged to define the Church in terms of its relationship to the world and to the nation as expressive of a Christian culture.

For Newman the Church must purge or regulate itself; its regulating principle was theology; and the laity are primarily its 'measure', its 'glass', or its 'matter'.[1] But Newman does not mean by theology an isolated scholarship which is confined to verbal analysis, exegesis, and recondite speculation. As he demonstrated in the *Apologia* theology, for its exercise, presupposes a response of the whole sensibility: it is more than what can be defined in words, since the prophetic office of the Church is the voice of the Spirit and is therefore 'commensurate with Revelation'.[2] Thus Newman speaks of theology as 'ever running into mysteries', and of its lines of thought as often coming 'to an abrupt termination'.[3] Its subject matter extends beyond the open and inexhaustible language of Scripture and includes the acts of charity and devotion of the whole people of God. If we recall Newman's point that religious pro-positions have a double function, as statements of theological truth and of religious fact, then the subject matter of theology is both the acts of a people and the explication of those acts. This is one of the reasons why, as Coleridge himself remarked, theology differs from history and philosophy in being both at once[4]; and a theology such as Newman conceives would, if it were to be able to function as the regulative principle of the Church, have to be representative of the life of the *whole* people of God and of their function to bring about the Kingdom of God.

That Newman was aware of the width of studies necessary for an

---

[1] See above, chapters 6 and 7, pp. 94, 115, 130.   [2] *V.M.*i, p. xlvii.
[3] *Diff.* ii, p. 81.   [4] Cited in Boulger, *Coleridge*, p. 229.

adequate theology is, as I have tried to show, the implication of his argument in the *Idea of a University* and in the *Apologia*. His change of mind about the Catholic university arises as much from a concern for theology as for the laity; since theology depends for its very life, relevance, and accuracy upon a diversity of schools and disciplines for which, even in Newman's day, the open university was the appropriate setting and source. Theology must take place within the context of the acts of the whole Church— 'the Church moves as a whole: it is not a mere philosophy, it is a communion'[1]—and it is for this reason that for Newman as for later theologians, theology is an ecclesial discipline, expressive of that tradition of the Church, of the past as well as of the present, that Möhler described as the living word of God.[2]

In fulfilling its theological function the Church shows itself as a language system, or what Coleridge describes as a *lingua communis*; its language 'is the armoury of the human mind; and at once contains the trophies of its past and the weapons of its future conquests'.[3] This dimension of the Church was the one least fully available to the nineteenth century. At the most, the language of the Church was seen by the Ultramontanes as a static list of propositions, a statement of the essence or deposit, to be imposed upon a graceless world. The deeper Catholic tradition was retained by Maurice, Coleridge, and Newman. For Coleridge and Maurice especially the language of the Church acted as a critical grammar or vocabulary of discrimination.[4] What Newman saw was the need to keep it perpetually in growth and relevance if it were to continue to fulfil its function of restoring all things to Christ, or—in Maurice's words—of realizing the Kingdom.

Yet, since a language cannot be understood or responded to as a living educt of the imagination apart from the community in which it has grown and is alive, so an effective theology presupposes a linguistic community which is the *whole* people of God. Newman was right to emphasize the essential role of the laity in the fullness of such a testimony: not only the Church but its language is foolish without them. Can the Church be said to be performing its pro-

[1] *W*. ii, p. 296.
[2] J. A. Möhler, *Symbolism* (1906), p. 279. That this was the view of the Second Vatican Council is confirmed by *Lumen Gentium*, para. 10.
[3] *BL*, p. 159.
[4] cp. Wittgenstein's remark in *Philosophical Investigations* (373) that Grammar tells what kind of object anything is and his parenthesis 'theology as grammar'.

phetic or theological function if the laity is held at arm's length? Newman's answer was no.

The relevance of Coleridge, Maurice, and their tradition for Newman's description of the Church and for the Catholic theology based upon it is that they show in some detail what are the consequences when the laity take an active part in the life of the Church. It is not only the relationships between priests and laity which change, but also the Church's description of itself in terms of its relation to the world and to the bringing about of the Kingdom of God. The world from which Coleridge and Maurice came was culturally much wider than that which, for the essential purposes of Church reform, the Tractarians narrowed and Roman Catholics kept narrowed; yet, as I have tried to show, there is sufficient common ground in their general sacramental view of the Church for the work of Maurice and Coleridge to throw useful light on the consequences of Newman's conception of the Church. What they do show is that although the Church structures a language, it is a language whose understanding is already determined by the world.

What I have tried to establish is that the difference between Maurice and Newman is ultimately one of priority. Newman is concerned primarily with those conditions internal to the Church which must first be fulfilled before the Church can convincingly show its authority to undertake the task for which it was instituted —by prescription and action to establish the Kingdom of Christ. It explains man to himself and verifies its explanations in deeds. Newman's concern was to work out the basis by which such actions and their explanations were verified and authorized, and what the principle was by which their continuing relevance and effectiveness could be regulated.

Maurice, whose threshold of self-evidence was so much higher, was content to start from what he found—a sacramental conception of the Church and a laity recognizing that conception and its responsibilities to the Church to a degree sufficient to allow Maurice to concentrate on relating the Church to the urgent social and political problems of the Industrial Revolution. He was able to take over Coleridge's conception of the double function of the layman who, in his capacity as a member of the Church and of society, becomes a member of what Coleridge called the 'clerisy'. Nowadays, the laity as the common element belonging both to Church and World is no longer required to exercise similar functions in each body. The layman's standing in the Church need not be necessarily that of his standing in the world; and this functional differentiation will increase as our society becomes more egalitarian. It is possible to conceive laymen who perform diaconal functions within the Church and unskilled functions within society[1]; and the creative element in so highly a technological society as ours is becoming is less and less likely to be the same as the organizing or directing element.

In the strains and tensions of this situation we do indeed meet a God who is hidden from us; but this is not a disaster, but an opportunity. If the laity is this common element, belonging to both worlds, in differing capacities then, having been taught the language which Christ has brought us, they must in their turn be prepared to bring themselves to bear upon the Church by informing, purifying, and making real its life and language. But this function can be performed only if the laity are educated to become bi-lingual, skilled not only in the language of their particular profession or trade, but also in the language of the Church. Coleridge's remark that 'not without celestial observations can even terrestrial charts be accurately constructed'[2] is true in a double sense, since not without terrestrial observations can celestial charts be understood and applied; and the role of the laity in the Church is not only to 'realize' the insights of the Church's language of worship and Scripture, but to be creative of theological development. Without such development what is revealed cannot be brought to bear upon the world.

When any Church accepts this form of the layman's contribution to its prophetic role, in its acts and deeds, that Church is able to enter into a relationship with the world which is more that of a soliloquy, a conversation with its *alter ego* or a sharing of concerns, than a collision with an alien element—the State. And the essential contribution of the Anglican tradition as developed by Coleridge and Maurice was to see the relationship with the secular world in terms of a building up by means of a give-and-take in a process of mutual confidence and co-operation. The presence of an element

---

[1] In Maurice's *Lectures on National Education* (1839), pp. 363–4, we read of his recommendation that the perpetual order of deacons should be revived, so that the religious responsibilities of teachers should be recognized by the Church; and he specifically refers to all teachers as members of what 'Mr. Coleridge has called a clericy'.

[2] *C & S*, p. 52.

common to Church and State—the laity or, in Coleridge's more exact terminology, the clerisy—blurred the outlines of what to Ultramontane minds appeared to be a necessary and inevitable clash between the absolute demands of God through his Church and the relative and contingent needs of the particular social or political problem on hand.

The contrast with the Ultramontanes is significant, because it indicates the real achievement of Christian Socialism. By preaching and organizing co-operation between all classes for the common good, Maurice and his associates helped to avert what seemed the inevitable and violent consequences of the collapse of the Chartist movement in 1848; and in so doing they contributed to that 'miracle of modern England',[1] viz., the extraordinary stability which, amid crises and revolutionary change, was England's precious and unique possession during the mid-nineteenth century. The prophecies of social revolution by Engels were thus frustrated in what seemed to be typical muddle-headed British fashion. Alexander Herzen wrote of the years after 1848: 'England teems with hundreds of associations of this kind: solemn meetings take place which dukes and peers of the realm, clergymen and secretaries, ceremoniously attend. . . . These philanthropic or religious gatherings fulfil the double function of serving as a form of amusement and acting as a sop to the troubled consciences of these somewhat worldly Christians. . . . The whole thing was a contradiction in terms: an open conspiracy, a plot concocted behind open doors.'[2]

The achievement of the Christian Socialists was to save religion from being identified with one kind of political order as on the Continent, so that opposition to a government of the right did not mean opposition to the Church, as it still seems to mean in some countries of the Catholic tradition. In one sense this effected a practical separation of Church and State; and radicalism could be Christian in England, where it was obliged to be atheist on the Continent. This is the sense in which it is possible to claim that the silent social revolution in this country was religious in origin rather than Marxist.

Obscure, ambiguous, and insulated as the insights of Maurice

---

[1] E. Halévy, *A History of the English People in* 1815 (1938), Bk. III, vol. 3, p. 10.
[2] Cited by Melvin Richter, *The Politics of Conscience* (1964), p. 299.

and his followers may have been it cannot be said of them what is now said of their contemporaries among the Roman theologians— that they were the prisoners of their hard and fast definitions: a theological method which is primarily concerned to safeguard the symbolic and metaphorical quality of religious language cannot be used as a basis for persecutions under canon law or for a syllabus of Errors. What it did permit was a wide tolerance of varying Christian theologies, whilst at the same time emphasizing that our obligation to ourself was our obligation to our neighbour; and that this implied social reform or, to put it in the words of one of Maurice's successors, that 'the great function of Christianity is to elevate man in his social condition'.[1]

In one sense, the influence of Maurice upon theology was to encourage it to perform a function which was logically impossible for the Ultramontane theologians, viz., by permitting the social and political developments of the age to operate *inductively* upon theological presuppositions and thereby to promote a development of theological ideas. The development was in the understanding that since we are members one of another, we can best *realize* Christ within us by putting first our obligation to our neighbour, so that we save our souls incidentally as we labour to improve the condition of industrial workers, the education of the poor, or the sanitation of cities.

To the extent that the Church permits the laity, by its acts and explications, to contribute to its theology, then that theology will become the expression of the 'pastorum et fidelium conspiratio', which is not in the pastors alone.[2] And within this limitation and in this sense, the Church is thereby allowing itself to be, in Maurice's words, 'purged by the nation'.

This argument has a further consequence. To ask what is the purgative or regulating principle of the Church is to put the question what is its *idea* in an empirically more satisfactory way; since to understand the extent to which the regulating principle— theology—is dependent upon its context for a healthy functioning is also to understand that a precondition for converting this, Newman's prescription, into fact is the development of an educated laity. It also explains why the formation of such a laity remained

---

[1] James Fraser, Bishop of Manchester (cited in Hudson and Reckitt, *The Church and the World*, vol. 3, p. 107).
[2] *O.C.T.F.*, p. 25.

Newman's chief practical concern throughout his life. But in fulfilling their double function in Church and World the laity also fulfil Pusey's prophecy—but in a sense somewhat different from what he intended—since through them there enters into the life of the separated Churches a common element.

XV

WHAT IS REVELATION?

(i) *Certainty and Certitude*

T HE key-note of Maurice's theological method is his relentless insistence that all the complex elements associated with Christian Revelation—the language of Scripture, the forms of worship, the acts of daily living—must be held together *initially* in a personal unity, because they are 'the very voice by which God speaks to his creatures'.[1] Maurice claims specifically that 'in this way there arose before me the idea of a Church universal, not built upon any human inventions or human faith, but upon the very nature of God himself'.

The effect of this 'method of personation' can be felt in the inevitable ambiguities and obscurities of his prose style—all the aspects of an insight must be held together; and he frequently requires a paragraph for one complex sentence. It also accounts for his hostility towards those contemporary theologians who, he considered, diminished the width of this prehensive unity and, in so doing, weakened both the reality of response and intensity of recognition. He was especially concerned to preserve the linguistic integrity of symbols and sacraments as ordinances which give knowledge of God's purpose in instituting them, and as being, therefore, both act and explication. This is the root of his opposition to the party strife which made Church unity impossible, and to the attempts by theologians to disjoin the sacramental act from its explanation by reducing faith in Christ to an assent to propositions or an obedience to moral maxims. This is to diminish 'the truth which dwelleth in us'.[2] We do not, he says 'speak of loving this lady and her children in the agreement with or assent to certain propositions'.

It was on these grounds that he collided with Mansel and continued to the end to collide with Newman. The collision with Mansel was permanently damaging to his reputation. Maurice

---

[1] *KC* II, p. 363.　　　[2] *The Epistles of St. John* (1881), p. 321.

considered the controversy to go to the heart of religious difference; but it is more properly a philosophical dispute about how we become certain of the truth of Revelation. What strikes us now is the extent to which these philosophical differences rest upon common ground in religion.

Mansel's Bampton Lectures for the year 1858 took Oxford by storm. Intended as a defence of Christian doctrine against the criticism of the Idealists, their impression now is of a re-statement of Butler. Mansel holds that religious consciousness rests upon the feeling of Dependence and the conviction of Obligation, and that these necessarily point to a Personal Being.[1] These are sufficient grounds for believing in God, but this is a very different thing from 'having sufficient grounds for reasoning about Him'. We must be content, with those regulative ideas of the Deity, 'which are sufficient to guide our practice'.[2] At this point Mansel appends a footnote reference to Berkeley's *Alciphron*,[3] which is presumably to the contention that we understand abstract general ideas as we apply them, and not as we try to make them logically more precise. Earlier on, Berkeley speaks of terms, such as the Trinity, which although they are significant signs need not suggest ideas represented by them, 'provided they serve to regulate and influence our wills, passions, or conduct'.[4] In other words—although we must first be assisted by Scripture to understand the Trinity, we cannot develop this understanding unless we will to live in a Trinitarian way. And it is clear from the drift of Mansel's argument that he is moving very close to a position adopted by some contemporary Christian philosophers, viz., that the verbal signs designating the Christian mysteries are directed primarily to the will in order to encourage a life of virtue; and their truth is verified in practice.[5]

Mansel draws the conclusion that 'Action, and not knowledge, is man's destiny and duty in this life'.[6] and that truth and falsehood are not properties 'of things in themselves, but of our conceptions'.[7]

[1] H. L. Mansel, *The Limits of Religious Thought*, the *Bampton Lectures for 1858* (fifth edition, 1867), p. 78.
[2] ibid., pp. 87, 90.   [3] Dialogue VII. 11.   [4] ibid., VII. 8.
[5] Cp. R. B. Braithwaite, *An Empiricist's view of the Nature of Religious Belief* (Cambridge, 1955), p. 32: 'A religious assertion, for me, is the assertion of an intention to carry out a certain behaviour policy . . . together with the implicit or explicit statement, but not the assertion, of certain stories.'
[6] Mansel, *The Limits of Religious Thought*, p. 105.
[7] ibid., cp. Ayer: 'It is only such things as statements or propositions, or beliefs or opinions, which are expressible in language, that are capable of being

Maurice published his objections to the Bampton Lectures in
1859 under the title *What is Revelation?*[1] The book is usually
regarded as the least satisfactory of his writings. He lacked skill in
controversy, and without intending to do so he gave the impression
of impugning Mansel's integrity. He had rashly concluded that
Mansell was merely 'a common-room wit and joker'[2]; but his
charge amounts to more than one of frivolity. It is, fundamentally,
to Mansel's language and tone; and this is always a field where
Maurice's full critical sensibility is most formidably employed.
Yet, of its very nature, such a charge can seem to question a
writer's integrity. In spite of Mansel's appreciative references to
Joseph Butler, Maurice finds little in his style of those qualities
which so characterize Butler—his 'tentative, experimental' approach, whereby he helps us to understand the sense of a word 'by
bringing us gradually into an experience of the fact which it
denotes'. Maurice speaks similarly of Anselm, and praises him for
securing 'his moral truth from all verbal invasions'. Mansel's
handling of Scripture, however, lacks any sense of its being a record
to which we must respond as a whole; and by reducing it 'to a
collection of opinions', or 'mottoes' intended 'merely to point a
sentence or confound an opponent', he has 'emasculated' the Word
of God and failed, therefore, to treat it with proper reverence.[3]
Such a practice is 'to intercept the direct communication between
God and His creatures which I believe the Bible bears witness of';
and Maurice feels that the climax of such a practice and doctrine
is reached when Mansel asserts that 'truth and falsehood are not
properties of things in themselves, but of our conceptions'.[4]

What the charge amounts to is that Mansel is thinning out the
depths and fracturing the unity of the Christian response in the
interests of a highly simplified leading idea, of which a contemporary form is that stated by Professor Braithwaite.[5] The most
fruitful of Maurice's strictures is when he uses the term 'rhetorical' of Mansel's celebrated passage on the Incarnation[6]; and it is
very revealing to notice how little of the substance of Mansel's

---

true or false, certain or doubtful. Our experiences themselves are neither
certain nor uncertain; they simply occur.' (*The Problem of Knowledge*, p. 52.)
  [1] *What is Revelation?* (1859). (*WR.*)
  [2] *Life* ii, p. 334.   [3] *WR*, pp. 168, 171, 211, 469, 478.
  [4] ibid., p. 345; Mansel, *The Limits of Religious Thought*, p. 105.
  [5] See above, p. 215.
  [6] Mansel, op. cit., p. 115; *WR*, p. 349.

argument is lost when the stately rhythms of his antitheses are reduced to the plain summary of the lectures affixed to the fifth edition.

The controversy never seems to do more than beg the question —what are the logical or linguistic difficulties which legitimately arise when we speak of religious belief as commitment to a divine Person; and how does that commitment, when assisted by Grace, characterize our knowledge? If Grace confers some special insight, to what extent is its expression related to the verification-procedures applicable to propositions? Such questions require a subtle probing; and the instincts of the undergraduates in Mansel's audience were probably correct—that beneath the dialectical rhetoric lurked an acceptably uncomplicated faith. Burgon's description of the lectures certainly confirms one's suspicions.[1]

The controversy with Mansel helps us to understand why Maurice rejected Newman's *Grammar of Assent*, when it was published in 1870.[2] He seizes on Newman's remark that 'certainty is a quality of propositions', without apparently attending to the force of the accompanying distinction that 'certitude is a mental state'[3]; and he goes on to deny that there can be any relationship between assent to theological statements and belief in religious truth on the grounds that an assent to propositions can never be related to the required assent to persons and things: apprehensions cease to be of things when they are expressed in propositional form and inevitably become notions.[4] Newman's account of how we learn step by step, proposition by proposition what is meant by the doctrine of the Holy Trinity in order that ultimately such growth of understanding will 'trigger off' a grasp of the truth as a

[1] J. W. Burgon, *Lives of Twelve Good Men* (1891), p. 339:
'The young men knew, of course, in a general way, what the champion of Orthodoxy was about. He was, single-handed, contunding a host of unbelievers —some, with unpronounceable names and unintelligible theories; and sending them flying before him like dust before the wind. And *that* was quite enough for *them*. It was a gladiatorial exhibition which they were invited to witness: the unequal odds against "the British lion" adding greatly to the zest of the entertainment; especially as the noble animal was always observed to remain master of the field in the end.'
[2] 'Dr. Newman's *Grammar of Assent*—a review', in *Contemporary Review*, Vol. XIV, May 1870, pp. 151–72.
[3] *GA*, p. 262; Maurice, art. cit., pp. 152, 168.
[4] Maurice, art. cit., p. 159.

whole is dismissed by Maurice in these words: 'How living objects
of trust become starved into notions.'[1]

Maurice specifically denies Newman's claim that in religion
propositions can be held in two ways—'either as a theological
truth, or as a religious fact or reality'.[2] Maurice in reply instances
the belief of the Jews: 'It is not an *assent* to a proposition. . . . It is
the *belief* in an actual personal Deliverer. . . . The devotion of the
Jews . . . rose directly to a living God, who discovered himself in
acts, not in propositions.'[3]

But, we must ask, can this distinction be drawn, since language
is used to clarify what we have experienced in order that we
recognize and know it for what it is? Had not God's actions upon
the Jews to be similarly recognized for what they were and clarified
in the language or propositions of the prophets? All that Maurice
has by way of an answer to this objection is given at the end of the
review, when he says: 'I fully admit, then, that the nations had, as
Dr. Newman says they had, a perception of God and of His purposes; but I submit to St. Paul's decision that their perceptions
came from a *revelation* of Him—a continued, daily, hourly revelation—not from the nature of things or from the nature of man
acting independently of a revelation.'[4]

Once more we are faced with having to maintain the integrity of
the sacramental vision; but what happens if (as now) the nation is
unable to embody or mediate these daily and hourly revelations?
And were all the events described in the Bible intended to be
taken as literally true? How do we distinguish between true and
false, literal and mythical? To deny the possibility of separating
our insight from the language in which it is expressed does not,
however, deny the possibility of theological discourse or development; since it does not follow from 'all paraphrasing diminishes'
that no paraphrase is possible, but only that all paraphrases are
approximations. Approximations are, however, the means of
developing an understanding of what they fail fully to express;
and this is what justifies a distinction between religious actions or
insights and theological explanations.

The highly charged language of metaphor and symbol in which

<hr />

[1] Maurice, art. cit., p. 164; *GA*, pp. 92 ff., 103.

[2] "The notion and the reality assented to are represented by one and the same
proposition, but serve as distinct interpretations of it.' *GA*, pp. 91–2.

[3] Maurice, art. cit., pp. 163–4.

[4] Maurice, art. cit., p. 170.

so much of Scripture is expressed requires to be interpreted as the basis of a more effective response; and such interpretations require a more objective validity than that of the private judgement which, even in ethical matters, is 'that highest of all teachers, yet the least luminous'.

Maurice's attempt to preserve the integrity of sacramental language by allowing no distinction between act and explanation denies the possibility of such an interpretation; and it also implies that certainty must be our starting point, and that its formulations must be self-authenticating; but can any language be self-authenticating? Is not an essential part of our understanding of any language an understanding of its rules and of how it has developed?—a book finds you only if you have been brought up to be found by it.

It was on these grounds that Newman insisted upon his distinction between religious acts and theological explanation; but he held the connection between them to be both necessary and organic; and his account of that connection also provides an answer to the other problem evaded by Maurice—what is the relationship between the idea of the Church Catholic and its local, empirical institution.

(ii) *'One complex act both of inference and of assent'*

What unites Newman, Maurice, and Mansel is their preoccupation with what their contemporaries regarded as 'the one danger of the present day' that of 'not believing in a Personal God'[1]; and the argument between them remains illuminating because it is conducted within a common philosophical tradition, of which Butler[2] is the determining influence, and to a lesser extent the Berkeley of *Alciphron*.[3] It accepts faith as being ethical in origin but as reveal-

---

[1] Entry in Bishop Samuel Wilberforce's diary, 20 April 1872, of a conversation with William Forster, whom he reports as saying: 'The one man I ever heard preach who really put that forward was Mansell [sic]: F. Maurice somewhat, but obscure in his statements' (*Life of Bishop Wilberforce*, by R. G. Wilberforce (1882), vol. iii, p. 396).

[2] Although Newman's debt to Butler is well authenticated, its strongest affirmation occurs in an unpublished letter to T. W. Allies: 'without of course comparing myself with Bishop Butler I may say that I am of his school'. (30 Nov. 1879.)

[3] Newman's denial in the *Apologia* (p. 120) that he had studied Berkeley probably refers to his epistemology, since Newman's own copy of Berkeley's works in the Oratory Library has passages marked by him. It is highly significant that these occur in *Alciphron*, Dialogues VI and VII, one of which is cited by Newman in *Miracles*, p. 10.

ing a personal relationship with God. Where Newman and Mansel differ from Maurice is on philosophical grounds: 'the vision which influences the heart'[1] will inevitably split into its constituent details.[2] These are isolated from each other in proportion to their intensity, yet the greater their isolation the greater the need to place them within the total order of signs which is the Christian Revelation.

This process of clarifying and unifying begins in rational explanation,[3] since knowledge is a precondition of the rightful exercise of the affections[4]; but its completion or ultimate ground is social: religious act and theological explanation cohere and develop within a community or polity (to use Newman's term).

It was this 'great principle of a social faith' which Maurice held the Oxford Movement to have recovered—'that we exist in a permanent communion which was not created by human hands, and cannot be destroyed by them'.[5] And it is in this sense that the theologies of Newman and Maurice are complementary. They provide compatible but not identical accounts of the same sacramental principle whose respective efficacy must be judged in terms of the priorities and questions they start from.

Maurice faces the social consequences of the Industrial Revolution; and his prior question is how to make religion relevant? Newman faces Bentham or, more exactly, the philosophical

---

[1] *Arians*, p. 144; *GA*, p. 83.

[2] This principle of limitation is probably the most fundamental of Newman's philosophical presuppositions. It is the basis of his philosophy of education, as expressed in the *Idea of a University*, as well as of his epistemology. It was this latter aspect—that we experience a unity but know only details, that the power to harmonise them is not our own, and that we must therefore accept apparent contradictions—which led Simpson to compare Newman and Mansel in a review of the Bampton Lectures (*Rambler*, 1858, vol. X, pp. 407–15). Newman discusses the comparison in a philosophical letter to Dr. Charles Meynell (20 Dec. 1859) which is referred to above in chapter 5, pp. 59 ff. It is ironical that in the very number of the *Rambler* in which Newman published his ill-fated article 'On Consulting the Faithful' (July 1859) there should have appeared a notice of the third edition of Mansel's Lectures in which he acknowledges the comparison with Newman and speaks appreciatively of the Oxford University Sermons, particularly of p. 351 where Newman warns against 'the ambition of being wiser than what is written'.

[3] *GA*, p. 106: 'Religion has to do with the real, and the real is the particular; theology has to do with what is notional, and the notional is the general and systematic.'

[4] *GA*, p. 91.

[5] In an open letter to Lord Ashley (1843), *Methods of Supporting Protestantism*, p. 10 (cited by Vidler, op. cit., p. 96).

rationalism which made the Revolution possible—and his priority is how do we become certain that religion is true? Maurice is concerned with relevance and with preserving the integrity of sensibility necessary for such acts of commitment. Newman is concerned with verification, and with the preconditions to be fulfilled before such sensibilities can be educated, and such acts authoritatively undertaken. Maurice's conservatism caused him to ignore the linguistic and epistemological difficulties which preoccupied Newman and Mansel; and his abiding suspicion of Romanism led him to ground the social dimension, not in its origins in the Church, but in its fulfilment in the nation—yet in a nation 'which recognises the Church'.

Such a qualification, however, not only reveals the prescriptive character of Maurice's idea of the nation, but also its disjunctive tendency. To what extent does society as a whole recognize the Church? And is not the 'nation' in Maurice's sense increasingly likely to stand for a determining *element*—whether Coleridge's clerisy, or Newman's socially wider 'enthusiastic laity'? Maurice's point is not wholly invalidated by such an objection, however, since his conception of the Kingdom brings out the eschatological function of the Church's relation to society: it is like a Pilgrim [1] drawing society on to develop its inherent tendencies by 'proclaiming what the state of things is which God has made, and which we are trying to set at nought'.[2]

The difference between Newman and Maurice lies in the extent to which each thinks it necessary to press the distinction between the social fabric and its motivation. American Catholic theologians have, for example, taken the principle that the State depends for its vitality upon motivation which it cannot by itself command[3] as grounds for arguing the separation of Church and State. And for Newman the distinction between social expedience and truth is so distinct as to require the motivating or prescribing function to be

---

[1] The Vatican Council Constitution, *On the Church* (I: 8) uses this term; and a considerable part of the argument in, for example, Harvey Cox, *The Secular City* (1966), is based on this notion of the Church as 'a word of motion' (op. cit., pp. 113, 144 f., 225).

[2] F. D. Maurice, *A Dialogue between Somebody, a person of respectability, and Nobody, the writer.* (*Tracts on Christian Socialism*, 1, 1850), p. 16.

[3] John Courtney Murray, S.J., *We Hold these Truths* (1960), pp. 212 and 201-15. For the extent to which this distinction informs the *Declaration on Religious Liberty*, see the same author's commentary, esp. on paras. 3 and 6, in *Documents of Vatican II* (1966), pp. 680, 684.

located not only in the people's *prior* membership of the Church, but more particularly in the Church's exercise of its prophetical office. It was to prescribe or propagate this truth that the Church was constituted; and since its security is lodged 'in the very fact of its catholicity',[1] the claim to act with Christian authority depends upon the extent to which individuals, theological schools, and local churches are prepared to universalize their actions and judgements. And, for Newman, this meant accepting the conditions of the Vincentian canon—*quod ubique, quod semper, quod ab omnibus.*[2]

This was not brought about by a crude imposition of authority from above—as Maurice imagined. It was more in the nature of a response to 'the secret life of millions of faithful souls'[3] nourished by acts of devotion, and formed by sensibilities 'found' by the words of Scripture and 'realized' by the discharge of their social responsibilities. What Newman presupposes from the start is an active laity fulfilling the duties of its double membership of Church and Nation, so that to the extent to which this membership is effective Christ's regenerative presence is functioning through the social structures of both Church and Nation; and the condition laid down by Maurice—that 'Christ came into the world to regenerate all human society'[4]—is *incidentally* fulfilled.

There is never any question of conformity to a system, in the limited Maurician sense, but to a body of persons to whom Grace has been promised. And, for Newman, this process—religious in origin, but theological in development—of conforming ourselves to the Church in its *idea* is completed by Grace: 'Grace gives certainty, reason is never decided.'[5]

For Maurice, however, certainty is what we must start with: the sole alternative to his enriched sensibility with its high threshold of self-evidence is scepticism. Newman, on the other hand, distinguishes certainty—which in the strict sense is a character of propositions and therefore verifiable[6]—from certitude—which is 'grown into'.[7] It is 'the bell of the intellect',[8] since it marks the act of judging a matter as a whole, of being determined by a body of proof which is treated 'as a body, and not in its constituent

[1] *Diff.* i, pp. 158, 166.   [2] See above, chapter 5, pp. 69 f.
[3] *O.U.S.*, p. 323.   [4] *TE*, p. 245.   [5] *D.M.C.*, p. 179.
[6] *GA*, p. 262.   [7] *Letters* XI, p. 110.   [8] *GA*, p. 176.

parts'.[1] It is certitude not certainty which religion demands, because its possession places us beyond the range of empirical questioning, enabling us to endure, and to persevere to the end.[2]

For Newman, therefore, religious certitude was the reward not the condition of faith, and although the image of Christ 'both creates faith, and then rewards it',[3] he held that an assent to religious objects 'as if they were objects of sight' was the privilege of a devout nation only—'but such a faith does not suit the genius of modern England'.[4]

Here is the essential ground of the difference between Newman and Maurice. For Maurice God is not concerned with the possibility or danger of error; for him the text is brighter and clearer than the comment.[5] Newman, however, remains unable to identify the certitude of Christ's presence to the believer with the certain knowledge of his teaching.[6]

But these are not denominational differences (as the controversy with Mansel shows). They have to do with philosophical notions about the nature of religious language and of sacramental language in particular.

Maurice feared that to permit a distinction to be made between the sacramental act and its explication was to risk a dissociation of religious sensibility. He therefore 'clung to the letter'[7] as he said; and by thus keeping faith with the language of ultimate concern reminded us that its characteristic expression is as 'these words in these positions': it is an order of words which we paraphrase at our peril. What he overlooked is that language is both for action and reflection, and to the extent that it preserves the trophies of our past conquests, it becomes thereby the weapons of our future conquests[8]: implicit in the symbolic concept is the capacity to grow, to develop and to apply itself to modes of being as yet unrecognized.

But a more serious error was to overlook the distinction between

---

[1] ibid., p. 222.   [2] ibid., p. 167.
[3] ibid., p. 354; *Letters* XVII, p. 243.   [4] ibid., p. 43.
[5] *H.*, p. lxxx; see above, chapter 5, p. 77.
[6] See the letter, already quoted, in chapter 12 above, p. 191, in which Newman says: 'I could not feed on words, without ideas. It is sheer Sewellism.' And immediately after his quip 'to sewellise, or to mauricise', he adds: 'Now I would say that the greater part of our Lord's teaching is *not* clear—and where it is clearest, it is most startling to the imagination'. (*Letters* XIV, p. 181.)
[7] Church, *Occasional Papers*, II, p. 323; see above, chapter 5, p. 70.
[8] See above, chapter 2, p. 18. (*BL*, p. 159.)

religious and poetic language, since in religion we claim, by means of 'a complex act both of inference and of assent',[1] to extract *true* statements from *a priori* assertions in symbolic and metaphoric form. And we verify these paraphrases in the lives of the saints and in terms of our relationship to that linguistic community we call the Church.[2]

In religion we begin within accepted institutions and ideas, but directly we apply them—as we must—and the momentum of change increases—as it will, then the question 'What is Revelation?' has to be answered in the form: 'How do we know our interpretations of it to be true?' Newman's achievement is to show how the sacramental tradition expressed by Coleridge and Maurice could be developed to answer contemporary Benthamite objections; and where it takes fuller account of the difficulties, his 'method of personation' may be considered to be philosophically the more adequate. It required him to conceive the Church as 'an open public union'[3]—as something more than an *idea* promoting a unity of sentiment,[4] but as something less than a counter society to the nation. His development of this common tradition towards communion with Rome was because he found—to use Maurice's words—'the barriers he thought would preserve us from Rationalism insufficient'.[5] It was this which obliged him to test the Establishment to destruction.

---

[1] ibid., p. 26. (*GA*, p. 374.)   [2] ibid., pp. 21 ff.
[3] See above, chapter 5, pp. 64 f.   [4] ibid., p. 71. (*Diff*. i, p. 335.)
[5] ibid., p. 81. (*H*., p. cxxviii.)

XVI

GENERAL CONCLUSION

To have established common links between Newman and that English tradition of which Coleridge and Maurice are the formative exponents is chiefly of value if it can be shown to have significance for the present day. And I wish to establish the bearing of my argument upon the more general problem of the relation of the Church to society. Briefly it amounts to this—that the Church cannot be conceived sacramentally, and in its *idea*, in isolation from society, because a relationship is already implied.

Three possible relationships of the Church to society have so far been discussed. They are both stages in the historical evolution of that relationship and possibilities which may recur. In a society which is or is considered to be actively hostile to Christian living, the Church will stand over against it in judgement—and this, the Ultramontane position, was also that of the first Tractarians. But in a society in which Christian principles are recognized as determining the pattern or ethos of its culture a more complex relationship is not only possible but necessary—and this was the position of the Establishment as interpreted by Coleridge and Maurice. There is, however, a third relationship—that of the Church to a society which no longer 'recognizes the Church',[1] and is to this extent separated from it, but is in the contemporary sense of the words open and pluralist. To the question—in which relationship is the sacramental idea of the Church best realized?—Newman answers by expressing a preference for the third and last form.

What I also wish to establish is that, in spite of its being so manifestly at odds with the relationship of Church to society customarily associated with Roman Catholicism, this preference is not mere idiosyncrasy, but is the one advocated by the published conclusions of the Second Vatican Council.

It is important to appreciate the grounds for the first relationship, however, since it is the most obvious way of conceiving the form

---

[1] See above chapters 13 and 15, pp. 196 and 221.

which a relationship between the sacramental idea of the Church and society should take. It was that adopted by the Ultramontanes, but also by the Tractarians in the first phase of the Movement, although—as Church points out—it seems to require a distinction between secular life and the life of religion which, even at the time, was no longer acceptable.[1] Yet the grounds for such a distinction are unequivocally expressed in Scripture, as when St. John speaks of the whole world as lying in wickedness or as being in the power of the evil one.[2] Newman had preached on this text, and had spoken of the Church as 'a body gathered together in the world, and in a process of separation from it'.[3] In 1860 he returned to the subject in a correspondence with his Professor designate of History at University College, Dublin, T. W. Allies.[4] This correspondence has been little noticed and never fully published; but it enables us to see how Newman would have answered the question: 'Is there a particular form of relationship to society in which the sacramental idea of the Church is best realized?'

Allies had contended that the Church benefits from being in that relationship to society which it had in medieval times; but Newman was not satisfied. Taking the passage from St. John as a basis, he argues that however much the world may be 'stamped with Christian civilization', it is still 'in maligno positus'. This seems to promise no advance on the position he adopted as a Tractarian—that whatever position the Church may hold in the fabric of society that society is still 'a worldly one', in which 'evil ever floats at the top'.[5] But the correspondence with Allies, if taken as a whole and related to the growth of Newman's idea of the Church, establishes a more complex argument, and one of great contemporary significance.

Nevertheless, it is important to realize how fundamental to a sacramental conception of the Church is its capacity to act as a separate body or polity. When, for example, the dogmatic constitution *On the Church* speaks of the Church as being 'in Christ like a sacrament or sign and instrument of a very closely knit union

---

[1] Church, *Oxford Movement*, p. 320.   [2] I John 5: 19.
[3] *P.S.* VII, p. 36 (8 March 1829).
[4] Partly published in M. H. Allies, *Thomas William Allies* (1907), chapter VI, pp. 105–46; the unpublished matter referred to is in the Archives of the Birmingham Oratory.
[5] *P.S.* VII, p. 36.

with God'[1] it goes on to emphasize that this inner nature is made known to us by metaphors and images of a particular kind: these are of the sheepfold, the field, the building in which the family dwell, and the temple.[2] It is significant that these are all metaphors and symbols of *unification* and of belonging face to face within a family. And they also characterize the Church as a liturgical community, which is 'the source and culmination of all Christian life'.[3]

It is easy to see how such metaphors can be cited to justify a purely defensive role for the Church as a besieged fortress standing in judgement upon the world. Such a role is forced on the Church when society persecutes Christians for being Christians or actively suppresses liberty of conscience. It was this role which the Ultramontanes considered themselves to have been obliged by circumstances to adopt.

The loyalty of Catholics to the Roman Pontiff in his political troubles predisposed them to be suspicious of the social changes which to us now seem to have been inevitable. To them the options still seemed open.[4] They hoped to restore Christendom to what they conceived to be its medieval norm by emphasizing the unity and authority of the Church—with Rome as its focus—at the expense of its freedom and diversity.[5] Instead, the Church fell victim to its own creeping Ultramontanism; and responsible statesmen, like Gladstone, could seriously conclude that the political consequences of the Decrees of the First Vatican Council were that Catholics must now be regarded as untrustworthy members of a modern state.[6]

In the absence of a theology such as Newman desired, and especially a university theology which would have been healthily critical and contextually significant,[7] such consequences were inevitable; as was the conception of faith as a system of fixed ideas.[8]

It is no wonder that the familial images of the Church became petrified at their patriarchal stage, and that their enclosing and

[1] *The Constitution on the Church of Vatican Council II*, ed. E. H. Peters (1965). (*Lumen Gentium*), Intro., para. 1.
[2] ibid., para. 6.   [3] ibid., para. 11.
[4] See above chapter 7, pp. 107 f. on Catholic opposition to Government inspection of their schools.
[5] See above chapters 6, 8, 10, pp. 96, 135, 169.
[6] See above chapter 9, p. 151.   [7] See above chapter 9, pp. 159 f.
[8] See above chapter 8, p. 135.

socially divisive tendencies became emphasized to the exclusion of other equally valid interpretations. But, on the credit side, it enabled that traditional conception of the Church to be preserved which is expressed by Ignatius of Antioch—that 'without the bishop there is not the name of a Church'. It enables a firm distinction to be made between the bishop—as the father or progenitor of the ecclesial family—and the layman who, although a member of the family and reunited to it by the common celebration of the liturgy, has stayed in the world and found his family circle there. The bishop and his assistant clergy have, by their devotion to the Church's mission to itself as polity or institution, removed themselves from the world: 'they live by the altar,' they turn their mission into their profession; and when they return to the world, they do so as explicit witnesses of Christ.[1]

It is the novelists of the time who can best show us how available such a patriarchal conception of the family still was to the nineteenth century. George Eliot, for example, stresses those characteristics of the family which make it the inescapable ground of our meeting face to face with those who, not of our own choosing, but purely by birth, are not merely our fellows, but our intimates. Such an enforced intimacy has its own deepening—usually in honesty and patience; and the clan is no place in which to nourish illusions about ourselves and our aspirations. However much its members may rise, individually or collectively, above the mental level of the previous generation, they remain tied to them by the strongest fibres of their hearts.[2] Here are the limitations but also the profound psychological compensations of what Maurice terms an 'organic' society,[3] viz., one in which the individual is educated morally by his placing within society and in the discharge of his duties towards its members.

It is these qualities which make possible that role for the family as being, above all, the place where the member receives justice—

---

[1] Karl Rahner, 'Notes on the Lay Apostolate', *Theological Investigations*, vol. ii (1963), p. 334 (*passim*).

[2] 'Heaven knows where that striving might lead us, if our affections had not a trick of twining round those old inferior things [the commonplace furniture of our early home]—if the loves and sanctities of our life had no deep immovable roots in memory.' George Eliot, *The Mill on the Floss* (Edinburgh, 1867), II. i, p. 136.

[3] *KC* II, p. 234, see above, chapter 13, pp. 196 ff.

'the right thing must always be done towards kindred'.[1] And, in what
is an implied reference to the Passover, George Eliot describes this
family characteristic as one which would be 'frankly hard of speech
to inconvenient "kin" but would never forsake or ignore them—
would not let them want bread but only require them to eat it with
bitter herbs'.[2]

Even on the narrower basis of the modern 'nucleated' family,
such relationships remain the only deep and abiding ones which
many people are capable of sustaining: we are narrowed by them,
but the narrowing deepens by intensifying and concentrating the
influences it transmits: it educates; and it is still a mark of successful places of education that they continue to resemble a family in
this respect.

George Eliot's family portrait should be set alongside Newman's
description of the patriarchal conditions and aspirations of the
Church in Ireland.[3] It had the same limitations, but also the same
virtues. Nevertheless, to apply the patriarchal analogy too literally or—to use Blondel's term—too monophoristically [4] is to sharpen
the distinction between clergy and laity. The bishop and his
priests are seen as those who live most intimately (and profitably)
within the family circle; while the laity are those 'inconvenient
kin' who are not at home as much as they ought to be, being too
much outside 'in the world', and too intimately in contact with the
sources of subversion. How else can one explain Ullathorne's
'horror of the laity' as disturbing the 'peace' of the Church,[5] and
Talbot's conceiving Newman to be 'the most dangerous man in
England' because of his intimacy with the laity?[6]

The limitations of this position are to be seen in its failure to
produce anything other than a negative definition of the laity: the
familial norm is the bishop and the priest, and the layman is defined
in terms of his relationship to them. If, as a Christian, he shows
any initiative, then he is treated as a 'suspect',[7] or as a species of
ecclesiastical suffragette. It is as if the only way to define a woman
was in terms of a man: this would imply a comparable dependence

---

[1] 'The right thing was to correct them severely if they were other than a credit
to the family, but still not alienate from them the smallest rightful share in the
family shoe buckles and other property.' Eliot, op. cit. IV. i, p. 250.
[2] ibid.   [3] See above, chapter 6, p. 97.
[4] See above, chapter 11, pp. 181 f.   [5] See above, chapter 7, p. 112.
[6] See above, chapter 7, p. 125.
[7] Simpson's term, see above, chapter 7, p. 112.

of women upon men and might be taken, as it once was, as grounds for justifying their subjection.

A further consequence is the division of the Church into a teaching magisterium and a passive inactive laity—a notion which, as Bishop B. C. Butler remarks, is ripe for re-examination.[1] What was overlooked was that such distinctions presuppose an initial unity—that of the whole people of God—and that 'professional' Christians are those whose episcopal or priestly function is their way of carrying out this universal function to redeem the world. That these distinctions presuppose an initial unity is affirmed by the unifying aspect of the familial images of the people of God. It was this aspect which Newman was alone in emphasizing, when he spoke of there being something in the *conspiratio* of pastors and faithful people, 'which is not in the pastors alone'.[2]

Karl Rahner argues that the cleric, in the strict sense, is the professional or institutionalized Christian, and the layman is the man who has discovered how to live as a Christian within the demands of his occupation; but that directly such implicit discoveries are made explicit, the layman is moving within the clerical condition, since his occupation is simultaneously the material of his being a Christian and the limit.[3] This leads Rahner to posit a threefold distinction between priests (or fathers), clergy, and laity; and his conception of the clerical condition as being one of overlapping roles and functions is strikingly close to that of the 'clerisy' as put forward by Coleridge and Maurice.[4]

That such necessary distinctions were not developed is the price that nineteenth-century Catholicism paid for its failure to encourage adequate schools of theology. Its neglect of what von Hügel called the arrears of some twelve generations[5] prevented a reasonable degree both of internal development and of adaptation to changing social conditions. The conception of the family described by George Eliot and still to be found as a Catholic norm in the backwoods was rapidly superseded, and it hardly, if

---

[1] Bishop Butler cites Rahner and Küng for a suggestion that Oecumenical Councils might be conceived as 'formally representative of the whole People of God, not only of the episcopate' (p. 5, note 7); and he goes on to suggest that 'the whole Church is, under different and correlative aspects, both *docens* and *discens*' (p. 110, note 22) in *Theology of Vatican II*.

[2] See above, chapter 7, p. 117.   [3] Rahner, op. cit., p. 324.

[4] See especially the discussion above in chapter 14, pp. 209 f.

[5] See above, chapter 11, p. 182.

ever, existed in the new towns of the Industrial Revolution. What
Newman could see was that to continue to conceive the Church in
exclusively patriarchal and therefore clerical terms in a world
which had outgrown such a basis was to lose sight of the purpose
for which the Church was founded—'to teach all nations'.[1]

It had the further effect of narrowing the Church into a sect,[2] so
that its social role appeared more that of a counter society to the
State than a sharer of mutual concerns.[3] In Europe such a posture
frequently converted the Church into a focus for unrest and
instability of an extreme right-wing and anti-liberal character.[4]
This is justified only for as long as society is deemed to be hostile
to Christian living, or where the Church's revolutionary role is
deemed to be primary—as in the early Church. In other and more
civilized circumstances it is a further example of that failure to
understand the nature of religious language and of the 'complex
act both of inference and of assent' which it requires.[5] Maurice's
mistake was, of course, quite different from that of the Ultramontanes. Theirs was what Blondel called 'monophorisme'[6]—
the taking of one interpretation—in this case of the family—as the
type of all family relationships, and assuming an undeveloping
relationship to a world which is always outside and alien to it. Yet
the Church is both the family to which the penitent must present
himself to be reconciled to Christ and the rehearsal community for
Christian living. Penitents become reconciled; rehearsals give place
to performances; children come of age—and the world becomes
their home.

Here is the ground for the second and more developed relationship of Church to society which is to be found so fully expressed
in Coleridge and Maurice. I now wish to consider to what extent it
is affirmed by the documents of the Second Vatican Council. When,

[1] See above, chapter 6, pp. 96–7. In an unpublished letter to Allies, 10 Nov. '63,
Newman writes: 'I am tempted to call both slavery and despotism in their idea
patriarchal power badly administered. Then 1. perhaps patriarchal power *on a
large field* will *ever* be badly administered. 2. Perhaps a race in the course of
centuries *outgrows* patriarchal power, which, *even were* it *well administered*, is
inexpedient for it.'

[2] See Newman's charge that Ward was turning the Church into a neo-
Novatian sect, in chapter 7 above, pp. 128 f.; and von Hügel's remarks on the
sect-principle in chapter 10 above, p. 178.

[3] See above, chapter 14, p. 210.
[4] See above, chapter 14, pp. 211 f.
[5] See above, chapter 15, pp. 218–9 *passim*.
[6] See above, chapter 11, p. 181.

in *Lumen Gentium*, the Church is spoken of as a Pilgrim,[1] an entirely new principle is introduced. Not only is a diametrically different conception of relationship to society implied from that of the Ultramontanes—that of drawing society on to develop its inherent tendencies[2]—but the Church is being conceived, in Coleridge's terms, as 'a medium between literal and metaphorical'.[3] By partaking of the reality it renders intelligible,[4] it acts as a living organ, or in Coleridge's term—'educt' of salvation,[5] having the power to bring the whole soul of man into activity.

This is the foundation of that *idea* of the Church to be found expressed in the common tradition of Coleridge, Maurice, and Newman; and the documents of Vatican II spell out this conception in details with which the student of that tradition will already be familiar. Christ is no longer conceived as being confined to a self-centred Church. Instead, its visible form or polity 'serve[s] the spirit of Christ, who vivifies it, in the building up of the body'; and this body—the Mystical Body of Christ—'*subsists* in the Catholic Church'.[6] The Catholic Church is no longer described in terms of a clerical hierarchy, but as the people of God. It is the people as a whole who exercise the functions of Christ as Prophet, Priest, and King: they 'participate in the one priesthood of Christ[7]; and 'the entire body of the faithful, anointed as they are by the Holy One, cannot err in matters of belief'.[8]

Although it is affirmed that the Church has been given an hierarchical structure from the moment of its constitution, and not after it, nevertheless, the hierarchy is now best seen as a function or service, rather than as an authority imposed in the manner of earlier times.[9] The rights of conscience having been con-

---

[1] 'The Church "like a pilgrim presses forward amid the persecutions of the world and the consolations of God"', *Lumen Gentium* I: 8.
[2] See above, chapter 15, p. 221.   [3] See above, chapter 3, p. 39.
[4] This is the terminology used by Coleridge when he discusses the symbolic *idea* of the Church (see above, chapter 2, p. 36). Its application to Newman's idea of the Church is discussed specifically in chapter 11 above, p. 180.
[5] *Lumen Gentium* I: 8.
[6] My italics. The distinction between 'subsisting in' and the hitherto more customary 'being identified with' should be noted.
[7] ibid. II, 10.   [8] ibid., para. 12.
[9] The hierarchical structure of the Church is intended for 'the constant growth of the people of God' (III: 18); and the function of the authority of Pope, bishops and priests is to embody the Church by serving it (III. 20). See Yves Congar, *Lay People in the Church* (new ed., 1965), p. 26.

ceded,[1] it follows that the Constitution *Lumen Gentium* should set its face against the juridical imposition of authority by re-emphasizing the principle that he who is the chief should become as the servant.[2] The Church does not cease to be a family in the sense of its action upon us at particular times and seasons, but the metaphor must give place to another as we try to grasp what is implied by its being 'in Christ like a sacrament'.[3] Newman's description of it as an equilibrium of functions to which we respond as a whole is very much closer to the kind of description given, particularly in the fourth chapter which is devoted specifically to the Laity. Here the laity are spoken of as partaking in the three offices of Christ as Priest, Prophet, and King; and the metaphor which now suggests itself is of the Church as a magnetic field of force, structured by the hierarchy, to which the terms bishop, priest, and layman apply as definitions of dynamic functions that are meaningful only in relation to the field as a whole: 'the very distinction . . . involves a connection, since pastors and the rest of the faithful are bound together by their common obligation'.[4] And this paragraph of the Constitution concludes with these words of St. Augustine on the bishop's authority: 'What I am for you terrifies me; what I am with you consoles me. For you I am a bishop; but with you I am a Christian. The former is a duty [the Latin reads *nomen officii*]; the latter a grace. The former is a danger; the latter, salvation.'

The layman's function is positively defined in terms of his calling to 'make the Church present and operative in those places and circumstances where only through them [the laity] can it become the salt of the earth'.[5] This function is to work from within the world 'as a leaven'[6]; but the layman has also to bring his experience to bear upon the Church, even to the extent of being sometimes '*obliged* to express their opinion on those things that concern the good of the Church'.[7] Here is that double function of the laity with which we have become familiar in Coleridge and Maurice; and the Constitution speaks of the need of the laity to 'learn how to distinguish' between these functions, and to reconcile them.

This interpretation is confirmed by the Constitution on the

[1] *Gaudium et Spes* (The Church in the Modern World), para. 16, in *Documents of Vatican II* (1966), p. 213.
[2] *Lumen Gentium*, para. 27.   [3] *Lumen Gentium*, Intro., para. 1.
[4] ibid., IV:32.   [5] ibid., para. 33.   [6] ibid., para. 31.
[7] ibid., para. 36 (my italics).

Church in the Modern World. Although it repeats the Apostle's warning that we must not be conformed to this world,[1] and continually affirms that the Church cannot be committed to specific social and political systems,[2] it speaks of the Christian as exercising a joint membership of the heavenly and earthly cities, and warns against a false opposition between secular work and religious life.[3] This it does under the general heading—'The Church and the World as mutually related'. The use of this term 'mutuality' to describe the relationship of the Church to the world (it is repeated in para. 76) is especially significant; and it has rightly been interpreted as marking a change in the attitude of the Church from that which the Ultramontanes came to adopt during and after the First Vatican Council. It brings us very close to the position of Coleridge and Maurice—that we meet the sacramental presence of Christ in that overlap between Church and World, or as the Church is embodied in a Christian people or nation. In this sense we can indeed see the Church as the 'be-friending opposite' of the world, and the laity as exercising the double functions of the clerisy; and —up to a certain point—the writings of Coleridge and Maurice give us a more developed understanding of what the Catholic Church will look like in itself and in relation to the world if, as I have argued, Newman's account of it is accepted as being that which the documents of Vatican II advocate.

This, the second type of relationship of the Church to society, is of course as old as the alleged Donation of Constantine: directly the practice of the Christian faith becomes socially acceptable or even desirable, then the Church appears committed to its social embodiment; and the Oxford Movement is one of many reactions through the Church's history which have been provoked by a desire to preserve its sacramental integrity. What separates Newman, not only from Coleridge and Maurice, but from his membership of the Church of England is the degree of importance he attaches to the dangers arising from a Church which is too much committed to society. This recurring danger is one of category confusion in which the immanence of the Church is over-stressed, and its transcendence so much obscured that it loses its essential self-determining power of development.

The action of Christ sacramentally through the Church is to

---

[1] *Gaudium et Spes*, para. 37.   [2] ibid., para. 42.
[3] ibid., para. 43.

deepen or, more exactly, to sanctify persons; and the Church's ultimate function is not to reform society but to redeem humanity —a function which is not irrelevant to social reform, but passes beyond it. It follows that much Christian discipline and terminology which is primarily for the formation of the Christian person is not directly applicable to social and political behaviour. Prayer, patience, obedience, and mortification have a social and political value, but they supplement, they do not replace expert knowledge or professional judgement: they are the performative utterances of the Pilgrim; they are undertaken in faith and satisfactorily understood only at the end of the Pilgrimage.

They point to a crucial distinction—that between acting from conscience, and from a calculation of the consequences. This—the choice between God's side and man's—is always obscured, the more certain Christians become of their position in society, since they may then seek to enforce a 'Christian' political ideology as a substitute for that more exacting discipline of the spirit which the depths and developing nature of Revelation require. This is what informs Coleridge's vision of the conflict between an older England and the new.[1] It is what Newman feared when he spoke of the nation's dragging down the Church to its own level.[2] It was the source of his objection to Kingsley's muscular Christianity, as it was of Maurice's collision with Ludlow over the future of the Christian Co-operatives. In a letter to Canon Longman, 28 May 1878, Newman is quite specific. He speaks of a movement which by 'assigning political or civil motives for social and personal duties' was withdrawing 'matters of conduct from the jurisdiction of religion'; and he goes on to speak of this general tendency as a form 'of what really is the Pelagian heresy'.[3] This is why, in his correspondence with Allies, he is sceptical about the claims of medieval society. What evidence, he asks, is there that more souls were saved 'under the Christian Theocracy than under the Roman Emperors, or under the English Georges?'[4] And he concludes: 'If not, cui bono the medieval system?'

Newman goes on to argue that a people 'will develop its faith in

---

[1] See above, chapter 3, pp. 42 f.   [2] See above, chapter 8, pp. 141 f.

[3] In T. Kenny, *The Political Thought of John Henry Newman* (1957), pp. 172–3. This was also the theme of Newman's Biglietto speech in Rome when he received his Cardinal's hat. See above, chapter 8 (ii), esp. p. 142 and note.

[4] Allies, op. cit., p. 113.

a corresponding state polity. This is the high sense of the word "nation", including both the *matter* and the *form* of a people.' Thus a Catholic nation establishes Catholicism, '*as a matter of course* . . . because it is a Catholic nation'. This is a spontaneous act of the people, not of the Church, whose relationship to such an establishment is 'but an accident'[1]; and it is this insight which Coleridge has but does not develop when, in *Church and State*, he speaks of the relation of the Church of Christ to the national Church and culture as being that of a 'blessed accident'.

This confusion of categories occurs whenever it is asserted that the Church depends upon some specific social order—whether of the Right, as in 'L'Action Française', or of the Left. It is to be found, as Newman himself pointed out, in the arguments for retaining the Pope's Temporal Power; but it is also to be found in theories of culture in which theological and sociological categories have become with the passage of time unconsciously assimilated.

Matthew Arnold, for example, claimed Newman as his authority for deducing the necessity for a cultural élite from the biblical text many are called, few chosen.[2] This is a particularly gross confusion of categories, in which the elect is permanently identified with a particular order or social class: many may be called, but it is God and not ourselves who chooses them. Coleridge and Maurice also fail to distinguish the Church from its embodiment in the nation to the extent of expecting it inevitably to reflect the existing class structure of Victorian England. The Church is served by being led —and by that class which has been educated to lead the nation. Maurice speaks of his 'horror of democracy', and writes: 'I must have Monarchy, Aristocracy, and Socialism, or rather Humanity, recognised as necessary elements and conditions of an organic Christian society.'[3]

Conversely, to decide that society must be *served*, or that conditions must be brought about which will render it *organic*, has its roots in the theological judgement that we live most fully when we are members one of another and exist in a relation of mutual service. The conception of the 'organic society' is one of the chief examples of this assimilation of theological and sociological categories. It is usually a generation or two back, and may correspond

[1] Allies, pp. 132–3.
[2] See De Laura, 'Matthew Arnold and John Henry Newman', in *Studies in Literature and Language* (Texas, 1965), p. 591.   [3] *Life* ii, pp. 131, 497.

to the world of lost innocence; but the Marxist conceives it apo-
calyptically as belonging to the future and to the withering away of
liberal institutions. In each case what determines the placing are
half-suppressed religious or metaphysical presuppositions; and
when terms like 'élite', 'service', and 'family membership' are
used unconsciously in overlapping language games, then they are
ripe for what Coleridge calls de-synonymization.[1] For the Christian, their origin in religious metaphor should oblige him to treat
them dynamically; and the history of his failure to do so is the
history of fanaticism—this 'final assimilation' of religious to social
forms has ranged from the Crusades, through the *politique* of the
Renascence papacy to muscular Christianity. It now applies to
Catholic anti-Communism.

The dialectic of Church and World, of social and theological
categories sets a limit to such aspirations and natural tendencies to
force the success of 'Christian' policies. In his collision with the
muscular Christians Newman noted their failure to allow for the
action of Grace which led them to 'do good that good might come,
that is, to act *in order* to their success, and not from a motive of
faith'.[2] Elsewhere he had referred to this as the sin of Balaam,
who ceased to be content to ascertain God's will, and attempted to
change it.[3] If we act from motives other than conscience or the
love of God, then, as Christians, we act from motives which are
defective, 'because they admit of being subjected to certain other
ultimate ends which are not religious'. And it is in this sense that
we can become too much attached 'to the world'.

Although it may be true that the Church contemplates 'not a
nation, but the men who form it; not society in the first place, but
in the second place',[4] does it follow that the Church can be
meaningfully defined in isolation from its social context? The
mistake has been to press the distinction, and to over-emphasize
the excluding character of its familial images. Not only F. D.
Maurice but Pope John saw that a personal relationship is also a
social responsibility; and the idea of the Church as the interaction
of the three offices of Christ can be fulfilled only when the Church

---

[1] See above, chapter 2, p. 17. Raymond Williams, in *Culture and Society* (1961),
pp. 253 f., 312 f., discusses the social and political consequences of allowing such
concepts to become hypostatized. See also his discussion of individualism in
The Long Revolution (1965), pp. 89–119.
[2] *Apo*, p. 386. See also *Diff*. i, p. 207, and chapter 8 (ii) above.
[3] *P.S.* (2 April 1837), IV, pp. 28–30.   [4] *Diff*. i, p. 207.

overlaps with the world, and there is a mutual interaction. To deny this is to deny the function of the laity to act not only as the leaven of the world, but as one of the agents of the development of the Church. Yet the laity are not the regulating principle of the Church, as Maurice, for example, seemed to suppose: what they are is the essential context of its regulation by theology. But the debate about the laity within the Roman Catholic Church is crucial for the development of a meaningful theology; since, in order to develop and to fulfil its role of Pilgrim, the Church must be able to recognize itself in society:

> Since the Church has a visible and social structure as a sign of her unity in Christ, she can and ought to be enriched by the development of human social life. The reason is not that the constitution given her by Christ is defective, but so that she may understand it more penetratingly, express it better, and adjust it more successfully to our times.[1]

To see the Church and the world in a dichotomous relationship is, therefore, mistaken; but there may well be phases of discontinuity.[2] The task of so relating the religious and social areas of our experience is an agonizing, dimly perceived, gradual process: it is like trying to make sense of the 'blips' on a radar screen; and we may prefer the illusory comforts of static slogans to this dialectic of life and growth. Yet to suppose that the relations of Church and World could be reduced to simple, clear, and direct causal sequences is to degrade a mystery into a problem. It was the mistake of the Ultramontanes and of the Neo-Scholastic social theologians; it was not Newman's.

Newman did not make this mistake, because he believed that to establish the Church socially was one thing, to verify it was another. In his correspondence with Allies already cited he touches directly on Maurice's argument that it was part of the Divine scheme that Christianity should subdue, first the individual, then the family, then the framework of society and so forth; but why, he asks, 'was the subjection of Literature and Science omitted in the progressive series of triumphs?' If Christianity fails to convince mankind that it is true, what is gained by showing that it works? 'If, then, Christianity has not compelled the *intellect* of the world, viewed in

---

[1] *Gaudium et Spes*, para. 44, p. 246. See also A. von Geusau in *The Committed Church*, ed. L. Bright and S. Clements (1966), p. 308.
[2] See *Diff.* ii, p. 204; see above, chapter 9, p. 152.

the mass, to confess Christ, why insist as a great gain on its having compelled the *social* framework of the world to confess Him?'

Again, Newman is arguing specifically against the claim that the Church fulfils its function by committing itself and its members to particular social and political forms; but his argument reaches into our own dilemmas: 'A medieval system now would but foster the worst hypocrisy,—not because this age is worse than that, but because imagination acts more powerfully upon barbarians, and reason on traders, savants, and newspaper readers.'[1]

We are back at the divergence between Newman and the Anglican tradition as represented by Maurice: the essential question posed by Christian Revelation is—how are we certain that it is true?

Newman's concern with verification caused him to adopt a new kind of relationship between Church and World which although not superseding either the first kind of relationship in which the family judges the world, or the second kind in which the family commits itself to leavening the world, requires a new degree of mutual autonomy. To compare Newman's position in the *Apologia* with that which he subsequently came to adopt in the *Letter to the Duke of Norfolk* is to see that his attitude to the emerging secular and open society underwent a considerable change. From disapproving condemnations of national apostasy Newman develops to a positive acceptance of a non-ideological, pluralist and open society.[2]

In doing so, Newman anticipates the main findings of the Second Vatican Council. These are that what verifies is Christ (not the Church as a purely social presence); and Christ 'vivifies'[3] the Church to the extent that it lives sacramentally—that is, as a personal unity or equilibrium, whose regulating factor is the action of the Spirit as it is made manifest through the Church's continuing attempt at explication. Newman did not regard this theological activity as being primarily directed at providing conclusive verifying arguments. Its purpose was, by correcting popular

---

[1] Allies, op. cit., pp. 113–14.
[2] cp. *Apo*, pp. 499–501, with J. Derek Holmes's discussion of Newman's refusal to condemn Bradlaugh's wish to affirm his allegiance on taking his seat in Parliament. Newman considered the Affirmation Bill to 'involve no religious principle'; and he refused to be drawn into the controversy. (*Historical Magazine*, March 1967, vol. 36, pp. 87–97).
[3] *Lumen Gentium* I:8.

superstitions and narrow ecclesiastical views,[1] to enable the Church effectively to address itself to persons as persons, and thereby to provide the means by which Christ verifies himself in us. For him, the Church is 'a sign and a safeguard of the transcendence of the human person'[2]; and his whole conception of the priestly function could not be more effectively summarized than it is in the words of the second chapter of the *Decree on the Ministry and Life of Priests* —that priests 'must treat all with outstanding humanity' by helping men to see 'what is God's will in the great and *small* events of life' (my italics), since it is only by this attention to personal detail that 'care of the faithful as individuals' can be 'properly extended to the formation of a genuine Christian community'.[3]

For Newman, therefore, the chief function of the regulative or purgative role of theology is to recall the Church to its sacramental function of embodying the personal presence of Christ; and his work can be seen as a reclamation of a personal, indwelling faith from sterile formalities and political conceptions. And in his opposition to the 'substitution of something human for the Divine', Newman shares in Maurice's protest against what the latter felt to be the chief heresy of the age—the setting up of 'religion against God'.[4] Newman is firmly at one with Coleridge and Maurice in seeing the relationship of the Church to society as pre-eminently one of fostering personal freedom, personal relations, and personal growth; and the stand which he took so notably in the matter, especially in the *Apologia*, accounts for something of the growing respect, even affection, he received from many who differed radically from him in matters of doctrine.

To this extent Newman was expressing within the Church of his adoption something of the English tradition—as Pusey foretold he would. As we have seen this witness was not wholly welcome at the time; but the Documents of the Second Vatican Council show how thoroughly what Newman stood for has permeated the theological thinking of contemporary Roman Catholicism. In summing up his impressions of the Second Vatican Council, Bishop B. C. Butler said that if oecumenical councils were to be given mottoes, then it is Newman's *cor ad cor loquitur* which he would choose; and

---

[1] Letter of Newman to Miss Froude, 28 July 1875 (*W.* ii, pp. 563–4).
[2] *Gaudium et Spes*, para. 76 (p. 288).
[3] *Presbyterorum Ordinis*, para. 6 (II) in *Documents of Vatican II*.
[4] *Life* i, p. 518.

he would apply it not merely to the dialogue between God speaking to his faithful servant, but to 'the heart of God to the heart of his Church; the heart of the Church to the heart of her God, and therefore to the hearts of all men of good will'.[1] The Council documents I have cited certainly confirm Newman's emphasis that the Church's function is, 'in the first place', to form and deepen persons; and we have seen to what extent Newman had to fight for this priority. He was not encouraged to develop the implications. The testimony afforded by Coleridge and Maurice, however, shows us in what manner persons so formed will bear upon their society; through them the Church works to *humanize* existing social, political, and industrial institutions. As Coleridge remarked, not even terrestrial charts can be accurately constructed without celestial observations [2]; and Maurice speaks of theology— or the truths about God—as essential for elucidating our social and political purposes.[3] Persons formed by the practice of a sacramental religion combined with the habit of theological reflection will tend to see things whole and in terms of their ultimate purposes; they will be less inclined to adopt short-term expedients or what Newman calls 'views'. The implication of Newman's argument about education, as well as Coleridge's, is that the religious man will tend to seek for the strong point or unifying principle not only in arguments, but also in the institutions by which he is formed, and which he develops.

It is hard, therefore, to restrict a concern for verification to the personal role of the Church: is not its social and political function somehow a correlative? It is often stated that Newman's attitude to such a question was unhelpfully negative; and it is true that in a private letter to Charles Marson, Newman admitted that 'he had never considered social questions in relation to faith'.[4] But Newman's caution had a deeper root than the indifference of one who was preoccupied with other matters. He was, as his treatment of Kingsley makes manifest, much more concerned to protect religion from a species of Pelagian exploitation in the interest of a particular social or political policy. To speak of a motive as being specifically religious is to direct our attention to purity of means, to recognizing

---

[1] B. C. Butler, 'Newman and the Second Vatican Council' in *Rediscovery of Newman*, p. 246.
[2] *C & S*, p. 52. [3] *Life* i, p. 373.
[4] In C. Marson, *God's Co-operative Society* (1914), p. 71.

the limits of our actions, and towards accepting the intervention of a power other than ourselves and our initiatives. When Christian life or the integrity of the Church is threatened Newman was clear that the Church had a political obligation—and said so [1]; but what should be the Church's function in a society, nominally Christian, officially tolerant, but facing rapid economic and industrial change?

Newman was prevented from dealing directly with this question; Maurice was not. He held that personal deepening was meaningless unless it affected the family and through the family the general structure of society. The break down of the social order by commercial and industrial exploitation, Maurice held to produce a false individualism, the antidote to which was for the Church to encourage those forces in society which would—to use Maurice's term—'socialise' the relationships of individuals thus condemned to unnatural degrees of alienation from each other and from their rightful social and political responsibilities. Kinship, togetherness, community, fraternity, a sense of belonging, roots—these are terms for that sense of being members one of another which itself leads a man to understand that ultimate dependence and relationship which is the presence of God to the believer. For Maurice to divide the person from his society was not only unreal but anti-Christian; and he is important for showing how a personal religion is what we achieve, not what we start from. To begin in our duty to our neighbour is what Maurice means by 'socialism'. That is not so very different from von Hügel's use of 'personalism'; and it is von Hügel who can help us to understand to what extent Newman, less directly and from a different starting-point, had reached Maurice's position.

In a sermon already referred to, [2] Newman speaks of our being embodied Christians first, and persons only as a result of that successful embodiment; and when von Hügel speaks of Newman as having taught him to glory in his 'appurtenance to the Catholic and Roman Church'[3] he is speaking of the Church as the social

[1] In the correspondence with Marson already cited, Newman quotes from *Arians* II. iii, p. 257, in support of this contention.

[2] MS. Sermon 213. See above, chapter 5, pp. 65 f. 'The body is the first thing and each member in particular the second.'

cp. *Lumen Gentium*, para. 9: 'It has pleased God to sanctify and save men, *not singly and without any mutual connexion*, but by constituting them as a people which should acknowledge him in truth and serve him with holiness' (my italics).

[3] *The Mystical Element of Religion* i, p. xxxi.

instrument which redeems us from a barren individualism. 'A human person,' he writes, 'begins more as a possibility than a reality.' He distinguishes the popular conception of a jealous God who demands to be loved alone from that of a God who is placed 'not alongside of creatures, but behind them, as the light which shines through a crystal and lends it whatever lustre it may have. He is loved here, not apart from, but through and in them.' And when the mystic speaks of the Bride of Christ, this 'never is, nor can be' any individual soul, but only the complete organism of all faithful souls, so that part of the condition of a healthy contemplative life is for the individual to practise 'the outgoing movement towards Multiplicity and Contingency', which involves our participation in 'the great sacred organisms of the Family, Society, and the Church'.[1]

This is the tradition which the documents of Vatican II have tried to re-express within the Church. The pastoral constitution on the *Church in the Modern World* speaks of the advance of the human person and of his society as 'hinging upon each other'; but what is most remarkable is its use of the term 'socialisation' to define this mutual relationship; and this term which appeared originally in Pope John's *Mater and Magistra* is twice repeated.[2]

Maurice called such kinship or 'socialisation', in the form of what was then thought to be its maximum feasible extent, a *nation*. Today, we have not only moved away from regarding the nation-state as an irreducible political entity, but the nation (to the extent that it is still a nation) has separated from the Church. Ought Christians to feel obliged to resuscitate the relationship, at least in terms of a Christian political ideology? Maurice's answer was to found the Christian Socialist Movement; yet, as we have seen, within a few years he had split it on the issue whether the Co-operative Societies which had been established should demand from their members a specifically Christian allegiance. Ludlow thought they should; Maurice, whose instincts in this matter would have been Newman's, thought not. What was at issue was the autonomy of secular activity; and in the end, because they were theologians, Maurice and Newman were on the same side.

Newman did not deny that a proper understanding of Christian theology should predispose us to accept certain social and political

[1] ibid., ii, pp. 353, 356, 365.
[2] *Gaudium et Spes*, paras. 25 (p. 224) and 75 (p. 286).

I

arguments and to reject others; and he certainly held that when Christians pursue illiberal and corrupting policies, this may well be a sign of their defective grasp of theological principles. He ascribed the idle, unemployed life of the young citizens of the Papal States, for example, to clerical rule and to the theological principles which were thought to require it.[1] But the source of Newman's restraint in his dealing with questions of the relation of Church to society is his acceptance—to a more marked degree than most of his fellow Catholics—of the evolving open and pluralistic society. As far back as 1833 we find him writing: 'I am become neither Whig nor Tory. In proportion as a Government disconnects itself with the Church, so does it cease to be the duty of a Churchman to be a Politician. . . .'[2]

Why Newman could contemplate the falling off of the nation from the Church with greater equanimity than his fellow Catholics —Roman or Tractarian—was because he rejected all ideological or 'divine interpretations'[3] of society. To say, therefore, that Christians were committed by their theological principles to bringing about a particular political structure or ideology was, for Newman, based upon a mistake about how we come to have knowledge of the world. It was in other words a category confusion. A distinction had to be made between what we had to grasp as a whole and with a full personal assent—the certain knowledge of God as mediated through the conscience—and what we could only grasp step by step—the probable deductions from our experience of the external world. This is Newman's distinction between real and notional assent; but it is also his distinction between theological knowledge and the autonomous knowledge of each particular science or mental discipline. The relationship between the sciences or between them all and theology is on the principle of 'live and let live'. Lines seemingly parallel may converge, but at leisure; comparisons and adjustments may be attempted and succeed, but not fusion; and although the ultimate principle is that truth cannot contradict truth, the only working principles that can be tolerated are those which arise from the desire to define relationships rather than to assimilate them: the philosophy of an imperial intellect is based,

[1] W. i, p. 604. 'Fancy the state of Birmingham if the rising generation had nothing to do but to lounge in the streets and throng the theatre.'
[2] Letter to W. Trower (16 April 1833) in R. D. Middleton, *Newman and Bloxam* (Oxford, 1947), p. 24.
[3] *Apo*, p. 128.

not on simplification, but on discrimination.[1] In the words of the poet, Robert Frost, 'Good fences make good neighbours'. Like the university the Church unifies, not theories about society, but persons. By explaining man to himself, the Church prevents him from succumbing to the expansionist tendencies of his specialism. He suffers personal and moral checks, and is likely to develop theological checks whenever the current accounts of his science seem to be attempting a total description of man. In Newman's time this was evidenced in the extension of the arguments about Evolution. The Christian who is a specialist ought to be able to specialize without fearing for the loss of his humanity; on the other hand tension and apparent contradiction between his specialism and his humanity are inevitable and must be borne. In a modern society the Church fulfils its family function in the manner of a college rather than of a patriarch; it constitutes itself the association of diverse persons who, formed as they are by their specialized undertakings and understandings, are unified by their common practice of the sacramental life. The specialist need lose neither his humanity nor his sense of social unity, provided he is willing to accept his state as that of being a member of 'divided and distinguished worlds', or more exactly of simultaneously distinct linguistic communities.

Although it is the same spirit which informs 'each variety of working',[2] it is a sectarian error to concentrate exclusively on one pole of the dialectic between unity and multiplicity. It is necessary to conceive theology and politics, for example, as autonomous and distinct universes of discourse; but it is also necessary to set this against the extent to which the meaning of a term in one context or language game depends for its sense upon how it is used in other contexts.[3] The highly abstract disjunction between Nature and Grace which informed the opposition to Newman's idea of a university is a prime example of what happens when Coleridge's

---

[1] For the details of this argument see above, chapter 6, pp. 87 f., and 93; and *Idea*, pp. 460–1.

[2] 1 Cor. 12.

[3] See Wittgenstein, *Remarks on the Foundation of Mathematics* (1956), IV, 2, p. 133: 'It is the use outside mathematics, and so the *meaning* of the signs, that makes the sign-game into mathematics.' See also its discussion by Peter Winch, 'Understanding a Primitive Society', in *American Philosophical Quarterly*, 1964, vol. 1, p. 321.

warning is ignored,[1] and theological definitions are held to be self-validating and unconditioned by their origins in a particular cultural situation. Far from freeing us from our culture, Newman's idea of the Church and the sacramental principle on which it rests oblige us to realize its disclosures and ascertain the meaning of its metaphorical and symbolic language by testing their fit with similar insights in such overlapping disciplines as philosophy, literature, and politics.

What we are freed from is the imperial fallacy that there is a once-for-all interpretation, a definitive ideology, a Queen of the sciences—and that theology or Marxism is its Queen; since the principle implies that both religious and social structures are but 'economies'[2] or paraphrases—they conceal while they suggest the living truth[3]—and while the function of the State is immediate and short-term, that of the Church is to provoke those 'further and deeper disclosures, of truths still under the veil of the letter, and in their season to be revealed'.[4]

Nor does a sacramental conception of the Church free us from an obligation to have opinions[5] or to be committed to programmes, since the performative nature of the response which it enjoins positively requires us to risk complicating our notions in action. This is what the Christian Socialists so rightly affirmed: it is not enough for us to criticize the world, we must change it; since to apply a Christian principle is a function of its understanding.

With this proviso, the principle stands that each discipline is a language with an appropriate range; but the extent of its legitimate application can be settled only by argument, collision, and experiment—as in a university, where a discipline exists on the university's terms and not its own. And it is in Newman's idea of a university

[1] 'What is Christianity at any one period? The Ideal of the human Soul at that period.' See above, chapter 3, p. 47.
[2] *Apo*, p. 128.
[3] See above, chapter 8, p. 146 and note.
[4] *Apo*, p. 128. Cp. Coleridge's remark that the purpose of the Church is 'another world, not a world to come exclusively, but likewise another world that now is' (*C & S*, p. 127. See above, chapter 3, p. 44).
[5] In a passage already referred to above in chapter 8, p. 146, but suppressed in the published version of the *Apologia*, Newman writes: 'and as certitudes about particular objects might be the duty of particular individuals, so also the particular opinions might be their duty also. This is the doctrine which in one shape or other lies at the bottom of most of my University sermons, of my Essay on Ecclesiastical Miracles, and of my Essay on Development of Doctrine' (*Apologia*, Oxford, 1967, p. 499).

that we shall find the model of his idea of the Church in relation to society: it too exists on society's terms and not its own, provided society conforms to the model of a university and remains tolerant and open. In such a condition, to paraphrase Newman's argument,[1] social science can be practised without 'bringing in Providence' or 'docete gentes'. Although the insights and proposals of social scientists, politicians or industrialists might seem to conflict with the truths necessary for salvation, ultimately, since truth cannot contradict truth, they will be shown to be mutually compatible— always provided that the argument can be kept open.

What Newman most feared in the new society he saw to be inevitable was not the defeat of religion in open dialogue, but the closing up of the dialogue in the supposed interests of social and intellectual progress. He feared that theology would be banished from the university because it was not a true knowledge but a form of intellectual perversion, turning 'the intellect away from what it can know, and [occupying] it in what it cannot'. The 'marvellous results' of science could lead to an all absorbing interest; and both mind and imagination could thus be indisposed to take theological studies seriously.[2] This point is developed in a sermon preached in 1873. The challenge presented is based on the assumption that faith is an intellectual mistake, since an absolute assent is rationally impossible. What was unique in the new society was a condition which Christianity had so far never experienced—'a world simply irreligious'.[3] In other words, what Newman feared about the new society was not its religious neutrality, but its acceptance of the Benthamite claim that religious discourse was meaningless, and that theological study was worse than a waste of time—it was positively harmful.

Both he and Matthew Arnold characterized this changed position as that of a Night Battle where 'friend and foe stand together'.[4] Its controversies being, as Newman remarks, of a verbal nature are, however, resolvable; but the Church would have to show, firstly, that its claim was true, and only secondly that it was socially viable. Yet, as has already been emphasized, this is a distinction between categories, not a dichotomy: it must be observed,

---

[1] See above, chapter 9, p. 159.
[2] *Idea*: 'A Form of Infidelity of the Day', pp. 389, 400, 403.
[3] *The Catholic Sermons of Cardinal Newman* (first pub. 1957), pp. 122-3.
[4] *O.U.S.*, pp. 200-1.

but not (as Coleridge warns) 'pressed onward into all its possible logical consequences'.[1]

Newman's preference for the neutral, open society was for the extent to which it left the Church free; since without a residual power of self-determination the Church (so he believed) could not achieve that equilibrium of functions on which its capacity depended to be the means, sacramentally, of verification. Too high a degree of commitment to an existing social order was as limiting as too clerical or familial a simplification of the autonomous nature of that relationship. Newman, Maurice, and Coleridge did not differ in their view of what the Church should be, so much as on the means by which it should be regulated to perform its sacramental function of showing Christ to the world. But such differences were then felt to be so irreconcileable as to justify a denominational position.

Although Newman had to work out his account of the Church before he could be sure of the manner of its relation to society, what I have tried to show is the extent to which he, Maurice, and Coleridge were members of a common tradition which, in some respects, was stronger than the grounds of their denominational difference. We are even more aware than they of the extent to which the Churches and their language of explanation are already and inevitably conditioned, even determined, by a prior cultural and social embodiment. Church and society have always met in the overlap of each other, even when they have failed to recognize the overlap for what it is. A qualitative change is introduced in the basis of denominational difference, however, when Christians agree to speak of the Church as the whole people of God; since to accept the laity as fully contributing to each of the three offices of the Church is for each denomination to accept an element already common to them all. This is to do more than to accept the context (the laity) to bear inductively upon the Churches' explanation of themselves, or to accept the criteria of the open society, it is to accept the seed of an inevitable unity. It is also to accept the implication that theology cannot function as an end in itself: it must become contextually significant. And it is for his unwavering testimony to this claim that Maurice is essential for this study.

In an age in which each denomination saw itself as essentially a professional body in an impassive context, Maurice stands out as a

[1] *AR*, p. 108.

pioneer of better times. A Church thus out of context, whose investigations and pronouncements are internal to itself is, in Wittgenstein's sense, 'like an engine idling'; its language becomes similarly ineffective and unreal; and its profession degenerates into a theological language-game which appears to be confined to the propounding of significant tautologies.[1] Propositions that 'we are saved by faith alone' or that 'England is the dowry of Mary' are not exempt from the requirement that meaning is a function of use, and that a language presupposes a community in which it lives and is developed. To the excesses of Marian devotion may be added the contemporary pre-occupations with the purely physical phenomena of mysticism—with inedia, levitation, stigmata, and other psychosomatic conditions. Von Hügel wrote *The Mystical Element of Religion* in order to show to what extent the mysticism of the saints presupposed an ecclesial tradition and institutional framework. And it is significant that it was for this purpose that he proposed his theory of the three elements of religion, making use as he did of Newman's account of the Church in terms of the three offices of Christ.

The method by which the *Syllabus of Errors* was compiled—a stringing together of passages divorced from their contexts—the confusions over what Modernism amounted to, and the invention of the heresy known as Americanism are further indications of a theology which has ceased to be healthily adverbial or adjectival. But, as Maurice was almost alone in pointing out, this was a disease which the Churches had in common: a theology which fails to structure and qualify the insights of the whole people of God as they work out their pilgrimage in terms of their daily occupations is unlikely to be able to cope either with Kingsley's muscular Christianity or with Maurras's Fascism. Seen in this perspective, the silence of the Catholic Church before the Nazis was inevitable.

Once theology is accepted as the regulating principle, not only of the Church's internal equilibrium but of its relation to society, and the laity are accepted as contributing both to the context and to the activity, then theology can no longer be undertaken as the language game of an enclosed professional order within the

---

[1] When Dickens was in Rome he noticed that those who succeeded in climbing the Scala Sancta on their knees gave the impression 'of having done a real good substantial deed which it would take a good deal of sin to counter-balance'. *Pictures from Italy* (Oxford, 1901–2), p. 158.

Church. And this is what it means to say that it must become con-textually significant. But there is more to such a claim than the obvious implication that theologians should invite questions from secular disciplines. The questions which secular disciplines ask of themselves may be of even greater importance for theology; and there are also those questions which they have tended to treat as closed to further opening. If the Church in its role as a Pilgrim 'pressing on' is under an obligation to develop its understanding of itself, who determines the agenda?

To take the obvious implication first. The traditional conception of Church authority based upon hierarchical imposition seems to have nothing in common with the secular notion of authority as a consensus which is elicited—as Newman discovered to his cost. The layman will ask to what extent an authority can be regarded as real if it is imposed without consultation; and he will wish to go further and ask (with Coleridge) whether we ought to accept an authority other than that which we impose upon ourselves. In Newman's time this gap between the two concepts of authority—ecclesial and secular—was painfully wide. It has since grown wider. Yet the problem goes deeper still. Newman could see that it was not for the Church to concede the autonomy of the secular, but to ask what this autonomy implied. The extent of the gap is shown by the different nature of the questions which each proposes to itself on the same issues.

In referring to the Church as a family, sheepfold, or ark, theo-logians speak, for example, as if the secular side of the analogy were plainly self-evident; but sociologists are by no means so certain about what is meant by family relationship or kinship. To talk of the local Church as a family and by this to imply an exclusive, face-to-face group is, therefore, to make a claim about what gives meaning to community relationships which is not self-evident.[1] And to go on to claim that whatever form the local church should take, its relation to the Church universal is mainly adminis-trative is already to have moved dangerously out of contextual significance. In a pluralist environment, in which one man plays many roles and belongs to inter-penetrating societies, to belong to the Church is not to belong to yet another club, it is to profess a

---

[1] Noel Timms, 'The Changing Family in Britain' in *The Committed Church*, pp. 91–114, esp. pp. 112–14.

common language—the Church is a society because it is a language.

An almost hypersensitivity to the dangers of dissociating these characteristics, assisted by Ludlow's expert diagnosis of the effects of social change, enabled Maurice to uncover what we now recognize to be the fundamental question—what is it to be a member of the Church? Is it, as he suggested, best defined in terms of what we affirm, or have we to include (as in the past) a requirement to agree on what we deny? Can theologians by themselves produce a definition of Church membership? To claim that theology must be contextually significant is to claim that such definitions must be worked out with sociologists and political thinkers. In such matters a Burke must sit down with an Aquinas; and a layman who, like Coleridge, was equally at home with Burke and Aquinas is an essential participant in such an investigation.

To say that the implication of Newman's idea of the Church is that theology ought to be contextually significant is another way of saying that the same questions ought to be asked by different people from within the standpoint of different disciplines: it is by means of the variety of the gifts that we understand the fullness of 'the same Spirit'.[1] But this is not to deny the right of initiation from within the Church to open up questions which a particular discipline prefers to keep closed. This was Coleridge's particular achievement when he attempted to show that the Benthamite conception of verification and meaningful language (with its implied dismissal of religious language as deception) was based upon a misconception of language which denied meaning to much of what we consider to be our greatest literature. Coleridge helps us to see what are the relevant questions for theology—what is it that validates or invalidates the language of ultimate concern? How do we know that there exists a reality to correspond? What are the conditions in which such language lives and is effective? Can all biblical metaphors and symbols be equally alive and available to successive generations?

It is the failure to see that this last question is one which has to be asked that may be detected behind such phrases as that God is dead or that England is the dowry of Mary—the terminology may have meaning only within a language which has itself been abstracted from a public language of a superseded secular culture.

[1] I Cor. 12:4.

A dowry belongs to a particular kind of marriage relationship no longer in general use; and a God that can die may be one we had expected to live in a somewhat naïvely direct and uncomplicated way. It is to Wordsworth's *Prelude* or Eliot's *Four Quartets* that the layman turns for an account of the God who lives to members of a modern society. And it is significant that when Newman is talking about what it means to be a person he frequently draws upon the language of Shakespeare, since, as he himself says, style is a thinking out into language, and literary achievement is the successful personal use of language.[1]

The relationship of the Church to society which can be elicited from Newman—in which each respects the autonomy of the other, yet requires the other for its mutual but autonomous development —has one further important consequence for the structure of the Church as we at present experience it. It requires an end to be brought to that division of the Church into two cultures—clerical and lay—with their separate systems of education and ways of life, since the consequences of this argument are that, once we speak of the Church as the people of God, we are presupposing a Church as wide as that of the open society and common culture which constitute its contemporary context. Only by itself becoming such 'an open public union' can the Church work for that unity which is ultimately the unity of all mankind: 'every kind of separateness' must be wiped out, we read in *Lumen Gentium*,[2] 'so that the whole human race may be brought into the unity of the family of God'.

It is therefore not a baseless vision to see that clergy and laity will have to pursue a common education for much longer than, in the past, was thought either necessary or desirable. And a convincing differentiation of function between them may well continue to elude us until such a common life and education are seen to be, ineluctably, the pre-condition. To realize the importance of the question—what ought *now* to be the form of Christian education in a common culture?—is also to realize that Newman's prescription in his Irish University Sermons is no mere piece of rhetoric. It is a precise definition of that education which, by enabling the Church to bear upon an open society, and the open society to bear upon the Church would end the threat of Romanism for good—and with it the principal objection to Newman's idea of the Church by the English tradition as represented by Coleridge and Maurice. To

[1] *Idea*, pp. 275–6.   [2] Para. 28.

produce intellectual laymen who are religious and devout ecclesiastics who are intellectual is indeed to destroy a diversity of centres and a contrariety of influences.[1] A common education such as Newman envisages is a seed; its growth is determined by many minds working openly together; and it is to the inheritors of such minds that the appropriate institutional forms will be revealed. These, while preserving our life-giving diversity, will make us one in Christ.

[1] *S.V.O.*, p. 13.

APPENDIX

'How much of Coleridge had Newman read?'

COLERIDGE'S works in the Library of Birmingham Oratory appear to have been annotated by Ambrose St. John and Joseph Bacchus. This and evidence such as that cited in chapter 2 above [1] indicate something of a Coleridgean tradition in Newman's Oratory.

Ward cites Newman's assertion in old age that he 'never read a line of Coleridge' [2] as an example of how in later years his memory became seriously at fault. Not only are there the references in Newman's early letters, [3] but in the *Apologia* Coleridge is commended for preparing the ground for the Oxford Movement. [4] Similar citations are both well distributed through Newman's working life and of a kind which only a thorough acquaintance with Coleridge's chief works could produce.

Newman's use of the *Treatise on Method* in preparing his discourses on university education has been discussed in chapter 2 (i) above [5]; and Coleridge is again specifically commended in the Appendix. [6]

In his second University Sermon, [7] Newman speaks of a 'remarkable passage' in the *Biographia Literaria* [8] as 'anticipating' his argument. Coleridge's point—that belief in God rests not upon an intellectual but a moral certainty—also anticipates the later argument from the illative sense in the *Grammar of Assent*. It is therefore significant that in the course of establishing this argument, Newman should quote [9] that maxim in *Aids to Reflection* [10] which speaks of there being 'something in the human mind which makes it know' that God exists.

Perhaps the most unexpected piece of evidence is the discovery among Newman's private papers of nine holograph letters from Coleridge to H. J. Rose. Known to the editor of the *Letters* only by transcripts in the possession of the Coleridge family, they cover the

[1] P. 33 and note.   [2] *W*. i, p. 58.
[3] *Moz.* ii, pp. 39, 54; 93, 156.
[4] *Apo*, p. 195 (first made in April 1839, *Essays* I, pp. 268–9).
[5] Pp. 23–5.   [6] *S & N*, p. 387.   [7] *O.U.S.*, p. 23.
[8] This, to vol. i, p. 199, must be to the first ed., 1817 (*BL*, p. 97).
[9] In *GA*, p. 231.
[10] Aphorism XII (*AR*, p. 54). A copy of the 1839 ed., bequeathed in the will of W. H. Scott is in that part of Newman's library he kept in his room. It is heavily scored, but probably by Scott.

years 1816–19,[1] and may have been bequeathed to Newman after Rose's death in December 1838. Coleridge's references to Rose show that he had 'a high opinion both of his Head and Heart', that he attended the Philosophical Lectures, and that they discussed philosophy, theology, the *Lay Sermons*, and the *Treatise on Method*. In one of the letters Coleridge remarks that 'a true system of Philosophy (= the Science of Life) is *best* taught in Poetry as well as most *safely*'.[2] He prepared a corrected edition of *The Friend* which he gave to Rose.[3]

Rose, who had a considerable correspondence with Newman, was regarded by Dean Burgon as the real founder of the Oxford Movement.

[1] *Collected Letters*, ed. E. L. Griggs (1959), vol. iv, nos. 1025, 1026, 1031, 1132, 1134–6, 1148. A letter dated 26 Jan. 1819—'to miss seeing you is at all times a disappointment'—remains unpublished.

[2] 28 Sept. 1816.

[3] The subject of an article in the *Times Lit. Supp.*, 14 June 1957.

BIBLIOGRAPHY

I MANUSCRIPT SOURCES

At Birmingham Oratory

1. Personal Collection. Newman's Correspondence on
   (a) *The Rambler* (1859) with
      (i) R. Simpson, Lord Acton, Archbishops Wiseman and Manning, Bishop Ullathorne (part at Downside);
      (ii) Dr. Gillow (part at Ushaw College, Durham).
   (b) the University question (1863–72) with Monsell, Spenser Northcote, Sir Justin Shiel, Lord Howard.
   (c) Church and State (1860–7) with T. W. Allies.
   (d) the oecumenical consequences of re-publishing his works (1868–70) with W. J. Copeland.
   (e) the Preface to the *Via Media* and its background (1874–80) with Lord Blachford, Lady Simeon, Dr. Jenkins, and Baron von Hügel.
2. MSS. Sermons, 121; 156; 157; 213. (A.50.2; A.17.1)
   MS. Lecture *On the Sacraments*. (A.50.3)

3. Preparatory work for 'Office and Work of Universities', including analysis of Coleridge's *Treatise on Method*. (D.5.15) 'On Necessary exceptions in fact to the Rule that Education must not be Mixed' (1867). (B.4.3)
4. Working papers and drafts, *Apologia*. (D.1.5; A.32.1)
5. Working papers and MS. of Preface (7 March 1877), *Via Media*. (D.5.8)
6. Letter on Matter and Spirit, 1 Sept. 1861. (A.46.3a) Discursive Exercises on Metaphysical Subjects. (D.E.M.S., Sundries, A.46.3)
7. Letter to Charles Meynell on Mansel's arguments (20 Dec. 1859). Letter from R. H. Hutton comparing Newman and Maurice (28 Feb. 1863).

At Pusey House, Oxford

Lectures on *Types and Prophecies* (1836), partly republished in *The Rediscovery of Newman* (q.v.)

At Downside Abbey

Letter written by R. Simpson for Montalambert's *Le Correspondant* but never published (c. April 1859).
Correspondence on the *Rambler* (1859) between Simpson, Acton, and Ullathorne.

II PRINTED SOURCES WITH MANUSCRIPT ANNOTATIONS

At Birmingham Oratory

Working copies of *Essay on Development*, London, 1845 (D.6.7), and *Scope and Nature of University Education*, Dublin, 1852 (A.16.5).
F. D. MAURICE, *Kingdom of Christ*, London, 1838, 3 vols.
GEORGE BERKELEY, *The Works*, 3 vols., London, 1820.
S. T. COLERIDGE, *Aids to Reflection*, London, 1839 (bequeathed by W. H. Scott)
— *Biographia Literaria*, 2 vols., London, 1847.
— *Church and State*, London, 1839 (inscribed 'Ambrose St. John, 1839').

At Pusey House, Oxford

R. W. Church's copy of F. D. Maurice, *Subscription No Bondage*, London, 1835.

At Downside Abbey

A. GASQUET, *Lord Acton and his Circle*, London, 1906. Copy annotated by Edmund Bishop in Bishop Library.

III PRINTED PRIMARY SOURCES

Part One: S. T. COLERIDGE

(a) IN WORKS, LETTERS, AND NOTEBOOKS

The Notebooks of Samuel Taylor Coleridge, ed. Kathleen Coburn, vols. 1,2,–, London, 1957–.

Unpublished Letters, ed. E. L. Griggs, 2 vols., London, 1932.

Collected Letters of Samuel Taylor Coleridge, ed. E. L. Griggs, 4 vols., 1785–1819, Oxford, 1956, in progress.

The Table Talk and Omniana of Samuel Taylor Coleridge, Oxford, 1917.

The Friend, a series of Essays (1809–10), London (Bohn), 1866.

Biographia Literaria (1817; second ed., 1847), London (Everyman), 1952.

Philosophical Lectures, 1818–1819, ed. Kathleen Coburn, London, 1949.

Coleridge's Treatise on Method as published in the Encyclopaedia Metropolitana (1818), ed. A. D. Snyder, London, 1934.

On the Constitution of the Church and State according to the Idea of each (1830); and *Lay Sermons* (1) *The Statesman's Manual* (1816), (2) '*Blessed are ye that sow beside all waters*' (1817), ed. H. N. Coleridge, London, 1839.

Aids to Reflection (1825) and *Confessions of an Inquiring Spirit* (1840), London (Bohn), 1904.

The Literary Remains of Samuel Taylor Coleridge, ed. H. N. Coleridge, 4 vols., London, 1836–9.

Coleridge on Logic and Learning, ed. A. D. Snyder, Yale U.P., 1929.

Inquiring Spirit, a new presentation of Coleridge from his published and unprinted prose works, ed. Kathleen Coburn, London, 1951.

Shakespearean Criticism, ed. T. M. Raysor, 2 vols., London (Everyman), 1960.

(b) IN RELATED WORKS

BOULGER, JAMES D. *Coleridge as Religious Thinker*, Yale U.P., 1961.

CHAMBERS, E. K. *Samuel Taylor Coleridge, a biographical study*, Oxford, 1950.

HORT, F. J. *Coleridge, an essay*, Cambridge Essays, 1856.

MILL, J. S. *Bentham and Coleridge* (1838; 1840), ed. F. R. Leavis, London, 1962.

MUIRHEAD, J. H. *Coleridge as Philosopher*, London, 1930.

WORDSWORTH, WILLIAM. *The Prelude*, London, 1850.
—'Letter to Mathetes' (in *The Friend*, Introduction to pt. III).
See IV (Wittgenstein).

Part Two: J. H. NEWMAN

(a) IN WORKS, LETTERS, AND JOURNALS

The Arians of the Fourth Century (1833), London, 1871.
Tracts for the Times, by Members of the University of Oxford, Nos.
1–90, 6 vols., Oxford, 1833–41.
Parochial and Plain Sermons, 8 vols. (1834–43; republished 1868),
London, 1877.
Lectures on the Doctrine of Justification (1838), London, 1890.
Sermons bearing on Subjects of the Day (1843), London, 1873.
Fifteen Sermons preached before the University of Oxford (1843), 1880.
An Essay on the Development of Christian Doctrine (1845), ed. C. F.
Harrold, New York, 1949.
Discourses addressed to Mixed Congregations (1849), London, 1876.
Certain Difficulties felt by Anglicans in Catholic Teaching, two volumes,
vol. 1, 1850; vol. 2 (including *Letter to the Duke of Norfolk*, 1875),
London, 1876.
Present Position of Catholics (1851), Dublin, 1857.
*Discourses on the Scope and Nature of University Education addressed to
the Catholics of Dublin*, Dublin, 1852.
Sermons preached on Various Occasions (1857), London, 1881.
On Consulting the Faithful in Matters of Doctrine (the texts of 1859 and
1871), ed. John Coulson, London, 1961.
Apologia pro Vita Sua (1864):
    (i) the two versions of 1864 and 1865, ed. Wilfrid Ward, Oxford,
        1913.
    (ii) (new ed.), with introduction and notes by M. J. Svaglic, Oxford,
        1967.
    (iii) (French edition), ed. M. Nédoncelle (q.v.), Paris, 1967.
Verses on Various Occasions (1868), London, 1903.
An Essay in aid of a Grammar of Assent (1870), ed. C. F. Harrold, New
York, 1947.
Two Essays on Biblical and on Ecclesiastical Miracles (1870), London,
1890.
Discussions and Arguments on Various Subjects, London 1872.
Essays Critical and Historical, two volumes (1871), London, 1890.
Historical Sketches, three volumes (1872), London, 1891; 1891; 1872.
The Idea of a University defined and illustrated (1873), London, 1925.
The Via Media of the Anglican Church (two volumes, 1877), London,
1895, 1901.

Stray Essays on Controversial Points (private), 1890.

My Campaign in Ireland, Part I (printed for private circulation only), 1896.

The Catholic Sermons of Cardinal Newman, published for the first time, ed. Birmingham Oratory, London, 1957.

John Henry Newman: Autobiographical Writings, ed. Henry Tristram, London, 1956.

Letters and Correspondence of John Henry Newman during his life in the English Church, ed. Anne Mozley, 2 vols., London, 1891.

Correspondence of John Henry Newman with John Keble and Others, 1839-45, ed. at the Birmingham Oratory, London, 1917.

The Letters and Diaries of John Henry Newman, ed., Charles Stephen Dessain of the Birmingham Oratory, vols. xi (Oct. 1845) ff.; London, 1961——, in progress.

WARD, WILFRID. *The Life of John Henry Cardinal Newman, based on his private journals and correspondence*, 2 vols., London, 1921.

(b) IN OTHER BIOGRAPHICAL AND RELATED SOURCES

ALLCHIN, A. M. see COULSON and ALLCHIN.

ALLIES, MARY, H. *Thomas William Allies*, London, 1907.

COULSON, JOHN. Introduction to J. H. Newman, *On Consulting the Faithful in Matters of Doctrine*, London, 1961

— and ALLCHIN, A. M. *Newman: A Portrait Restored*, London, 1965.

— — *The Rediscovery of Newman, An Oxford Symposium*, London, 1967.

CROSS, F. L. *John Henry Newman*, London, 1933.

CULLER, A. D. *The Imperial Intellect, A Study of Newman's Educational Ideal*, London, 1955.

DELAURA, DAVID J. *Matthew Arnold and John Henry Newman*, Studies in Literature and Language, Texas, 1965.

DESSAIN, C. S. *John Henry Newman*, London, 1966.

KENNY, TERENCE. *The Political Thought of John Henry Newman*, London, 1957.

MACDOUGALL, H. A. *The Acton-Newman Relations*, New York, Fordham, 1962.

MCGRATH, FERGAL. *Newman's University: Idea and Reality*, London, 1951.

MARSON, C. *God's Co-operative Society*, London, 1914.

MIDDLETON, R. D. *Newman and Bloxam*, Oxford, 1947.

(c) IN PERIODICALS

BLEHL, V. F. 'Newman's Delation—some hitherto unpublished letters', in *The Dublin Review*, 486 (winter 1960-1), 296-305.

CAPES, J. M. 'A Parallel and a Contrast', *The Gentleman's Magazine*, new series IX, 2 (1872), 33–44.

HOLMES, J. DEREK. 'Cardinal Newman and the Affirmation Bill', *Historical Magazine of the Protestant Episcopal Church*, New York, xxxvi, No. 1 (March 1967).

NEWMAN, J. H. 'Letter to J. S. Flanagan', *Journal of Theological Studies*, ix (1958), 324–35.

Rambler, The. XI (1859); I, New Series (1859).

(d) IN CRITICAL AND RELATED STUDIES

NÉDONCELLE, MAURICE. 'L'apologia de Newman dans l'histoire de l'autobiographie et de la théologie' in *Studies presented to Romano Guardini on his 80th birthday*, Echter-Verlag, Würzburg, n.d. See *Apologia*.

TREVOR, MERIOL. *Newman*, vol. i, *The Pillar of the Cloud*; vol. ii, *Light in Winter*, London, 1962. *See* IV (Acton, von Hügel).

Part Three: F. D. MAURICE

(a) IN WORKS AND LETTERS

Subscription No Bondage, or the Practical Advantages afforded by the Thirty-Nine Articles as Guides in all the Branches of Academical Education, by Rusticus, London, 1835.

The Kingdom of Christ: or Hints on the Principles, Ordinances, and Constitution of the Catholic Church in Letters to a Member of the Society of Friends, 3 vols., London, 1838.

The Kingdom of Christ, new edition based on the second edition of 1842, ed. Alec R. Vidler, 2 vols., London, 1958.

Has the Church, or the State, the Power to Educate the Nation (Lectures on National Education), London, 1839.

The Epistle to the Hebrews; being the substance of three Lectures, with a Preface containing a review of Mr. Newman's Theory of Development, London, 1846.

The Religions of the World (1846), London, 1877.

Sermons on the Prayer Book, and the Lord's Prayer (1848), London, 1893.

Dialogue between Somebody, a person of respectability, and Nobody, the writer (F. D. Maurice). Tracts on Christian Socialism, no. 1, London, 1850.

Theological Essays (1853), third edition, London, 1871.

Sermons on the Sabbath Day, London, 1853.

The Epistles of St. John, a series of Lectures on Christian Ethics (1857), London, 1881.

What is Revelation? A series of sermons on the Epiphany: to which are added letters to a student of theology on the Bampton Lectures of Mr. Mansel, London, 1859.
The Friendship of Books and other Lectures, London, 1874.
MAURICE, FREDERICK. *The Life of Frederick Denison Maurice, chiefly told in his own letters*, 2 vols., London, 1884.

(b) IN PERIODICALS

CAPES, J. M. 'A Parallel and a Contrast', *The Gentleman's Magazine*, new series IX, 2 (1872), 33–44.
MAURICE, F. D. 'Dr. Newman's *Grammar of Assent*—a review', *Contemporary Review*, xiv (1870), 151–72.

(c) IN RELATED WORKS

CHRISTENSEN, TORBEN. *Origin and History of Christian Socialism 1848–54*, Universitetsforlaget I Aarhus, 1962.
GLOYN, C. K. *The Church in the Social Order*, Pacific University Press, 1942.
MANSEL, H. L. *The Limits of Religious Thought*, the Bampton Lectures for 1858, fifth edition, London, 1867.
MASTERMAN, N. C. *John Malcolm Ludlow, The Builder of Christian Socialism*, Cambridge, 1963.
RAMSEY, A. M. *F. D. Maurice and the Conflicts of Modern Theology*, Cambridge, 1951.
RAMSEY, IAN T. *On being sure in Religion* (the F. D. Maurice Lectures), London, 1963.
RECKITT, M. B. *Maurice to Temple, A Century of the Social Movement in the Church of England*, London, 1947.
VIDLER, A. R. *F. D. Maurice and Company*, London, 1966.

IV GENERAL SOURCES

(a) IN BOOKS

ACTON, J. E. D., Baron. *Historical Essays and Studies*, London, 1907.
— *Selections from the Correspondence of the First Lord Acton*, ed. J. N. Figgis and R. V. Laurence, London, 1917.
— *Letters to Mary, Daughter of the Rt. Hon. W. E. Gladstone*, ed. Herbert Paul, London, 1904.
— 'The Munich Congress' (*Home and Foreign Review*, No. 7, Jan. 1864, 209–44) as republished in Acton, *Essays on Church & State*, ed. Douglas Woodruff, London, 1952, pp. 159–99.
— *History of Freedom and other Essays*, London, 1907.
ALTHOLZ, JOSEF. *The Liberal Catholic Movement in England*, London, 1960.

BACON, FRANCIS. *Bacon's Essays, including his moral and historical works*, London (Chandos ed.), 1892.

— *Novum Organum* (as reprinted in *Modern Classical Philosophers*, ed. Benjamin Rand, Boston, 1908).

BERKELEY, GEORGE. *Works*, ed. G. Sampson, 3 vols., London (Bohn ed.), 1898.

BLONDEL, MAURICE. *Letter on Apologetics* and *History and Dogma* (ed. and translated by Alexander Dru, and Dom Illtyd Trethowan), London, 1964.

BRIGHT, L., and CLEMENTS, S., edd. *The Committed Church*, the seventh Downside Symposium, London, 1966.

BRAITHWAITE, R. B. *An Empiricist's view of the Nature of Religious Belief*, Cambridge, 1955.

BURGON, J. W. *Lives of Twelve Good Men*, London, 1891.

BUTLER, B. C. *The Theology of Vatican II* (The Sarum Lectures 1966), London, 1967.

BUTLER, CUTHBERT. *The Vatican Council 1869–1870* (1930), London, 1962.

BUTLER, JOSEPH. *The Analogy of Religion, etc.*, with an introduction by Samuel Halifax, London, 1834.

CHADWICK, OWEN. *From Bossuet to Newman, the Idea of Doctrinal Development*, Cambridge, 1957.

— *The Victorian Church*, I, 1966– , London, in progress.

CHURCH, R. W. *The Oxford Movement, Twelve Years 1833–1845*, London, 1891.

— *Occasional Papers 1846–1890*, ed. Mary C. Church, 2 vols., London, 1897.

CHURCH, M. C. *The Life and Letters of Dean Church*, London, 1895.

CONGAR, YVES. *Lay People in the Church* (1957), new ed., London, 1965.

COULSON, JOHN. (ed.) *Theology and the University, an Ecumenical Investigation*, the sixth Downside Symposium, London, 1964.

COX, HARVEY. *The Secular City*, London, 1966.

DABIN, PAUL. *Le Sacerdoce royal des fidèles dans la tradition ancienne et moderne*, Bruxelles, 1950.

DESCARTES, R. *A Discourse on Method* (inc. *Meditations on the First Philosophy*), London (Everyman), 1946.

DOWNSIDE SYMPOSIA. (*See* Coulson ed., Bright and Clements edd.)

EUSEBIUS. *The Ecclesiastical History*, trans. H. J. Lawlor and J. E. L. Oulton, London, 1927.

Gaudium et Spes. See *Vatican II*, documents of.

GILLOW, JOSEPH. *A literary and biographical history or Bibliographical Dictionary of the English Catholics* (5 vols.), London, 1885.

18+N.C.T.

HALES, E. E. Y. *Pio Nono*, London, 1956.
HALÉVY, ELIE. *A history of the English People in 1815*, 3 vols., London, 1938.
HÄRDELIN, ALF. *The Tractarian Understanding of the Eucharist*, Uppsala, 1965.
HOBBES, THOMAS. *Leviathan*, ed. Michael Oakeshott, Oxford, 1946.
HOOKER, RICHARD. *The Laws of Ecclesiastical Polity*, ed. Henry Morley, London, 1888.
HUDSON, C. E., and RECKITT, M. B. *The Church and the World, being materials for the Historical Study of Christian Sociology*, 3 vols., vol. iii. *Church and Society in England from 1800*, London, 1940.
HÜGEL, F. VON (Baron). *Selected Letters*, London, 1927.
— *The Mystical Element of Religion as Studied in St. Catherine of Genoa and her friends*, 2 vols. (1908), second ed., 1923.
— *Letters from Baron Friedrich von Hügel to a Niece*, ed. Gwendolen Greene, London, 1928.
— *Essays and Addresses on the Philosophy of Religion*, (i) first series, 1921; (ii) second series, 1928.
HUTTON, R. H. *Essays on some of the Modern Guides to English Thought in Matters of Faith*, London, 1891.
LIDDON, H. P. *Life of Edward Bouverie Pusey*, 4 vols., London, 1893.
Lumen Gentium. See *Vatican II*, documents of.
MALCOLM, NORMAN. *Ludwig Wittgenstein, A Memoir*, London, 1958.
MILL, J. S. *Autobiography*, Oxford (World's Classics), 1949.
— *Bentham and Coleridge*, ed. F. R. Leavis, London, 1962.
MITCHELL, WILLIAM FRASER. *English Pulpit Oratory from Andrewes to Tillotson*, London, 1932.
MÖHLER, JOHN ADAM. *Symbolism, or exposition of the Doctrinal Differences between Catholics and Protestants*, London, 1906.
MURRAY, JOHN COURTNEY, S.J. *We hold these Truths, Catholic Reflections on the American Proposition*, London, 1961.
PATTISON, MARK. *Essays*, ed. H. Nettleship, 2 vols., Oxford, 1889.
PURCELL, E. S. *The Life of Cardinal Manning*, 2 vols., London, 1896.
RAHNER, KARL. *Theological Investigations*, 3 vols., London, 1960– .
RICHTER, MELVIN. *The Politics of Conscience, T. H. Green and his Age*, London, 1964.
SPRAT, THOMAS. *History of the Royal Society* (1667), second edition, London, 1702.
TILLICH, PAUL. *Dynamics of Faith*, London, 1957.
— *The Protestant Era*, London, 1951.
TREVOR, MERIOL. *Apostle to Rome*, the life of St. Philip Neri, London, 1966.

Vatican II, documents of:

(i) *Dogmatic Constitution on the Church (Lumen Gentium),* ed. E. H. Peters, London, 1965.

(ii) *Pastoral Constitution on the Church in the Modern World (Gaudium et Spes);*
Decree on Ecumenism (Unitatis Redintegratio);
Decree on the Ministry and Life of Priests (Presbyterorum Ordinis);
Declaration on Religious Freedom (Dignitatis Humanae);
in *The Documents of Vatican II,* ed. Walter M. Abbott, S.J., London, 1966.

WHITEHEAD, A. N. *Science and the Modern World,* Cambridge, 1927.
— *Aims of Education,* London, 1932.
WILBERFORCE, R. G. *Life of Bishop Wilberforce,* 3 vols., London, 1882.
WILLIAMS, RAYMOND. *Culture and Society 1780–1950,* London, 1961.
— *The Long Revolution,* London, 1965.
WITTGENSTEIN, LUDWIG. *Tractatus Logico—Philosophicus* (1922), London, 1955.
— *Philosophical Investigations,* Oxford, 1953.
— *Remarks on the Foundation of Mathematics,* London, 1956.
See MALCOLM, N.

(b) IN PERIODICALS

BEALES, A. C. F. 'Catholic Higher Institutes', *Dublin Review,* 1962, No. 491, 82–4.
DRU, ALEXANDER. 'Blondel's *La Semaine Sociale*', *Downside Review,* 81 (1963), 226–45.
JONES, R. F. '17th Century Scientific Prose', *Publications of the Modern Language Association of America,* xlv (1930), 992 ff.
WINCH, PETER. 'Understanding a Primitive Society', *American Philosophical Quarterly,* I (1964), 307–24.

INDEX

Acland, *Sir* Thomas Dyke, 58 n.4

Acton, *Sir* John, *first Baron Acton*, 102, 105, 118, 121–2, 133–4, 136, 138, 139, 152, 155–6, 172

The Advancement of Learning (Bacon), 5

Aids to Reflection (Coleridge), 19, 31, 61, 67 n.2, 192, 254

Aims of Education (Whitehead), 93

Alciphron (Berkeley), 12, 215, 219

Allchin, Arthur Macdonald, 59 n.2, 67

Allies, Thomas William, 144 n.3, 150, 160 n.1, 161 n.1, 187 n.1, 219 n.2, 226, 235

'Americanism', 249

The Analogy of Religion (Butler), 66 n.6

Anselm, *Saint*, 216

Antonelli, Giacomo, *Cardinal*, 140. n.2

Apologia pro Vita Sua (Newman), 55, 57–8, 66, 68, 71, 72, 73, 75, 76, 113, 125, **136–147**, 176, 191, 204, 207, 208, 219 n.3, 237, 239, 240, 246, 254

Apostle of Rome, the Life of St. Philip Neri (Trevor), 99–100

The Arians of the Fourth Century (Newman), 125–6, 153 n.4, 220, 242 n.1

Aristotle, 10

Arnold, Matthew, 80, 110, 129, 144, 173 n.1, 236, 247

Arnold, Thomas, 131

Assent: one complex act both of inference and of assent, 29, 219–224, 231, 244. *See also under* Berkeley, Certitude, Wordsworth 'spots of time'

Athanasius, *Saint*, 56

Augustine, *Saint, Bishop of Hippo*, 16, 73, 115, 118, 122, 233

Authority: in Church, 51, 74, 76–7, 93–4, 97–8, 99–101, 117, 132, 164, 167, 168, 169, 209, 233, 250;

best exercised when it 'commits the Church least', 153, 156; ecclesiastical, and the university, 97–8, 100–1; Church's pastoral, in university, 87, 90, 91–2; papal, 81, 122, 140, 152–6, 169, 175; for Ultramontanes, exercised in imitation of secular power, 172. *See also under* Conscience, Infallibility

Autobiographical Writings (Newman, ed. Tristram), 57, 91 n.3, 97, 124, 131, 132

Autobiography (Mill), 30

Autonomy: intellectual, and theology. *See under* Theology
of conscience, in Acton. *See under* Conscience
of studies, fundamental to university. *See under* University

Ayer, Alfred Jules, 215 n.7

Bacchus, Joseph, 254

Bacon, Francis, 4–5, 7, 16, 17

Baptism, 189–90, 191 n.5

Barnabò, Alessandro, *Cardinal*, 127–8

Bedini, Gaetano, *Archbishop*, 123

Bellarmine, Robert, *Cardinal*, 152–3

Bentham, Jeremy, 3–4, 8, 11, 13, 15, 16, 17, 18, 25, 38, 50–1, 60, 81, 220–1, 224, 247, 251

Berkeley, George, *Bishop of Cloyne*, 11–12, 13, 17, 26, 154, 215, 219

Bethell, Augustus, 156

Bible: Matthew xx: 16, 236; John x: 9; John xiv: 6, 21; Romans xii: 2, 234; I Corinthians iii: 202; I Corinthians xii: 245; Hebrews, 77; I John v: 19, 226. *See also* Revelation, Scripture

Biographia Literaria (Coleridge), 9, 10, 11, 17 n.3, 18, 19, 20, 22, 208, 223, 254

Bishop, Edmund, 105 n.2, 118

Church—*continued*
theology is equilibrating or regulating principle, 81, 87, 130, 167,
168, 171–3, 175–6, 179, 181–3,
203, 207, 212–13, 233, 238, 239-
240, 248, 249–50; perpetually in
movement between essentialist
and existentialist poles, 134; University, as model for, *see under*
University
Church and Christ: as embodiment of,
139; even when silent, 141; as
In-Dwelling of, 78, 79, 81, 172,
198; as Body of, 166, 169, 181,
188, 204, 232; as presence of, in
the World, 49, 50, 58, 62, 64–5,
183, 206, 240, 248; as three
offices of, 101, 166–7, 168, 170,
171–2, 173, 176, 177, 179, 198,
203, 207, 210, 222, 232, 237–8,
248, 249
Church and Society: purpose distinct
from State's, 71; distinguished
from Establishment, 39, 62, 66,
68, 69, 84, 187, 225, 234; as embodied in nation, 39, 40, 43,
45–6, 47, 49, 66–7, 182, 236; as
related to nation 38–48, 74, 79,
83, 110, 196, 201, 204, 205, 207;
mutual relationship to World,
49, 234, 238; as be-friending
opposite, 41, 44, 110, 148–9, 234;
blessed accident, 41, 110, 236;
sharing of concerns, 210–11, 231;
happy anomaly, 83; relationship
of sacramental Church to Society,
144, 147, 148, 156–7, 164, 169,
178, 187, 207, 219, **225–53**; three
forms of relationship generalized,
225–53
in politics, uncommitted to specific
systems, 234, 235, 236, 237, 239,
244; a redeeming not a reforming
role, 235, 241
in its double aspect, 40, 68–9, 170,
173, 204, 206; abuses, 170, 206;
Coleridge on its apostasy, 45, 75;
provinciality, 129, 130; as sect
190, 231. *See also under* Novatianism, Romanism
Church of England, 47, 55, 69, 70,
145; role as *via media* rejected by
Newman, 72–3; as representing

national ethos, 150–1, 163, 204–5,
225; seen by Newman as liable
to corruption by political and
social pressures, 141–2
Church, Richard William, *Dean of
St. Paul's*, 35, 39, 69, 70, 192,
223, 226
Civilization, 41
Clergy: narrowing of Church upon,
'apostasy', 45, 75; separation
from laity 'fearful', 96; and
laity, Rahner on, 229–30
need for unity with laity *see under*
Common culture, Conspiratio,
Education
Clerisy, 42, 43–4, 46, 49–50, 110, 230,
234
Coleridge's description of, 42, 43–4,
46, 49–50, 209, 211, 221, 230,
234; referred to by Maurice, 210;
compared to double function of
laity in Newman, 110. *See also
under* Laity
Coleridge, Derwent, 190–1
Coleridge, Henry Nelson, 47
Coleridge, Samuel Taylor, **1–51**, 57,
81, 86–7, 129, 137, 139–40,
143, 150 n.6, 156, 166, 167, 168,
179, 190–2, 195, 198, 204 n.2,
206, 207, 208, 209, 210, 211,
224, 225, 230, 231, 232, 233,
234, 235, 236, 237, 240, 241,
246 n.4, 248, 252, 254–5
on language as intermediate between
matter and spirit, 9, 18–19, 36, 39,
42, 58, 232; claims of, for poetic
language dependent on prior
assumptions about religious language, 14, 21, 22, 26, 31, 32, 34,
38, 42, 49; interests in language
paralleled by those of Wittgenstein, 9, 10, 14–18; on language as world-revealing, 20,
31, 34; on poetry, 18–22; claims
of, for poets, 20; cause of obscurities in, 14, 22, 191. *See also
under* Language, Lingua communis, Realizing principles
on Bentham, 8–9, 251; on education, 24; on Middle Ages, 43, 44;
'Platonism' of 60. *See also under
the titles of individual works*
Collegiality, 203–4

18*

Maurice—*continued*
248–9; and the regeneration of
society, 79, 182, 195–6, 222; the
Church 'a house not made with
hands', 78, 214, 220
and the Bible, 75–6, 77, 192; and
our being *found* by Scripture
192; on unity of elements of
Revelation, 214
primary emphasis on family and
nation, 195–6; Newman's objection, 238
his theological method, 200; 'only
a digger', 202, 204; tendency
to regard as norm Church establishment of his time, 205; inductively influenced by social
and political change, 212; unity
of elements of Revelation keynote
of theology of, 214
dictated his writings, 193; charge of
obscurity, 191–3, 214; high
threshold of self-evidence, 222–3;
compared to 'certainty' in Newman, 222–3; shrank from the
political involvement he recom-
mends for fear of compromising
Church, 202–4 (*see also under*
Motives); insulated insights am-
plified rather than developed,
193; strength, one of affirmation,
192–3, 200; on Christian Socialism, 201–2. *See also under*
Christian Socialism, Church,
Language, Nation *and under the
titles of individual works*
Maurras, Charles, 236, 249
Method *see under Treatise on Method*
Meynell, Charles, 59, 220 n.2
Mill, John Stuart, 40, 41, 46, 190
n.7, 191
on Bentham, 3, 8, 30; on Coleridge,
3, 8, 191; on Wordsworth, 30
Minimising: principle of, 153, 156;
'what commits Church least',
153. *See also under* Authority
Modernists, 181, 249
Möhler, Johann Adam, 93, 133, 180,
208
Molina, Luis, 153
'monophorisme', 181, 229, 231. *See
also under* Essentialism
Monsell, William, 127, 138, 150

Montalambert, Charles Forbes René,
Comte de, 111
Motives: religious and social, for ac-
tion distinguished, 141, 142–3,
202–4, 235–9; religious, of social
vitality, 221
Mozley, Anne, 72, 83, 110, 117 n.1,
141
Mozley, James Bowling, 191 n.5
Munich Brief, 91 n.3, 135–6, 138,
139, 146
Munich Congress, 1863, 132–6, 140,
147, 155 n.1
Munich theologians, 133, 135
Murray, John Courtney, 221
My Campaign in Ireland (Newman),
163
The Mystical Element of Religion (von
Hügel), 175, 177, 200 n.2, 242,
249

Nation: Maurice on, 195, 196, 197,
199, 201, 203, 204, 205, 218, 221,
222, 243;
Newman on, 204, 218, 221, 222,
236. *See also under* Church and
Society, Clerisy, Coleridge,
Maurice
Nationalty, 41, 44
Nature and Grace, 84, 89, 96, 98, 99,
141, 142, 171, 222, 245
Nédoncelle, Maurice, 146 n.1, 170,
206
Neri, Philip, *Saint*, 92, 98–100, 178
Newman, John Henry, 34 n.4, 35, 47,
49, 50, 214, 217, 218, 219, 220,
232, 240
reception into Roman Catholic
Church and ordination, 83, 85;
too simple a view, initially, of
Roman church? 83–4; as bridge
between two churches, 56–7, 75,
240; refusal to repudiate the
tradition in which he had been
formed, 55, 98, 100, 137, 145,
161, 240; *via negativa*, 101, 132,
136, 140, 148, 167, 179; willingness to face the consequences of
his conclusions, 55–6, 148; and
the Church Fathers, 67–8, 104,
115; 'Platonism' of, 60–1; empiricist epistemology, 59 n.2,
76, 220 n.2, 221; spiritual rigour,

Newman—*continued*
58; on atheism implicit in blind acceptance of authority, 151; not interested in 'splendid conversions of great men', 132; on the Irish clergy, 96–7, 229; on the English Catholic clergy, 110 n.5; responsiveness of, to charge of 'Romanism', 75, 94, 139–40; on a *mixed* society, 97, 135, 149, 150, 151, 156–64, 208, 225, 239, 248, 252; use by, of term 'open university' 161, 162, 163; and habit of the Roman system of evaluating theological matters in political terms, 127, 128–9, 140, 174 n.1, 206; on Italians' capacity to disjoin religion from morality, 84; antipathy of, to imperialism, 143, 144; opposed to Crimean War, 144; reservations on laymen writing theology, 105 n.1, 163 n.3
and our personal encounter with Christ, 58, 64, 66; evangelical grasp of the indwelling presence of Christ to believer, 58, 64, 177; view of the Person as 'temple' of Christ, 93–4
on the Church, 3, 33 n.2, 39, 57–8, 62, 83, 179–83, 188, 209, 221–2, 224, 232 n.4, 246; concept of Church's verifying power based on study of the Arians, 83; explains Church by harmonic analogy, 172. *See also under* Church
Scripture 'disappoints', 75–6, 174 n.2, 194; on Revelation, 59
reservations on restoration of English hierarchy, 103; makes annotated translation of Munich Brief, 136; and First Vatican Council, 151, 154–5
foundation of the Birmingham Oratory, 85, 99–100; project of Oxford Oratory, 156, 157, 158, 160, 161 n.1; split between Birmingham and London Oratories, 99–100
education 'from first to last' Newman's line, 131; and the Dublin Catholic University project, 85–100, 102, 113–14, 131; perseveres in this project in deference to Holy See, 97; and Manning's Kensington Catholic University College, 158; university as model for idea of Church, 87, 93, 101, 167, 203, 245–6, 247; conceives of university and church as republican rather than monarchical, 87, 98; on the 'gentleman', 89–90, 91; on liberal education, 86, 88, 89–90, 92–3, 115–6, 241. *See also under* Education, University.
'occasional' character of major writings, 86, 105–6, 113–4, 132; takes over *Rambler*, 102–5, 110, 118; interview with Ullathorne over *Rambler*, 112–13; correspondence with Gillow in 1859, 119–121; after *Rambler* episode withdraws into silence, 124–5, 131; answer to Kingsley subsumed, in *Apologia*, into unified affirmation, 137, 145; influence of Acton's letter on development of *Apologia*, 138–9; *Apologia* as apologia for the 'silent church', 136, 138, 140, 146; *Apologia* challenges authority to repudiate a defender, 139, 152; heals breaches with old friends, 148–50, 151, 240; later revisions to *On Consulting the Faithful*, 126; oecumenical intention of, in republishing his works, 149–50, 165, 169 n.2; Preface to *Via Media* confronts the Newman of 40 years earlier, 165, 169, 170–1; also attempts to conciliate Ultramontanes, 166, 174; asked to retract *Letter to the Duke of Norfolk*, 165
and Coleridge, 3, 23, 24, 25, 43, 49–50, 55, 57, 58, 60, 61, 62, 63, 64, 81, 86–7, 129, 137, 139–40, 143, 150 n.6, 156, 166, 167, 168, 179, 206, 207, 208, 209, 224, 225, 232, 233, 234, 235, 240, 241, 246 n.4, 248, 252, **254-5**; divided from Coleridge by distinction between conscience as divine agent and as moral principle, 156; first reads Coleridge in 1835,

Propaganda, Sacred Congregation of, 96 n.1, 123, 124, 126–8, 138, 157
Purgatory, 79–80
Pusey, Edward Bouverie, 34 n.4, 56–7, 62, 67–8, 131, 144, 163, 189–90, 191, 213, 240

Rahner, Karl, 229, 230
The Rambler, 102–131, 142 n.2, 220 n.2. *See also* Home and Foreign Review *which succeeded it*
Ranke, Leopold von, 152
'realize': use of term, by Newman, 145
Realizing principles, 19, 25–7, 31–2, 38, 61, 192
 how recognized, in Wordsworth's 'spots of time', 27, 28–9, 30, 31, 32. *See also under* Idea, Coleridge on *and* Language, analytic and fiduciary usage distinguished
Reason: implicit and explicit, distinguished, in Newman, 24 n.3; and understanding, in Coleridge, 67 n.2
The Rediscovery of Newman (ed. Coulson & Allchin), 59 n.2, 67
Religions of the World (Maurice), 78, n.8
The Republic (Plato), 33
Revelation, 214–15, 216, 218, 220, 224, 239
Rogers, Frederic, *Lord Blachford*, 67 n.2, 171
Roman Catholic Church: as viewed from within English tradition, 39, 45, 46, 49, 55, 56, 69, 71, 73; Newman's experience of, leads to his *via negativa*, 83, 88, 89–90, 91 n.3, 95–8, 101, 123, 124–5, 131; narrow 'provinciality' of, 129, 130
'Romanism', 75, 77, 78–9, 83, 94, 129, 137, 139–40, 141, 166, 169, 173, 179, 181, 190, 198–9, 205, 221, 252
Rose, Hugh James, 254–5
Rousseau, Jean Jacques, 7
Royal Commission on Elementary Education, 106–9, 118

Sacrament and symbol, 3, 4, 8, 9, 11,

17, 21, 22, 23, 26, 32, 35, 36, 37, 43, 57–8, 63, 64, 67, 68, 180, 195, 198, 215, 218, 219, 220, 223, 224, 226–7. *See also under* Symbol
St. John, Ambrose, 33 n.2, 124, 125, 127–8, 160, 191 n.5, 254
St. Paul and Protestantism (Arnold), 80
Scherr, Gregor von, *Archbishop of Munich*, 135. *See also under* Munich Brief
Schillebeeckx, Edward, 182
Scripture, 38, 75–6, 77, 172, 173, 174, 189, 192, 214, 215, 216, 218. *See also under* Bible, Revelation
Second Vatican Council *see* Vatican II
The Secular City (Cox), 221 n.1
Sensibility: dissociated, 7; how unified, 7, 32–3, 34
Sermons bearing on Subjects of the Day (Newman), 70, 142, 150, 170
Sermons preached on Various Occasions (Newman), 95, 98, 99
Sewell, William, 191, 223 n.6
Shakespeare, William, 18–19, 21, 131, 139, 252
Shiel, *Sir* Justin, 157
Simeon, *Lady* Dorothea, 151
Simpson, Richard, 96, 102, 104, 105, 111–12, 118, 127, 220 n.2, 229
Society: sacramental of God's presence, 194, 195. *See also under* Church and Society, Plural Society
Society for the Promotion of Working Men's Associations, 202
Spanish theologians, 134–5
Sprat, Thomas, *Bishop of Rochester*, 5–6
'spots of time' *see under* Realizing principles, Wordsworth
State: purpose of, distinguished from that of Church, 71–2; Coleridge on, 33; 'as much God's creation as the Church', 190
The Statesman's Manual (Coleridge), 36, 41, 42, 195
Stephen, *Sir* James, 3
Stokes, Nasmyth Scott, 107–8, 110
Stray Essays on Controversial Points (Newman), 67 n.2

Unity—*continued*
of knowledge, basis of university, 88

University: Newman on, **85–101**, 130–1, 156, 171; for Newman, an embodied idea, 93; model for his idea of the Church, 87, 93, 101, 167, 203, 245–6, 247; Catholic, Newman's change of mind, 156–64, 208; 'open', Newman's preference for, 97, 156–64, 208, 252; conceived as equilibrium of functions, 87, 91, 94–5, 161–2; restrictions on Catholic attendance at, 157–8; education of clergy at 94–5, 130–1, 133, 162, 252–3 (*see also under* Common culture); intellectual emphasis distinguishes from seminary, 158, 159, 160, 163 n.3. *See also under* Newman

University Sermons see Fifteen sermons Preached before the University of Oxford

The Vanity of Dogmatizing (Glanvill), 6

Vatican I, 75, 134–5, 151, 153, 154–5, 156, 160, 165, 169, 182, 227, 234

Vatican II, 50, 134, 154, 165, 166, 175, 182, 204 nn.2, 3, 208 n.2, 221 n.1, 225, 226, 231–4, 238–43, 252

Verification: principle of, 3, 30, 34, 35, 39; the fundamental question, 50–1, 55, 81–2, 221, 224, 238, 239; Newman denies that to establish Church socially is to verify it, 238, 241. *See also under* Church, as verifying community, Truth

Verot, Augustin, *Bishop of Savannah*, 155 n.1

Verses on Various Occasions (Newman), 144

The Via Media of the Anglican Church (Newman), 33 n.2, 63, 94, 143, 161, 162, 165, 166, 169, 170, 171–2, 173, 174–5, 176, 200 n.2.

See also under Lectures on the Prophetical Office

Vincent of Lérins, *see:*

Vincentian canon, 69–71, 73, 80, 222
application by Newman, in *Tract XC*, 69–71, terrestrially and chronologically, 73, 130

von Hügel, Friedrich, *Baron*, 34 n.4, 169, 174, 175, 176–8, 180, 182, 200, 230, 231 n.2, 242–3, 249
interest of, generally in religion, Newman's specifically in the Church, 175, 177; direct influence on, of Newman, 176, 177, 242–3; proposes translation of Newman into German, 176

Ward, Wilfrid, 164, 254

Ward, William George, 100, 128–9, 161, 191 n.5, 231 n.2

We hold these Truths (Murray), 221

What is Revelation? (Maurice), 216

Whately, Richard, 57, 193 n.4

Whitehead, Alfred North, 27, 93

Wilberforce, Henry William, 113

Wilberforce, Samuel, *Bishop*, 219 n.1

Williams, Raymond, 237 n.1

Wiseman, Nicholas, *Cardinal, Archbishop of Westminster*, 103, 104, 105, 111, 124, 131, 157

Wittgenstein, Ludwig, 9–10, 20, 146 n.1, 208 n.4, 245 n.3, 249
moves from analytic to fiduciary attitude to language, 14, 17, 18

Wood, J. F., 144 n.2

Words: as deeds, 17; not things, but living powers, 19

Wordsworth, William, 11, 18, 20, 22, 27–30, 31, 32, 43, 252
'spots of time', 27, 28–9, 30, 31, 32. (*See also under* Assent)

Workers: and religion, 197, 199–200, 201–2

Working Men's College, 197, 203–4

World: as reconciled to Christ, 187, 189, 195, 222. *See also under* Church and Christ, Church and Society, Maurice

Worship, 65–6